Linked Data

Linked Data

STRUCTURED DATA ON THE WEB

DAVID WOOD
MARSHA ZAIDMAN
AND LUKE RUTH
WITH MICHAEL HAUSENBLAS

MANNING
Shelter Island

For online information and ordering of this and other Manning books, please visit
www.manning.com. The publisher offers discounts on this book when ordered in quantity.
For more information, please contact

> Special Sales Department
> Manning Publications Co.
> 20 Baldwin Road
> PO Box 261
> Shelter Island, NY 11964
> Email: orders@manning.com

Manning Publications Co.	Development editor: Jeff Bleiel
20 Baldwin Road	Copyeditor: Linda Recktenwald
PO Box 261	Proofreader: Elizabeth Martin
Shelter Island, NY 11964	Typesetter: Gordan Salinovic
	Cover designer: Marija Tudor

ISBN 9781617290398
Printed in the United States of America
1 2 3 4 5 6 7 8 9 10 – MAL – 18 17 16 15 14 13

brief contents

contents

2 RDF: the data model for Linked Data   27

3 Consuming Linked Data   60

foreword

Linked Data: Structured data on the Web the book is just what Linked Data the technology has needed. It is a friendly introduction to the use and publication of structured data on the World Wide Web.

Linked Data was part of my initial vision for the Web and is an important part of the Web's future. The Web took off as a web of hyperlinked documents which were exciting to read, but which could not effectively be used as data.

And, yes, in fact, much of the Web is data-driven, and the data has been hidden on files inside the server. In slides from my wrap-up talk at the very first WWW conference in 1994, I pointed out that while documents talk about people and things, such as a title deed saying who owns a house, the system was not capturing the data—the actual ownership fact—in a way that could be processed. As the Web evolved, and became more driven by data, there has been frustration that changing, hidden data is not exposed to the reader. Linked Data standards allow you to publish data in a way that can be read by people and processed by machines so that previously hidden flows of data become evident.

Linked Data may not be as exciting as a hypertext Web to read, but it is more exciting in terms of making everything work more effectively, from business to scientific research. Machines can read, follow, and combine Linked Data much more effectively than they can perform those actions using other forms of data currently on the Web.

The role of machines has previously been subservient to the role of people in the technology used to allow people to communicate. Now machines are beginning to become active participants in the communication. Linked Data allows machines to become more useful partners in our daily lives.

Linked Data has come of age in the last couple of years. In the last two years we have seen Google announce its Knowledge Graph and adopt the JSON-LD serialization format for Gmail, and produce a large set of terms for general use at schema.org; IBM announce that the DB2 database will become a Linked Data server; and Facebook expose Linked Data via its Graph API. Other large companies and government organizations have followed suit. We have needed a book like this one to introduce Linked Data development to a new and wider group of programmers. *Linked Data* will provide you with the questions to ask, even if it doesn't answer them all. It is a great place to begin your study and kick-start your development.

I have known Dave Wood for just about a decade. We met when he started his work with the World Wide Web Consortium. We later worked on a Web research project together. Dave has worked tirelessly to develop Semantic Web and Linked Data frameworks since the late 1990s. As a developer, he is well-placed to show others how it is done.

The building blocks of Linked Data are not particularly new. The original proposal for the World Wide Web that I wrote in 1989 for my bosses at CERN included hyperlinks with semantics. The proposal read, in part, "The system we need is like a diagram of circles and arrows, where circles and arrows can stand for anything." In fact, the Enquire program I had written in 1980 captured the relationships between things in a graph. That was the vision. Now Linked Data is delivering on this vision, by adding meaning that computers can process.

As we all know, in the basic hypertext Web, the arrows we ended up with all stood for the same thing: "There is some interesting information over here!" Linked Data extends the "document Web" by allowing arrows to stand for anything we can name with a URI. Hyperlinks gain the semantics they need, and, in the process become much more useful.

The Web of hypertext-linked documents is complemented by the very powerful Linked Web of Data. Why linked? Well, think of how the value of a Web page is very much a function of what it links to, as well as the inherent value of the information within the Web page. So it is—in a way even more so—also in the Semantic Web of Linked Data. The data itself is valuable, but the links to other data make it much more so.

I believe that the Web should evolve to serve all of us, regardless of our nationality, language, economic motivation, or interests. Linked Data is just one part of that evolution. It is not the end—it is just another part of the beginning. There is still plenty to do, so come join us in building the next generation of the Web!

TIM BERNERS-LEE

DIRECTOR OF THE WORLD WIDE WEB CONSORTIUM (W3C)

3COM FOUNDERS PROFESSOR OF ENGINEERING, MASSACHUSETTS INSTITUTE OF TECHNOLOGY

PROFESSOR IN THE ELECTRONICS AND COMPUTER SCIENCE DEPARTMENT, UNIVERSITY OF

SOUTHAMPTON UK

preface

We love the Web and we love the way it's evolving from the rather simple web of linked documents of the early 1990s into the framework for the world's information. Representing data on the Web is an obvious, but slightly harder, next step.

We each came to the Web in our own ways but came to Linked Data nearly together. David found the Web as a programmer and later as an entrepreneur, Marsha as an educator, and Luke as a student. Marsha and David are old enough to have started computing with punch cards and paper tape. The Web was a very welcome degree of abstraction from ones and zeros.

David was introduced to the Web at Digital Equipment Corporation's fabled Western Research Lab in California in 1993. It was an eye-opener. One of the first large websites showed photos of thousands of pieces of artwork held by the Vatican. Another showed a list of projects that Digital researchers were working on and linked to each of their own individual web servers for detailed documents. David was hooked. Tellingly, it was the project website that he found most interesting. If only you could link into databases and spreadsheets the way you could link to documents.

Marsha also found the Web in the early days, when Gopher was the primary search tool and Web browsers worked in a terminal, and she kept up to date with its rapid changes in order to teach new generations of computer scientists. Her career has lasted long enough for her to see the incredible changes wrought by the invention of spreadsheets and databases on decision making, and this fostered an interest in moving data to the Web.

Marsha gave David the chance to teach at the University of Mary Washington just as the Linking Open Data project was starting. Luke took the first class offered to U.S. undergraduates on Linked Data in 2011, followed by an independent study and an internship, all with David. He was eventually hired by David to work on Linked Data projects.

Luke and David contribute to the Callimachus Project, an open source Linked Data platform described in this book. We've used it to build applications for a variety of organizations, from U.S. government agencies and pharmaceutical companies to publishers and health-care companies. Each of those projects is based on the creation, manipulation, and use of Linked Data.

We decided to write a Linked Data book for Web developers because there simply wasn't one. We all had to learn Linked Data from the specifications or by readying academic papers. There are some other books on Linked Data (David edited two of them), but none are aimed specifically at developers. We thought that our combination of real-world development experience and experience teaching technology would result in a useful book. We hope you agree.

It's our privilege to work with a loosely affiliated international group of people working to bring data to the Web. We hope that you'll read this book and then join us. We can't wait to see what the Web will become next.

acknowledgments

We would like to extend our gratitude to the original members of the Linking Open Data project, many of whom are quoted in this book. We would like to thank Michael Stephens, Jeff Bleiel, Ozren Harlovic, Maureen Spencer, Mary Piergies, Linda Recktenwald, Elizabeth Martin, and Janet Vail, and the rest of the team at Manning Publications for working so hard to make this book a success.

We also owe thanks to the following reviewers who read and commented on our book through its many iterations and multiple review phases: Alain Buferne, Artur Nowak, Craig Taverner, Cristofer Weber, Curt Tilmes, Daniel Ayers, Gary Ewan Park, Glenn McDonald, Innes Fisher, Luka Raljević, M. Edward Borasky, Michael Brunnbauer, Michael Pendleton, Michael Piscatello, Mike Westaway, Owen Stephens, Paulo Schreiner, Philip Poots, Robert Crowther, Ron Sher, Thomas Baker, Thomas Gängler, and Thomas Horton.

Special thanks to Zachary Whitley, our technical proofreader, for his careful review of the final manuscript shortly before it went into production, and to Tim Berners-Lee for contributing the foreword.

The book was greatly improved by those who contributed to the Author Online Forum, the Public LOD mailing list, and the W3C RDF Working Group. Sincere thanks to the readers who participated in the Manning Early Access Program (MEAP) and left feedback in the Author Online forum. Their comments had a strong impact on the quality of the final manuscript. Lastly, we would like to thank the organizers of the Cambridge, New York City, Washington D.C., Northern Virginia, and Central Maryland SemWeb meet-ups for letting us make presentations on the book.

Dave would like to thank Bernadette, who is always there for him when he starts some silly project, as well as his coauthors for making the creation of this book much less of a silly project.

Marsha would like to extend her gratitude to her husband, Steven, who believed in her and encouraged her to pursue this new venture. A special thanks to her coauthor, David, who solicited her participation and had faith that she could extend her previous teaching experiences into written communications. Thanks to both Luke and David for making writing this book a rewarding experience.

Luke would like to thank Dave and Marsha for including him in this process and teaching him so much about technology—and about the world. He would also like to thank his parents, Rick and Tania, for instilling in him the importance of education and trying new things, and his wife Laura for her constant support.

about this book

Linked Data is a set of techniques to represent and connect structured data on the Web. This book shows you how to access, create, and use Linked Data. Linked Data has one amazing property: it can be easily combined with other Linked Data to form new knowledge.

Linked Data makes the World Wide Web into a global database that we call the Web of Data. Developers can query Linked Data using a query language called SPARQL from multiple sources at once and combine those results dynamically, something difficult or impossible to do with traditional data-management technologies. The examples in this book are intentionally drawn from public sources, but the techniques illustrated can just as easily be used with private data. You may be unfamiliar with some of the resources that we use, but they're readily accessible on the Web, and we encourage you to check them out as you encounter them. We apologize in advance for any inconsistencies between the screen shots and URLs referenced in the text and the actual content when you visit those sites on the Web. The Web is a rapidly changing entity, and no printed matter can absolutely represent that. We do promise that all the screen shots and URLs were correct as we entered production.

The techniques of Linked Data enable us to more easily share our knowledge with others. Literally anything can be described by Linked Data. Linked Data on the World Wide Web may be found, shared, and combined with other people's data. Unlike traditional data-management systems, Linked Data frees information from proprietary containers so anyone can use it. As with any data, the consumer is responsible for evaluating its quality and utility. We use sources whose data we trust.

Intended audience

Linked Data: Structured data on the Web should be read by application developers who want to appreciate, consume, and publish Linked Data. This book assumes that you have a basic familiarity with fundamental web technologies such as HTML, URIs, and HTTP. We introduce you to Linked Data, place it in context, outline its principles, and show you how to use it by walking you through the process of finding, consuming, and publishing Linked Data on the Web. We illustrate this process with real-world applications of gradually increasing complexity.

Roadmap

This book has eleven chapters, divided into four parts, a glossary, and two appendixes.

Part 1 "The Linked Data Web" provides an introduction to the fundamentals of Linked Data, the Resource Description Framework (RDF) data model, and the common standard serializations used in representing this data. It guides the reader in identifying and consuming Linked Data on the Web.

- Chapter 1, an introduction to Linked Data, places it in context, outlines its principles, and shows you how to use it by walking you through a Linked Data application.
- Chapter 2 introduces the Resource Description Framework and its relationship to Linked Data. We describe the RDF data model along with the key concepts that you're likely to use in your own Linked Data. In closing this chapter, we address common issues of file types and web servers and provide techniques for resolving those issues.
- Chapter 3 acquaints you with the distributed nature of the Web and how data and documents are interlinked. You become aware of the relationship between the Web of Documents and the Web of Data. You learn how to find and consume Linked Data on the Web.

Part 2 "Taming Linked Data" emphasizes techniques for developing and publishing your own Linked Data and enhanced searching techniques for aggregating such data. You learn how to use the SPARQL query language to search for relevant Linked Data datasets and aggregate the results.

- Chapter 4 covers methods of creating, linking, and publishing Linked Data on the Web using the Friend of a Friend (FOAF) and Relationship vocabularies.
- Chapter 5 introduces the SPARQL query language for RDF. SPARQL enables you to query the Web of Data as if it were a database, albeit a very large one with many distributed datasets.

Part 3 "Linked Data in the wild" illustrates how to use RDFa to achieve search engine optimization of your web pages. It introduces you to RDF databases and illustrates the differences between these and the traditional RDBMS. We illustrate how you can best share your datasets and projects on the Web and optimize the inclusion of your projects and datasets in Semantic Web search results.

- Chapter 6 illustrates how to use Resource Description Framework in Attributes (RDFa) to enhance your HTML web pages to achieve enhanced results from search engines. You're introduced to the GoodRelations business-oriented vocabulary and similar techniques using schema.org.
- Chapter 7 introduces RDF databases and the differences and benefits of such data stores over RDBMS. In general, integrating information already in RDF format is painless. But data that you need and would like to use is often stored in non-RDF sources. This chapter illustrates how non-RDF data can be transformed into RDF for ease of integration into other applications.
- Chapter 8 provides an introduction to all the ways that new Linked Data should be described and linked into the larger Linked Data world. It describes and applies the Description of a Project (DOAP) vocabulary to describe projects, the Vocabulary of Interlinked Datasets (VoID) to describe datasets, and semantic sitemaps to describe the Linked Data offerings on a site. This chapter also presents guidelines to publishing your data on the LOD cloud.

Part 4 "Putting it all together" pulls all the concepts covered in parts 1, 2, and 3 together. We develop a complex, real-world application using an open source application server for Linked Data and help you summarize the process of preparation to publication of Linked Data.

- Chapter 9 introduces the Callimachus Project, an open source application server for Linked Data. We show you how to get started with Callimachus, how to generate web pages from RDF data, and how to build applications using it.
- Chapter 10 summarizes the process of publishing Linked Data from preparation to publication. We identify and clarify easily overlooked steps, like minting URIs and customizing vocabularies.
- Chapter 11 surveys the current state of the Semantic Web and the role of Linked Data. We identify some interesting applications of Linked Data and attempt to predict the future direction of the Semantic Web and Linked Data.

The appendixes provide supplementary information.

- Appendix A is a quick reference to the development environment setups of the tools used in the book.
- Appendix B is a guide to interpreting SPARQL query results formats.
- A glossary lists and defines terms used in this book.

How to use this book

We expect you to get the most from this material by reading the chapters in sequence, downloading and executing the sample applications, and then trying modifications of the applications to increase your understanding of the concepts. In those applications where you need particular software tools, we guide you in locating and obtaining those resources. We expect this book to provide you with a foundation to appreciate, consume, and publish Linked Data on the Web.

Code conventions and downloads

All source code in this book is in a `fixed-width font like this`, which sets it off from the surrounding text. In many listings, the code is annotated to point out the key concepts. In some cases, source code is in `bold fixed-width` font for emphasis. We have tried to format the code so that it fits within the available page space in the book by adding line breaks and using indentation carefully. Sometimes, however, very long lines include line-continuation markers.

Source code for all the working examples in the book is available from http://LinkedDataDeveloper.com or from the publisher's website at www.manning.com/LinkedData.

A Readme.txt file is provided in the root folder and also in each chapter folder; the files provide details on how to install and run the code. Code examples appear throughout this book. Longer listings appear under clear listing headers, shorter listings appear between lines of text.

Author Online

Purchase of *Linked Data* includes free access to a private Web forum run by Manning Publications where you can make comments about the book, ask technical questions, and receive help from the authors and from other users. To access the forum and subscribe to it, point your browser to www.manning.com/LinkedData. This page provides information on how to get on the forum once you're registered, what kind of help is available, and the rules of conduct on the forum.

Manning's commitment to our readers is to provide a venue where a meaningful dialog between individual readers and between readers and the authors can take place. It's not a commitment to any specific amount of participation on the part of the authors, whose contribution to the AO remains voluntary (and unpaid). We suggest you ask the authors challenging questions lest their interest stray!

about the cover illustration

The caption for the illustration on the cover of *Linked Data* is "Grand Vizier," or prime minister to the king or sultan. The illustration is taken from a collection of costumes of the Ottoman Empire published on January 1, 1802, by William Miller of Old Bond Street, London. The title page is missing from the collection and we have been unable to track it down to date. The book's table of contents identifies the figures in both English and French, and each illustration bears the names of two artists who worked on it, both of whom would no doubt be surprised to find their art gracing the front cover of a computer programming book...two hundred years later.

The collection was purchased by a Manning editor at an antiquarian flea market in the "Garage" on West 26th Street in Manhattan. The seller was an American based in Ankara, Turkey, and the transaction took place just as he was packing up his stand for the day. The Manning editor didn't have on his person the substantial amount of cash that was required for the purchase and a credit card and check were both politely turned down. With the seller flying back to Ankara that evening, the situation was getting hopeless. What was the solution? It turned out to be nothing more than an old-fashioned verbal agreement sealed with a handshake. The seller simply proposed that the money be transferred to him by wire and the editor walked out with the bank information on a piece of paper and the portfolio of images under his arm. Needless to say, we transferred the funds the next day, and we remain grateful and impressed by this unknown person's trust in one of us. It recalls something that might have happened a long time ago.

We at Manning celebrate the inventiveness, the initiative, and, yes, the fun of the computer business with book covers based on the rich diversity of regional life of two centuries ago, brought back to life by the pictures from this collection.

Part 1

The Linked Data Web

What is Linked Data? What is the Resource Description Framework (RDF)? What is the relationship between RDF and Linked Data? How is data expressed using RDF? Why is publishing 5-Star Linked Data beneficial? Where do you find Linked Data, and how can you use it in your own applications?

In these first three chapters, we'll explore these questions and others. We'll introduce you to Linked Data, place it in context, outline its principles, and show you how to use it by walking you through your first Linked Data application. We'll expose you to the multiple facets of consuming Linked Data from the Web. We'll find Linked Data on the Web both manually and through the use of special tools. We'll illustrate how you develop programs that retrieve Linked Data from one source and use those results to retrieve additional data from a different data source.

Introducing Linked Data

This chapter covers

- An introduction to Linked Data
- The Linked Data principles
- Linked Data foundations
- Anatomy of a Linked Data application

What would you do if your boss told you to produce web pages for 1,500 television and radio programs each day, in multiple languages and character sets, with a staff of a handful of people? What if you needed to publish web content for every band and the songs they record, updated each day? How about web pages for each animal species and its habitat, inclusive of its endangerment status, when your organization doesn't have that information?

The development team at the British Broadcasting Corporation (BBC) faced all three challenges at once during a period of budget cuts. Very soon we'll show you how they solved all three using Linked Data.

Linked Data makes the World Wide Web into a global database that we call the Web of Data. Developers can query Linked Data from multiple sources at once and combine it on the fly, something difficult or impossible to do with traditional data-management technologies. Imagine being able to gather any data you require in a single step! Linked Data can get you there. We know this may seem impossible, and it is with traditional techniques, but we'll demonstrate how it works.

In this chapter, assuming that you have a basic familiarity with fundamental web technologies such as HTML, URIs, and HTTP, we introduce you to Linked Data, place it in context, outline its principles, and show you how to use it by walking you through your first Linked Data application.

We may reference resources that you don't instantly recognize, such as MusicBrainz—the open music encyclopedia. Don't worry. We provide URLs to help you gather the context you'll need to be productive.

1.1   Linked Data defined

The World Wide Web is full of data. Data is published in formats such as PDF, TIFF, CSV, Excel spreadsheets, embedded tables in Word documents, and many forms of plain text. These files are linked to and from HTML and other documents. They are, in a sense, data that you can link to. But this kind of data has a limitation: it's formatted for human consumption. It often requires a specialized utility to read it. It's not easy for automated processes to access, search, or reuse this data. Further processing by people is generally required for this data to be incorporated into new projects or allow someone to base decisions on it.

We'd rather have a universal way for anyone to read and reuse data on the Web. You don't want to just link to the files that data comes in; you want data that you can link into. You want your data to link to related data. You want to foster reuse between people who may never meet.

This book will introduce you to a new way to consume, reuse, and publish data on the Web so that it may be reused by automated processes on either side of enterprise firewalls. The way to do this is called Linked Data. The term *Linked Data* refers to a set of best practices for publishing and connecting structured data on the Web using international standards of the World Wide Web Consortium.

You already know some of the techniques we use for Linked Data because you understand HTTP, URIs, and hyperlinks. You want to publish data on the Web, and you use URIs to identify data elements and the relationships between them. You can use those URIs to hyperlink between data elements the way web pages are hyperlinked. Linked Data is just data but it's on the Web and structured the way the Web is structured. These ideas are collected into the *Linked Data principles*, described in more detail in section 1.4.

The more principles you adhere to, the better your Linked Data. The 5-Star scoring system of Linked Data is:

★   Data is available on the Web, in whatever format (for example, a scanned image).

★★   Data is available as machine-readable structured data (for example, an Excel spreadsheet).

★★★ Data is available in a non-proprietary format (for example, CSV).

★★★★ Data is published using open data standards from the World Wide Web Consortium.

★★★★★ All of the above apply, plus links to other people's data.

The 5-Star system is cumulative. Each additional star presumes that your data meets the criteria for the previous steps. Linked Data developers pride themselves on creating 5-Star Linked Data. Anything less gives you more work to do, perhaps in converting data into 5-Star format, creating additional links, or trying to convince your data sources to create better data. By creating 5-Star Linked Data, you're making the world a nicer place.

The World Wide Web Consortium (W3C) defines standards for the Web, including an open data model and several formats for that model. This chapter will introduce you to the Resource Description Framework (RDF), which is used for the best quality Linked Data.

A paraphrasing of the 5-Star system is given on the W3C coffee mug shown in figure 1.1.

Linked Data (pardon the repeated definition) is a set of techniques for the publication of data on the Web using standard formats and interfaces. We also call data that conforms to those techniques Linked Data.

For example, much of the content in Wikipedia can be thought of as structured data. A Wikipedia article may have a box in the upper right of the page with information like names, dates, places, and links to other content. The DBpedia project (http://dbpedia.org) extracts this structured data from Wikipedia articles and puts it on the Web. Once the data is published in accordance with the Linked Data principles, it is Linked Data and may be used by others who have access to the data.

Figure 1.1 The 5-Star Linked Data mug, available from cafepress.com. The mug may be ordered either with the "Open" and "Open license" labels or without them; Linked Open Data uses both, Linked Data uses neither. Sales of the mugs benefit the W3C.

Linked Data has one amazing property: it may be easily combined with other Linked Data to form new knowledge. That is the best reason to explore and use Linked Data. Traditional data-management techniques have resulted in separation of most of our data into silos that can't be readily recombined. We need to write programs to find, access, convert, and combine data from silos before we can get on with any particular job. Linked Data makes that sort of work much easier because it's easy to combine Linked Data from multiple sources.

Another useful feature of Linked Data is that it's self-documenting. You can immediately figure out what a term means by resolving it on the Web. This makes Linked Data a wonderful new technique for data sharing.

So, imagine that you're gathering data from a variety of sources to perform an analysis or make a mash-up. You could grab data from DBpedia and other Linked Data from elsewhere on the Web and throw it all together to make the data set you want.

The rest of this chapter presents programming ideas from the public Web, but don't let that convince you that all Linked Data needs to be public. Linked Data techniques are also widely deployed behind enterprise firewalls on private networks. Everything you learn in this book can be deployed with public or private data or a mix of the two.

1.2   *What Linked Data won't do for you*

You might be wondering whether Linked Data is too good to be true. It's not. Linked Data is built on the Web and has the same benefits and problems that the Web does.

Linked Data is no silver bullet. It won't protect you from issues of data quality or from service failures. Nothing inherent to Linked Data improves the efficiency of distributed queries. The same goes for changing definitions of schema terms. If the meaning of your terms changes in time, your data might be more difficult to understand in the context in which it was developed.

But Linked Data does provide you with new ways to manage these existing data-management challenges.

Data quality is a problem in every data-management system. Dirty data in a relational database or on a website can very rapidly be turned into dirty Linked Data. You'll find that Linked Data is most often published in ways that aren't specific to a particular application. That can expose data cleanliness issues that weren't previously transparent and at the same time make them easier to spot. Many sites structure their reuse of Linked Data so that it may be reviewed and even curated before it's used, as you'll see with the BBC example later in this chapter. Others don't and put up with dirty data as a consequence. As always, the choice is yours.

What will you do if you're using Linked Data from a service on the Web and that service shuts down or becomes temporarily unavailable? Most people won't build production services that query distributed data in real time, for issues of both reliability and efficiency. You can treat your local copy of some remote data as a sort of cache. The failure of a remote service just means that your data may not be up to date until the service returns to operation or a replacement is found.

What about changing schema terms? Linked Data schema terms are identified using HTTP URIs, so it's relatively easy to migrate to another URI if the meaning of a term changes. Even if you don't change a URI for a term, you can (and should) generally record some information about where and when the definition of terms was valid. There are even ways to check for equivalent terms. Linked Data offers several layers of flexibility to help you with changing schemas.

You might think about these challenges in the context of the Web. Early hypertext systems were implemented on single machines and could therefore ensure that each link resolved to a valid resource. A resource that was being linked to, that was aware it was being linked to, could count those links and automatically link back. Hypertext researchers were nearly unanimous in their dislike for the early Web precisely because it didn't have those handy features. Instead, the Web had frequent 404 error messages when links failed to resolve. But the Web had some important features that other hypertext systems didn't have, especially scalability and distributed authorship. Those features turned out to be much more important to us than link management.

Linked Data is analogous because it doesn't resolve long-standing problems with distributed data management. Worse, it even introduces new problems, such as requiring that at least some data elements be named with complex-looking web addresses that make data formats harder to read and write. As with the Web, we're going to make the case in this book that the benefits strongly outweigh the detriments. Specifically, we're going to show you how Linked Data can be used to maintain the context that's so often lost when you publish data via other mechanisms. You can even layer that context back onto your data after the fact, which in turn allows new ways for your data to be used by people you may never meet. As with the Web, we think you'll come to love it once you understand it.

1.3 Linked Data in action

The techniques of Linked Data give us a new answer to an age-old question: how can we share our knowledge with others? Linked Data is a general-purpose concept. Literally anything can be described by Linked Data.

Linked Data places structured data on the World Wide Web so that it may be found, shared, and combined with other people's data. Linked Data frees structured data from proprietary containers so anyone may use it.

1.3.1 Freeing data

For most of history we confused information with the containers it came in. Even though all we really cared about was the information inside the containers, we built institutions dedicated to the preservation of the form, not the information. The earliest libraries protected scrolls, rolls, and books, not the words inside. Librarians limited access to the containers so they would last longer.

Eventually, we freed content by turning it into bits of information that could be shipped around the internet. That has many advantages, but we recognize that libraries and bookstores will never be the same. This book was being written during the year that Borders, one of the largest bookstore chains in the United States, declared bankruptcy and shuttered hundreds of stores. Local libraries have drastically changed their offerings, now providing, in addition to books, internet access, as well as music and videos and audio books for checking out. Libraries hold classes, rent space to clubs, and desperately try to maintain relevance to constituents in the face of Google, Apple, and Amazon.

Music has undergone the same transition, from selling containers to selling bits of information that may be played on a variety of devices, from iPods to computers to home stereos. All of these things happened because of the World Wide Web.

Where is your data in the age of the Web? Your data, like the books and music of a few years ago, is mostly stuck in proprietary containers, such as relational databases and spreadsheets. Your data is generally read via the containers in which it was created, whether relational databases or spreadsheet programs. Your data is hierarchical, and so are the systems that support it. The BBC worked around this problem in a novel way by both pulling information from the Web and curating it to ensure its accuracy.

Yet, because hierarchical data doesn't combine easily, you have information silos. Artificially separating information into containers means you have to combine the information in your head when you want to use data from more than one source. If you try to combine information from various sources, you generally lose track of where the components came from.

Sometimes you want your data to be in proprietary containers and protected from prying eyes. Your personal financial information is a good example. But you still want to perform financial transactions via the Web, and it would be easier if your bank used common formats to move your data, just as they already use HTTP to serve web pages. Other times you want your data to be open and free, such as when you wish to determine which factories near your house are polluting or which artist produced a new hit song.

How can you free your data like you freed your books and music? One answer is to move data to the World Wide Web. Just as the Web enables you to link related documents, it allows you to link related data, especially if everyone shares a common data format and means of accessing it.

1.3.2   *Linked Data with Google rich snippets and Facebook likes*

You have almost assuredly seen the benefits of Linked Data, although you may not have realized that Linked Data was behind them. Facebook's Like button,[1] Google's enhanced search results, and the BBC's beautiful wildlife and music pages are all examples of Linked Data in action.

For instance, Google introduced rich snippets[2] (figure 1.2) in 2009, which provide enhanced search results.

Salad - **Thai** Green **Mango Salad** Recipe

★★★★★ 5 reviews - Total cook time: 20 mins
You asked for a one-page printable version of my step-by-step Green **Mango Salad** recipe, so here it is! This salad will blow you away with its ...
thaifood.about.com/od/thaisnacks/r/greenmangosalad.htm -
Cached - Similar

Figure 1.2   Google's rich snippets provide nicely formatted search results that increase user click-through rates by 15–30%.

---

[1]   Facebook developers, Like button plugin, https://developers.facebook.com/docs/reference/plugins/like/.

[2]   Google webmaster tools, "About rich snippets and structured data," June 5, 2013, https://support.google.com/Webmasters/bin/answer.py?hl=en&answer=99170.

The rich snippets program is powered by a form of Linked Data known as the Resource Description Framework in Attributes (RDFa). RDFa is a way of encoding meaning in web pages and will be covered later at length. It's one format for Linked Data. For example, a telephone number on a web page is readable by people, but by marking up the number with HTML attributes that are hidden in a browser's display, Google's search engine can also determine that it is a telephone number. Google can use that information to construct more targeted search results. Best Buy, the large consumer electronics retailer, has reported that the use of RDFa resulted in the a 15%–30% increase in click-through rate for its Google results.

Facebook introduced its Like button in April 2010. When a user clicks a Like button on a web page, that user's Facebook profile is updated to show that they liked the thing that page talks about—be it an article, a movie, or a restaurant. The Like button (figure 1.3) is powered by RDFa.

RDFa is part of a family of standards for describing structured data known as the Resource Description Framework (RDF). RDF is *not* a data format; RDF defines a simple way of expressing relationships between arbitrary data elements that may be serialized in a variety of standard formats. RDF provides a common data model for Linked Data and is particularly suited for representing data on the Web. Linked Data uses RDF as its data model and represents it in one of several syntaxes. There is also a standard query language called SPARQL. The RDF data model will be described later in this chapter and more fully in chapter 2. Later chapters will show you how to use both the data formats and the query language in your Linked Data projects.

👍 Like   f   Joanne Spear, Mark West and 91 others like this.

Figure 1.3   The Facebook Like button can be placed on any page on the Web. Facebook uses this to connect pages outside Facebook to the Facebook social graph.

1.3.3   *Linked Data to the rescue at the BBC*

Now let's turn our attention to the BBC and how its development team used Linked Data to gather information from the Web, ensure its accuracy, and reuse it to automatically create deep and complex websites.

The data needed by the BBC already existed on public services scattered around the Web. The BBC realized that it could collect and repurpose some of this data to more rapidly build its new sites.

The BBC uses Linked Data to generate web presences for three of its web properties: BBC Programmes (http://www.bbc.co.uk/programmes), BBC Music (http://www.bbc.co.uk/music), and Wildlife Finder (http://www.bbc.co.uk/nature/wildlife). Web presences for more than 1,500 daily television and radio broadcasts are created in BBC Programmes alone. To make such a tall order practical, the development team uses public data that already exists on the Web.

The BBC collects, filters, and reuses Linked Data from various sources, including the World Wildlife Fund, MusicBrainz (http://musicbrainz.org/), and the DBpedia project. For example, DBpedia extracts structured data from Wikipedia (the parts of a

Wikipedia page you see in the upper-right corner of their pages) and converts it into Linked Data, as shown in figure 1.4. The BBC then uses DBpedia's Linked Data to enhance information presented about musical artists and wildlife species discussed in its broadcasts. Linked Data gathered from other sites is managed in a similar way. Because Linked Data shares a common data model (discussed in chapter 2), the data from those sites may be immediately combined.

In using Linked Data, the BBC has turned traditional content-management concepts on their heads. If BBC editors find an error or need to make a change, instead of making the change on their own site, they often make the change on someone else's website. BBC editors curate third-party Web content to make their own site more factually correct, while improving our common knowledge resources. Of course, the BBC editors can do this only because they are allowed to write into sites like Wikipedia.

The BBC's use of the Web of Data is both innovative and immensely useful to its audience. Before BBC Programmes started using Linked Data, only a few of the network's most popular broadcasts had a Web presence.

Developers outside the BBC also benefit from the organization's approach by being able to access and reuse Linked Data published by the BBC. Have you ever wanted to make a new web page from information you found on multiple web pages? Linked Data gives you a standard way to do just that.

The self-descriptive nature of Linked Data has many positive side effects. A not-so-obvious one is that of serendipitous reuse. A Linked Data publisher might expose

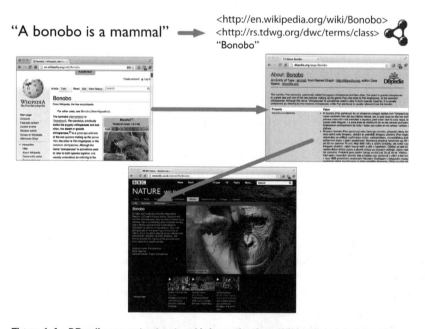

Figure 1.4   DBpedia converts structured information from Wikipedia's info boxes into Linked Data. The BBC uses content from DBpedia and other Linked Data sources to create three of its web properties (BBC Wildlife Finder is shown).

their data with a certain goal or purpose in mind, but it's up to you to determine how and in which way you want to use the data.

The Wikimedia Foundation, which operates Wikipedia, didn't know that the BBC wanted to use their data. The volunteer editors of Wikipedia didn't think about the BBC when they created an article about bonobos. The BBC didn't coordinate with DBpedia in order to use their data, nor did the academics who created DBpedia coordinate with Wikipedia when they created DBpedia. We say that Linked Data enables *cooperation without coordination.*

The BBC found the data they wanted to use on the Web, probably via a traditional full-text search engine like Google or perhaps using a Linked Data search engine like Sindice (http://sindice.com). Linked Data made their job relatively easy once they found the information they needed.

The remainder of this book will show you how organizations large and small can use Linked Data to enhance their content, integrate data from other sites, and allow their data to be reused by others.

1.4 The Linked Data principles

Linked Data uses the Resource Description Framework data model and other standards related to RDF, just as it uses HTTP. Linked Data is built upon RDF but is not the same as RDF. Linked Data is separated from RDF by the four Linked Data principles:

- Use URIs as names for things.
- Use HTTP URIs so that people can look up those names.
- When someone looks up a URI, provide useful information, using the standards (RDF*, SPARQL).[3]
- Include links to other URIs, so people can discover more things.

NOTE Tim Berners-Lee, the inventor of the Web and the progenitor of the Linked Open Data project, proposed the four Linked Data principles. You can read more about his thoughts at http://www.w3.org/DesignIssues/ LinkedData.html.

Let's look at each of the four rules in order.

1.4.1 Principle 1: Use URIs as names for things

The first Linked Data principle deals with identifying things. If you can't identify a thing, you can't talk about it. The underlying technology we'll use to identify things is probably already familiar to you. You may know it by its full name: *Universal Resource Identifiers* (URIs). URIs used to name things in Linked Data are a generalized version of the URLs used to locate web pages in the browser. In other words, all URLs are URIs but not the other way around. A URI is a universally unique name; a URL is a special type of URI that resolves on the Web.

---

[3] The term *RDF** is sometimes used to refer to the entire family of RDF standards.

You're already familiar with HTTP URLs. They're the type of URLs most commonly found on the Web. You type one into your browser's address bar, and you get a web page back. Your browser can also handle other types of URLs, such as those for the File Transfer Protocol (FTP), whose URLs start with ftp://. You might also have seen the file: URL used for accessing files on your local disk.

Just as URLs unambiguously locate web pages so that everyone arrives at the same document when typing in a certain URL, Linked Data's use of URIs provides the means to name things unambiguously.

> **NOTE** When you look at the URI specification (RFC 3986, available via http://tools.ietf.org/html/rfc3986), you might wonder why it's called Uniform Resource Identifier there rather than Universal Resources Identifier. This has historical reasons, and if you're interested in the details, read Tim Berners-Lee's design document, "Web Architecture from 50,000 feet," www.w3.org/DesignIssues/Architecture.html.

To sum up, in order to be able to talk about things, you must be able to identify them. You use URIs to identify things in Linked Data. A thing can be virtually anything: concrete things like a book, a person, or a gene, but also more abstract things like love or war, or even other data representations such as a certain row in a CSV file or a table in a relational database.

You can actually find a URI for the concepts love and war. The DBpedia project has modified URLs from the Wikipedia entries to create http://dbpedia.org/page/Love and http://dbpedia.org/page/War. Linked Data describing those concepts can be found via links at the bottom of those pages.

1.4.2   *Principle 2: Use HTTP URIs so people can look up those names*

It's good to be able to talk about things on a worldwide scale and unambiguously. But you could be tempted to use other identification schemes to name things. For example, books are commonly identified by International Standard Book Numbers (ISBN). The ISBN for Charles Dickens' *The Old Curiosity Shop* is 0140437428. You could make a URI out of that like isbn:0140437428. Now, try to paste this URI into your browser and see what happens. The browser will complain that it doesn't know how to handle it, because it isn't a type of URI that it implements. This is what the second Linked Data principle is all about. If you use HTTP URIs, you can choose to make them resolvable on the Web.

1.4.3   *Principle 3: When someone looks up a URI, provide useful information*

Any HTTP URI can be typed into a web browser, and the browser will know what to do with it. It parses the URI to find the host and port number to use and then attempts to establish an HTTP connection. It requests the resource identified by the path portion of the URI. If the remote server responds affirmatively by returning a resource representation such as a web page, then that particular URI is also a URL. It's resolvable on the Web. The third rule recommends that your identifiers resolve on the Web often, if not all the time. When you create a URI to name a thing, you should either refer to an existing web resource or make up your own. In either case, you want your URIs to resolve to useful descriptions about the thing you've named.

For example, consider Galway Airport. Listing 1.1 gives the URI for the Galway Airport as http://dbpedia.org/resource/Galway_Airport. Try putting that into a web browser, and you'll get redirected to a human-readable version of an RDF document that describes the airport. If you'd like a much friendlier version of the same information, scroll to the bottom of the page and you'll see a link to Wikipedia: http://en.wikipedia.org/wiki/Galway_Airport.

> **Listing 1.1   Example schema for the figure 1.6 spreadsheet in Turtle format**

```
@prefix rdf: <http://www.w3.org/1999/02/22-rdf-syntax-ns#> .
@prefix rdfs: <http://www.w3.org/2000/01/rdf-schema#> .
@prefix dc: <http://purl.org/dc/terms/> .
@prefix loc: <http://www.daml.org/2001/10/html/airport-ont#> .
@prefix eg: <http://example.com/> .
@prefix qb: <http://purl.org/linked-data/cube#> .
@prefix xsd: <http://www.w3.org/2001/XMLSchema#> .
@prefix sdmxa: <http://purl.org/linked-data/sdmx/2009/attribute#> .
@prefix sdmx-measure: <http://purl.org/linked-data/sdmx/2009/measure#> .
```

Prefix information (to abbreviate the way you write long URIs)

```
<http://example.com/my_temperature_data>
    rdfs:label "Temperature observations";
    rdfs:comment "Temperature observations at Galway Airport";
    loc:location <http://dbpedia.org/resource/Galway_Airport>;
    dc:creator "Michael Hausenblas".
```

The location (Galway Airport)

The spreadsheet's URL

A short human-readable label

A longer human-readable comment describing the resource

The author's, or creator's, name

```
eg:day a rdf:Property, qb:MeasureProperty;
    rdfs:label "day"@en;
    rdfs:subPropertyOf sdmx-measure:obsValue;
    sdmxa:unitMeasure <http://dbpedia.org/resource/Day> ;
    rdfs:range xsd:date .
```

The precise definition of what you mean by "day"

```
eg:temperature a rdf:Property, qb:MeasureProperty;
    rdfs:label "temperature"@en;
    rdfs:subPropertyOf sdmx-measure:obsValue;
    sdmxa:unitMeasure <http://dbpedia.org/resource/Celsius> ;
    rdfs:range xsd:decimal .
```

The precise definition of what you mean by "temperature"

The DBpedia project turns structured data in Wikipedia into RDF. Later we'll show you how to access the RDF. For now, notice that we used a URI to name the airport, that we used an HTTP URI, and that it resolves to a readable description of the place in question.

1.4.4   *Principle 4: Include links to other URIs*

What makes Linked Data "linked"? Just as web pages are more useful if they contain hyperlinks to related information, data is more useful if it links to related data, documents, and descriptions. The fourth rule makes this idea explicit: Your data becomes Linked Data when it links to related resources. Because you used resolvable HTTP URIs to publish your data (you did, right?), other people can link to your data. The ability to follow these links allows people to surf the Web of Data just as they can surf the Web of Documents.

An example of this principle at work can be seen in listing 1.1. That listing includes links to the DBpedia description of Galway Airport and the unit of measure for days.

1.5   *The Linking Open Data project*

Most of the data that we'll use in this book is freely available on the Web. It's rather amazing to think that open-content projects as diverse as encyclopedias and dictionaries, government statistics, information regarding chemical and biological collections and endangered species, bibliographic data, music artists and information about their songs, and academic research papers are all available using the same data format and reachable using the same API! This is all due to the Linking Open Data (LOD) project.

The LOD project[4] is a community activity started in 2007 by the W3C's Semantic Web Education and Outreach (SWEO) Interest Group (www.w3.org/wiki/SweoIG). The project's stated goal is to "make data freely available to everyone."

The collection of Linked Data published on the Web is referred to as the *LOD cloud*. A recent attempt at visualizing the LOD cloud is shown in figure 1.5.

NOTE   *LOD* is typically pronounced by saying each letter, like "ell oh dee."

Here are some quick facts regarding the LOD cloud.

- The LOD cloud has doubled in size every 10 months since 2007 and currently consists of more than 300 datasets from various domains (http://lod-cloud.net/state/). All of this data is available for use by developers!
- As of late 2011, the LOD cloud contained over 295 datasets from various domains, including geography, media, government, and life sciences. In total the LOD cloud contained over 31 billion data items and some 500 million links between them.
- The LOD cloud has grown so large that no attempt was made to visualize it in 2012.
- More than 40% of the Linked Data in the LOD cloud is contributed by governments (mainly from the United Kingdom and the United States), followed by geographical data (22%) and data from the life sciences domain (almost 10%).
- Life sciences (including some large pharmaceutical companies) contribute over 50% of the links between datasets. Publication data (from books, journals, and the like) comes in second with 19%, and the media domain (the BBC, the *New York Times*, and others) provides another 12%.
- The original data owners themselves publish one-third of the data contained in the LOD cloud, whereas third parties publish 67%. For example, many universities republish data from their respective governments in Linked Data formats, often cleaning and enhancing data descriptions in the process.

---

4 "Linked Data—Connect Distributed Data across the Web," http://linkeddata.org/.

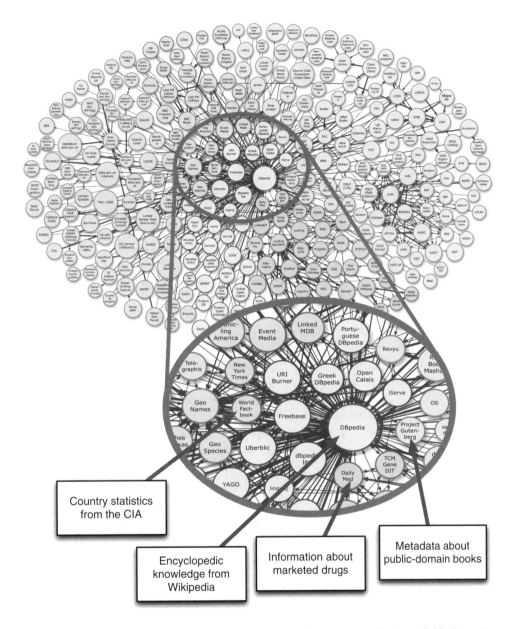

Figure 1.5   The Linked Open Data cloud in late 2011. The circles represent freely available datasets and the arrows represent links between them.

1.6   *Describing data*

The LOD cloud is not just a collection of data silos. Linked Data offers something not found in systems like relational databases or content management systems: *discoverability*. Imagine your client provides you with a spreadsheet that contains certain data. In order to use this data in your application, you'd need to know what the columns

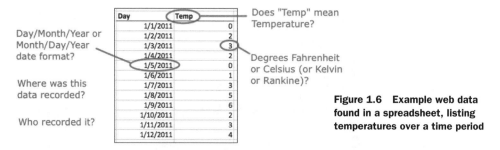

Figure 1.6   Example web data found in a spreadsheet, listing temperatures over a time period

represent. Typically, looking at a column header gives you an idea of what's going on, as shown in figure 1.6.

The problem with the data in the figure is that without more information from the person who created it, you really don't know what it means.

You could call your client and ask if the temperature is given in Celsius, or you might guess it from the range of the values. Too often the information you seek is no longer available—it was lost or the person who knows is not around. Descriptive column headers would help but still not give you all the information you'd like to have, such as where the data was collected and who collected it. You'd rather have the sort of schema information shown in figure 1.7.

Whereas figure 1.6 demonstrates a problem with most spreadsheet data—its lack of context—figure 1.7 solves that problem with annotations that provide sufficient context for some new person to understand the author's intent.

Linked Data can provide the schema information for your spreadsheet and also allow you to publish the data itself in an open, extensible format. It also provides you a way to link to other, related data, anywhere on the Web, in an unambiguous way. *Dereferenceable identifiers*, web addresses, are used for both schema information and data resources. Web addresses provide you a way to get to schema documentation and to related data. You simply follow the links, just like on the rest of the Web. This is discoverability in action.

Linked Data places itself in context by following the precepts of the Web: data elements are named using HTTP URIs, and those URIs can be resolved to discover more information about them. Importantly, and it bears repeating, Linked Data should contain links to other information on the Web. These Linked Data principles are discussed in detail in section 1.4.

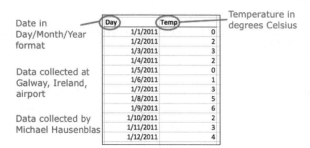

Figure 1.7   Example schema information for the data in figure 1.6

The Linked Data principles provide a common API for data on the Web. This is much more convenient for developers than the many separate (and differently designed) APIs currently published by major websites such as Flickr, Twitter, or Amazon.

Listing 1.1 demonstrates how you might use Linked Data to create a schema for the spreadsheet data shown in figure 1.6. Don't worry that it looks unfamiliar or even complicated! It's actually quite easy, and we'll show you how it's created and read. Once you get used to it, it's much easier to understand than, say, XML or other people's code. You only need to follow a few simple rules.

You needn't go through listing 1.1 character by character quite yet (unless you want to). We presented it to give you a feel for what Linked Data looks like and how it's published (as a file or in a database, either of which may be queried via the SPARQL query language).

Let's dive more deeply into the code. We mentioned that Linked Data uses RDF as a data model. A single RDF statement describes *two things and a relationship between them*. Technically, this is called an *Entity-Attribute-Value* (EAV) data model, although Linked Data people often call the three elements in a statement the *subject*, the *predicate*, and the *object*. Those terms correlate directly to an entity, an attribute, and a value. For example, we might want to say that the title of this book is *Linked Data*. Figure 1.8 shows how that can be done in RDF by using the URI for the book, a well-known relationship defining the title property, and a literal string for the name.

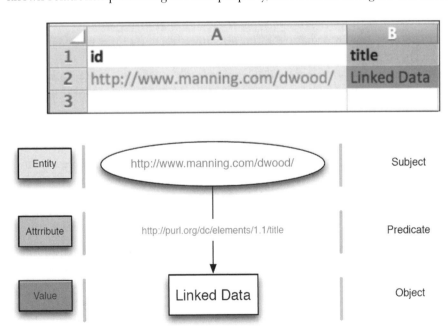

Figure 1.8 Example RDF statement

An entity (or subject) can be anything that we can name by a URI, such as a person, a book, a car, or a web page. In this case, the subject is the URI that uniquely identifies this book. An entity's attribute (or predicate) relates the subject to another entity or provides information about the entity itself (which we call a property of the subject). In this case, we're using a relationship for the book's title as the predicate and the book's title as the object. Relations and properties are the objects of an RDF statement. Through this standardized data model, an API is created that's consistent over all Linked Data sources. In other words, you only have to learn the Linked Data model once and you can use any kind of data source that complies with it. Anytime you want to know what a predicate means, you can type its URI into a web browser and look for information about it.

This statement excerpted from listing 1.1 shows a simple "triple," or RDF statement:

```
<http://example.com/my_temperature_data> rdfs:label "Temperature observations";
```

`<http://example.com/my_temperature_data>` is a URI representing and perhaps pointing to our sample spreadsheet, which forms the entity (subject) of an RDF statement. The two components in `rdfs:label "Temperature observations";` are the attribute (predicate) and the property (object) of the first RDF statement. In this case, we're saying that the spreadsheet may be given a human-readable label of `"Temperature observations"`.

`rdfs:comment "Temperature observations at Galway Airport";` provides another attribute and property for the same subject, which forms another RDF statement. We can keep adding information about our spreadsheet that way until we're finished.

There's no restriction in RDF about what you can link to or describe. That's why RDF is a framework for *describing resources*. RDF statements tend to create graphs of metadata. In other words, they needn't form hierarchical relationships. You'll often hear the term *RDF graph* because of this.

1.7   *RDF: a data model for Linked Data*

Linked Data is structured data. To be more precise, we're talking about structured data based on a certain data model: the Resource Description Framework data model as defined by the W3C (http://w3.org/). As a convention, we identify things using HTTP URIs and then provide information about them when an HTTP URI is resolved.

Just like on the "normal" Web (which we tend to call the Web of Documents to separate it from the Web of Data), resolving an HTTP URI generally means to perform an HTTP GET request on it. A GET request is the simplest of the actions that a client can take using HTTP. A GET request is issued by a client to say to a server, "Please send me back whatever you know about the URI I'm giving you." You could use a web browser to do that or a command-line web client such as the curl utility, which is an abbreviation for "Client for URLs."[5] You can get the DBpedia page for a bonobo (based on the Wikipedia page for the same subject) in HTML format at http://dbpedia.org/page/Bonobo.

---

[5] The download wizard for curl, a cross-platform command-line web client, http://curl.haxx.se/dlwiz/.

DBpedia allows you to download the Linked Data about a bonobo by changing "page" to "data" and appending the appropriate file extension:

```
$ curl -L http://dbpedia.org/data/Bonobo.n3
```

In this case, the file extension .n3 is one of several used for Linked Data. The publisher of a URI has the right to create it however they like, subject only to certain rules in the HTTP specification regarding legal characters. In the previous code snippet, DBpedia decided to call its server dbpedia.org. The commonly used style www.dbpedia.org redirects to dbpedia.org. The organization chose to put all its HTML entries under the page/ path and to assign each entry the same identifier used in Wikipedia (in our snippet's case, Bonobo). They also chose a convention to construct their Linked Data URLs.

The `curl` command means "Resolve the URI and put whatever comes back from the server onto the standard output (the –L means to follow any HTTP redirects encountered)." If you execute this command in a console, it will print RDF data describing a bonobo in a serialization called N3. That's because the given URI identifies the concept of a bonobo, and you expect to get back a Linked Data description of a bonobo when you resolve it.

You'll see a lot of Linked Data in this book, and almost all of it will be in a format known as Turtle. Turtle is a minimal syntax for representing the RDF data model and is meant to be easy to read. Turtle is a subset of N3, so DBpedia chooses to use the .n3 file extension for both formats. Chapter 2 covers more detail on RDF data formats.

The entire data dump is too big and not interesting enough to show here, but in the following listing you can see an excerpt that will give you an idea of what it looks like. Just be aware that if you try the given `curl` command, the data you will get back will be larger and you may need to look through it to find the part we extracted for this example.

> **Listing 1.2   Excerpt of the Linked Data about bonobos in Turtle format**

```
@prefix dbpedia:        <http://dbpedia.org/resource/> .
@prefix dbpedia-owl:    <http://dbpedia.org/ontology/> .
@prefix foaf:           <http://xmlns.com/foaf/0.1/> .

dbpedia:Bonobo     rdf:type     dbpedia-owl:Eukaryote ,
                   dbpedia-owl:Mammal ,
                   dbpedia-owl:Animal .                      Name of the animal in
                                                             English ("A Bonobo has
dbpedia:Bonobo     foaf:name    "Bonobo"@en ;      ◁─────    a name of 'Bonobo'")
                   foaf:depiction <http://upload.wikimedia.org/wikipedia/
    commons/a/a6/Bonobo-04.jpg> ;
```

If you're familiar with key-value structured data (as you find in configuration files), then you might already have guessed how it works.

We deal with a thing in listing 1.2 called `dbpedia:Bonobo`. That thing has a name of "bonobo" in the English language. There is a picture (a "depiction") of it at a URL on Wikimedia.org, and it's of several types: It's an animal, a mammal, and a eukaryote.

The prefixes at the top of listing 1.2 are just ways to shorten URIs for easier reading.

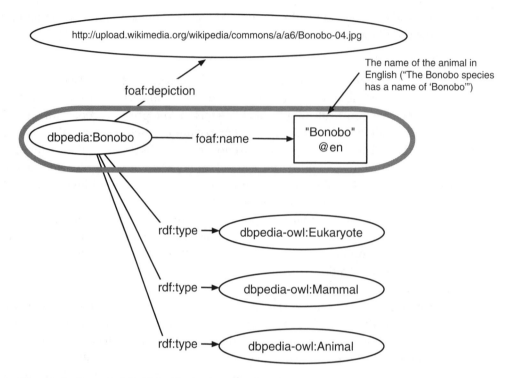

Figure 1.9   Excerpt of the Linked Data about bonobos shown as a graph

Another way to represent this RDF data snippet is shown in figure 1.9, this time visualized as a graph. In RDF, you either have literal values, such as the animal's name, or you have a link to another thing, such as its picture.

The take-home message from this section is simple. When looking up an HTTP URI for a Linked Data resource, you can expect to receive structured data in some RDF serialization format. We'll mostly show you data in the RDF serialization format called Turtle because it's easiest to read.

1.8   *Anatomy of a Linked Data application*

Now that you're equipped with the Linked Data principles and an overview of RDF, it's time to peer beneath the covers of a Linked Data application. You'll look closely at an existing Linked Data application published on the Web and examine the publicly accessible information about it, such as its HTTP endpoints, HTML source code, and associated JavaScript.

The application you'll explore is the U.S. Environmental Protection Agency's Linked Data service. As of this writing, the EPA publishes data about 2.9 million facilities in the United States and roughly 100,000 chemical substances as Linked Data. About 1% of the facilities have reported annual estimates of pollution for more than 25 years, and that information is also available as Linked Data. Figure 1.10 shows a typical facility page.[6] This one is for the Browns Ferry nuclear power plant near Decatur, Alabama.

NOTE The Linked Data application described in this section was in quality control testing at the time this book was printed. A portion of the EPA Linked Data site has been duplicated at http://linkeddatadeveloper.com so you can see how it was created.

The first thing to note is that the underlying data comes from several different systems. The Wikipedia Foundation has collected pictures and abstracts about many of the larger facilities, including Browns Ferry. The EPA doesn't hold that information itself. The page also contains general information about the facility, such as its mailing address and reports of pollution it generated. Mailing addresses and pollution information are held in different EPA databases, and they weren't designed to work

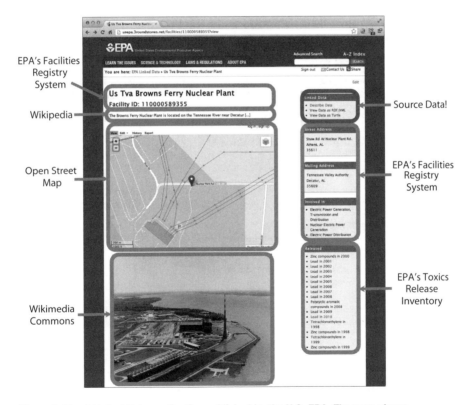

Figure 1.10 A Linked Data application published by the U.S. EPA. The page shown describes the Browns Ferry nuclear power plant near Decatur, Alabama. Note the different data sources combined to form the page.

---

6 Source of the page reproduced in figure 1.10, http://linkeddatadeveloper.com/facilities/110000589355?view.

together. Linked Data was used as a common data language, a *lingua franca*, to facilitate combining that information.

1.8.1 Accessing a facility's Linked Data

Next, you should try clicking the links in the upper-right corner of the page under the heading Linked Data. All three links will show the data used to create the page, each one using a different Linked Data format.

The top link is labeled Describe Data and goes to an HTML view of the raw data that's nicely laid out. This view is not a standard Linked Data mechanism, so you can safely ignore it for now. It comes from a Linked Data server called Callimachus that we use for our examples in chapter 9. The next two links give you access to the underlying Linked Data in two commonly used standard formats: RDF/XML and Turtle. RDF/XML is, unsurprisingly, an XML format. Turtle is a much less verbose syntax and is easier for people to read.

If you look at the HTML source code for the Browns Ferry page, you'll see how the Linked Data is accessed. The following listing shows the relevant HTML and listing 1.4 shows the JavaScript click handlers.

Listing 1.3 HTML for Linked Data elements shown in figure 1.10

```
<h3>Linked Data</h3>
<ul>
    <li><a href="?describe">Describe Data</a></li>          Link to "Describe
    <li><a href="#" id="rdfxml">View Data as RDF/XML</a></li>   Data" function
    <li><a href="#" id="turtle">View Data as Turtle</a></li>
</ul>                                                         Link to RDF/XML
                                          Link to Turtle click  click function
                                          function handler       handler
```

Listing 1.4 JavaScript click function handlers for HTML elements shown in listing 1.3

```
jQuery(function($) {
    $('#rdfxml').click(function(event) {
        event.preventDefault();
        var request = $.ajax({
          url: '?describe',
          headers: { Accept : "application/rdf+xml" }        Set the HTTP
        });                                                   request header for
                                                              RDF/XML format
        request.done(function() {
            var win = window.open('', document.URL);
            win.document.write('<pre>\n' + request.responseText.replace(/</g,
  '&lt;').replace(/>/g, '&gt;') + '\n</pre>');
        });

        request.fail(function() {
            alert("We're sorry, the request could not be completed at this
  time. Please try again shortly.");
        });
    });
```

```
$("#turtle").click(function(event) {
    event.preventDefault();
    var request = $.ajax({
        url: '?describe',
        headers: { Accept : "text/turtle" }
    });

    request.done(function() {
        var win = window.open('', document.URL);
        win.document.write('<pre>\n' + request.responseText.replace(/</g,
    '&lt;').replace(/>/g, '&gt;') + '\n</pre>');
    });

    request.fail(function() {
        alert("We're sorry, the request could not be completed at this
    time. Please try again shortly.");
    });
});
});
```

Set the HTTP request header for Turtle format

A careful reading of listing 1.4 will show you that the Linked Data for the Browns Ferry page is accessed using the *same URL*. The URL was nearly the same as the URL used for the default HTML rendering of the page (the HTTP query string ?describe was added), but that's an implementation detail of the particular server involved. The details of URL construction aren't important here and may vary across sites.

Different HTTP Accept headers were used in the three requests.

- For HTML, use Accept: text/html
- For RDF/XML, use Accept: application/rdf+xml
- For Turtle, use Accept: text/turtle

Accept headers are used to inform a server what type of formats a web client can accept. This is known as HTTP content negotiation and is often referred to as *conneg*. Not all Linked Data sites provide data access via conneg, but many do.

Conneg allows you to request the data directly instead of relying on a web page author to make links for you. You can get the Linked Data for the Browns Ferry page in Turtle format by performing an HTTP GET on the URL and using the Accept header for Turtle:

```
$ curl -L -H 'Accept: text/turtle'
    http://linkeddatadeveloper.com/facilities/110000589355?describe
```

The ability to get access to the underlying data used to create a web page is a hallmark of Linked Data applications. Most Linked Data applications expose their data for further reuse. Users of a Linked Data site can decide whether they like the way information was presented or grab the data and create their own. They can even build a more complicated application by combining that data with data from other sites or other applications. *Linked Data frees data from application UIs.*

1.8.2 *Creating the user interface from Linked Data*

We said that the Browns Ferry page was built entirely from Linked Data. Let's look at the data to see how the UI was created. A small extract of the Linked Data will be enough to prove the point. The next listing shows an extract that contains information used to create the map, show the picture of the plant, and show a URI used to get information about the street address. Again, if you try the given `curl` command, the data you'll get back will be larger and you may need to look through it to find the part we extracted for this example.

Listing 1.5   Extract from the Browns Ferry nuclear power plant Linked Data

```
@prefix foaf: <http://xmlns.com/foaf/0.1/> .
@prefix place: <http://purl.org/ontology/places#> .
@prefix vcard: <http://www.w3.org/2006/vcard/ns#> .

<http://linkeddatadeveloper.com/facilities/110000589355> place:point_on_map
    "34.710917,-87.112"^^place:latlong ;
foaf:depiction
<http://upload.wikimedia.org/wikipedia/commons/a/ab/Browns_ferry_NPP.jpg> ;
vcard:adr
<http://linkeddatadeveloper.com/addresses/
    shawrdatnuclearplantrdathensal35611usa> .
```

Latitude and longitude of the facility

Street address URI

URI of the facility's picture on Wikimedia Commons

The page uses OpenStreetMap (http://openstreetmap.org/) to draw the map. The OpenStreetMap API uses a latitude and a longitude to create a map for a point. The latitude and longitude are available in the data, and that makes it easy to make the call to the OpenStreetMap API.

The picture is even easier to include because the URL for the image we want is also in the data. A simple HTML `image` tag using that URL in its `src` attribute is all we need to include the image.

Now for the fun part. We want to display the street address and can see on the page that the address is Shaw Rd. at Nuclear Plant Rd., Athens, AL 35611. But the data only shows a URL for the street address. How can we get to the details of the information for the address? By resolving its URL! Try this:

```
$ curl -L -H 'Accept: text/turtle' http://linkeddatadeveloper.com/addresses/
    shawrdatnuclearplantrdathensal35611usa
```

Resolving the address URL returns all the data for that address, including information that wasn't used in the UI. This illustrates another good reason for using Linked Data: more data is often available than is used in a particular interface. Linked Data allows you to find and use that additional information much more easily than other structured data technologies.

The full street address information is shown in the next listing. Note that it contains a county name (Limestone), a country name (USA), and other information that we didn't previously know.

Listing 1.6   Linked Data for the Browns Ferry nuclear power plant street address

```
@prefix rdf: <http://www.w3.org/1999/02/22-rdf-syntax-ns#> .
@prefix foaf: <http://xmlns.com/foaf/0.1/> .
@prefix vcard: <http://www.w3.org/2006/vcard/ns#> .
@prefix frs: <http://linkeddatadeveloper.com/id/us/fed/agency/epa/frs/schema#> .

<http://linkeddatadeveloper.com/addresses/
     shawrdatnuclearplantrdathensal35611usa> a vcard:Address ;
   vcard:street-address "Shaw Rd At Nuclear Plant Rd." ;
   vcard:locality "Athens" ;
   vcard:region "Alabama" ;
   frs:county_name "Limestone" ;                  <─── The county name
   frs:fips_county_code "01083" ;
   frs:state_code "AL" ;
   frs:state <http://linkeddatadeveloper.com/states/AL> ;
   vcard:postal-code "35611" ;
   vcard:country-name "USA" ;                      <─── The country name
   foaf:based_near <zip:35611> , <zip:35611> .
```

Next, let's look at how Linked Data applications can be distributed across multiple servers. There are lots of ways to segment data and applications. One of the easiest is by using the humble hyperlink to good advantage.

The Browns Ferry page contains reports of pollution in the lower right of the page under the heading Released. Click the link that reads "Lead in 2001." That's a report of lead pollution that was filed by the owners of the facility in 2001. Figure 1.11 shows the resulting page.

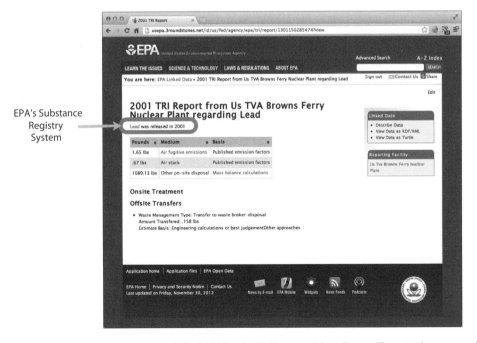

Figure 1.11   An HTML rendering of the 2001 lead pollution report from Browns Ferry nuclear power plant

Figure 1.11 summarizes the amount of lead pollution released from Browns Ferry during 2001. You can see a hyperlink to Lead circled in the upper left of the page. That link leads to a page describing the chemical properties of lead and synonyms for the chemical name. Chemical information comes from a completely different dataset and therefore forms a natural segmentation point for scaling.

The point here is subtle and intentionally hard to see: the page about the substance lead could be on any server. The humble web hyperlink allows you to segment your data and your Linked Data applications in any way you wish. They could all be on the same server or they could be on hundreds or thousands of servers. All you would need to do is to link to the appropriate locations. You could use the hyperlinks on your web pages directly from the Linked Data or redirect them as you wish by building new links from the Linked Data URIs. All the standard web tools and techniques apply to the creation of Linked Data applications.

1.9   *Summary*

Linked Data is a set of techniques for publishing and consuming structured data on the Web. It uses the Resource Description Framework as a data model and RDF serializations to express data representations. But Linked Data is not just RDF. Links play a central role in Linked Data. A Linked Dataset should (indeed, must) link to other Linked Data on the Web.

Linked Data uses HTTP URIs to identify things and HTTP to send descriptions of the things from a dataset to a Linked Data consumer, such as a browser or an application.

Linked Data is a general-purpose concept. Literally anything can be described using Linked Data. This chapter showed examples of Linked Data being used by large organizations on the Web and discussed the components of a real-world Linked Data application. Don't forget that Linked Data can also be used in private settings.

Writing applications using Linked Data is no more complicated that using native JSON or XML data sources, but Linked Data is more flexible and limits how many new APIs you need to learn.

RDF: the data model
for Linked Data

This chapter covers

- An introduction to the Resource Description Framework
- RDF as a data model for Linked Data
- RDF formats relevant to Linked Data
- Linked Data vocabularies

Linked Data couldn't exist without a consistent underlying data model. That data model is the Resource Description Framework (RDF). Some people have negative opinions about RDF because they consider it to be overly complicated. Those opinions were generally formed in the early days of RDF and relate to its first, and rather complicated, serialization format based on XML. We hope to show you that RDF is quite simple and introduce you to the variety of different serialization formats that make modern RDF easy to use.

We briefly introduced RDF in chapter 1 and mentioned that *a single RDF statement describes two things and a relationship between them*. Multiple RDF statements can connect to form graphs (not just hierarchies) of information. The only thing that might make RDF seem complicated is that most things and the relationships use URIs to name them.[1] RDF statements may be hard to read in the raw because URIs can be long. Fortunately, many RDF serialization formats have ways to write abbreviations for long URIs.

This chapter describes the RDF data model and how it relates to Linked Data. We'll start by examining the Linked Data principles again, this time as they build on and restrict what can be done in RDF. We'll then describe the RDF data model in some detail, including how to find, use, and create RDF vocabularies. RDF vocabularies provide schema information for RDF data and are analogous to the schema in a relational database. Finally, we'll show the four RDF serialization formats that are most commonly used with Linked Data. By the end of this chapter, you'll be comfortable with how Linked Data is written and will start to understand how to write your own.

> **NOTE** RDF is fully described in specifications published by the W3C at http://www.w3.org/standards/techs/rdf.

2.1   *The Linked Data principles extend RDF*

Let's revisit the Linked Data principles, described in chapter 1, in more detail so you can see how the RDF data model is used and how the Linked Data principles restrict that data model for use on the Web.

The first Linked Data principle is "Use URIs as names for things." RDF allows you to name things with either URIs or literals in the object position, such as <http://www.manning.com/dwood/> dc:creator "David Wood", but using URIs is more flexible in that it encourages linking and extension. Literals (such as strings, numbers, or dates) can't be subsequently used as subjects.

Figure 2.1 shows three RDF statements that share the same subject (http://www.manning.com/dwood/) and all use the same predicate (dc:creator). Two of the statements end in literal objects ("David Wood" and "Marsha Zaidman"). The third statement uses a URI in the object position: http://lukeruth.co/me.ttl#Me. That URI resolves on the Web to an RDF document describing Luke Ruth and provides a unique, worldwide, unambiguous web identifier for Luke.

The predicate dc:creator is shorthand for the fairly long URI http://purl.org/dc/elements/1.1/creator. You'll see how each RDF serialization format can abbreviate URIs in section 2.4 RDF formats for Linked Data. For now, note that you can abbreviate any URI you wish by splitting it into a prefix (like http://purl.org/dc/elements/1.1/) and a suffix (creator). You can then assign a short name to the prefix (dc: in this case), so dc:creator becomes synonymous with http://purl.org/dc/elements/1.1/creator. We'll continue to use both long URIs and prefixed URIs throughout our examples so you get used to seeing them. Similarly, any URI can be

---

[1] RDF 1.1 changed URIs to IRIs (Internationalized Resource Identifiers) in 2013. For our purposes, we generally mean the same thing when we say URI or IRI; the differences are subtle. When in doubt, remember that modern RDF and hence Linked Data use IRIs.

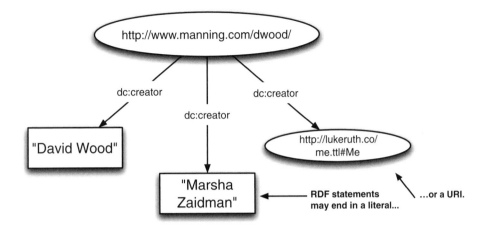

Figure 2.1 Objects in RDF statements can be literals or URIs

assigned a short prefix. The examples in the remainder of this chapter assume the prefixes listed in table 2.1.

Table 2.1 URI prefixes used in the examples, unless otherwise specified

Prefix	Namespace URI
dc:	http://purl.org/dc/elements/1.1/
foaf:	http://xmlns.com/foaf/0.1/
rdf:	http://www.w3.org/1999/02/22-rdf-syntax-ns#
rdfs:	http://www.w3.org/2000/01/rdf-schema#
vcard:	http://www.w3.org/2006/vcard/ns#

Figure 2.2 shows why we often prefer to use URIs as names for things. We can make other statements about Luke because RDF subjects must be URIs, such as his name and things he's interested in. We'd need to change David and Marsha's literals into URIs in order to make more statements about them in the same graph.

The second Linked Data principle is "Use HTTP URIs so people can look up those names." RDF itself doesn't specify the type of URIs to use. You could use an FTP: URI, an ISBN: URI, or even one that you make up yourself. Linked Data specifically requires the use of HTTP URIs so you can tie data into the Web. Linked Data URIs should be resolvable and intrinsically part of the Web.

Try resolving Luke Ruth's URI, shown in figures 2.1 and 2.2, by typing it into a web browser's address field. You'll find that it resolves to an RDF document in Turtle format and contains RDF statements about Luke. Even the tiny RDF graph in figure 2.1 is useful

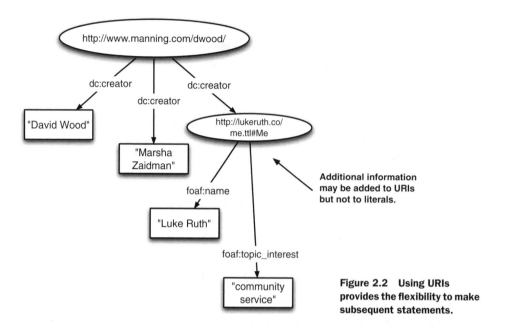

Figure 2.2   Using URIs provides the flexibility to make subsequent statements.

because it points you to more information about Luke. That's the power of Linked Data: getting a small amount of Linked Data leads you to more, maybe much more.

You should make up your own URIs when making your own data. You already know that they should be HTTP URIs. Here are some other guidelines:

- Name things with URIs most of the time.
- Use a DNS domain that you control.
- Use natural keys.
- Make your URIs neutral to implementation details.
- Be cautious with the use of fragment identifiers.

You've already seen how to name things with URIs. Let's look at the remainder of the guidelines in detail. If you own the DNS domain example.com, you can make URIs like http://example.com/some_stuff. Of course, you don't own the domain example.com, so you should use a domain you do own. Making URIs (also known colloquially as "minting" URIs) in someone else's DNS domain is considered extremely rude. Although it's true that RDF allows anyone to say anything about anything (just as the Web does), it's also true that you need to be careful about sources of data (the same as for sources of documents on the Web). Minting URIs that use your own domain and publishing them on your own domain help people to trust your data. This is part of the social contract inherent in Linked Data publishing.

Natural keys are human-readable categories and subidentifiers within a URI that reflect what the identifier describes. Try to use natural keys when creating your URIs so people reading your RDF in its source format (mostly developers) will be able to quickly understand what you're saying. For example, if you're trying to make a URI to describe a particular kind of rye bread loaf in a bakery, you could use a nonnatural key such as a product number (http://paulsbakery.example.com/984d6a) or natural keys (http://paulsbakery.example.com/baked_goods/bread/rye-12). Clearly, the URI with the natural keys is easier on everyone.

Neutral URIs avoid the exposure of implementation details in the URIs. Many, many websites use nonneutral URIs. When you see a site with a URI like http://example.com/index.aspx, you know that it uses Microsoft.NET's ActiveX Server Pages. If the site administrators change the web server infrastructure, all their URIs will change. That can be a problem for people who have bookmarked pages or who have written RDF that uses those URIs. Neutral URIs, by contrast, hide implementation details because exposing them does more harm than good. An example of a neutral URI is http://example.com/2013/03/20/linked-data-book, which does not expose what kind of technology is used to serve the content.

Fragment identifiers are the part of an HTTP URI that follows a hash symbol (#). Fragment identifiers are not passed to web servers by web clients like browsers. That means that if you try to resolve a URI such as http://example.com/id/vocabulary#linked_data, your browser will just send http://example.com/id/vocabulary to the server. The fragment identifier will be processed locally. This is an attempt to protect your privacy. Fragment identifiers are often used in HTML pages to point to a particular section, and there's no reason to tell web server operators which part of a document you particularly want to read. They have enough information about your browsing habits already! Fragment identifiers are used by many Linked Data vocabularies because the vocabulary is often served as a document and the fragment is used to address a particular term within that document.

But fragment identifiers won't work well for all data identifiers. What would happen if you were to ask a web server to see information about a resource named http://example.com/cars#porsche? The server would never receive the fragment #porsche and would thus be likely to return information to you about all cars! That's why we suggest that you use fragment identifiers with caution to avoid unexpected consequences. You don't need to think about what information gets passed to a web server if you avoid their use.

There are legitimate use cases for URIs with and without fragment identifiers. Unless you understand the ramifications inherent in the choice, we recommend that you avoid fragment identifiers when naming resources, but you can choose to use them when creating vocabularies. Figure 2.3 summarizes our URI creation guidelines.

The third Linked Data principle is "When someone looks up a URI, provide useful information." This principle relates Linked Data to related documentation and to anything else that's relevant to it on the Web. You've already seen this in action when you resolved Luke's URI from figure 2.1. You did, right? If not, you really should do it now. We'll wait. RDF doesn't require you to make your URIs resolvable, but Linked Data does because it's just so handy.

The fourth Linked Data principle is "Include links to other URIs." Linked Data isn't just data—it's data with links. Linking is what makes the Linked Data approach

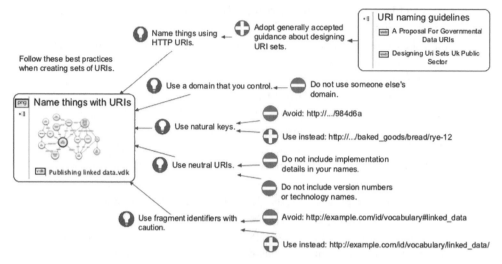

Figure 2.3   How to create your own URIs (credit: Richard Howlett)

better (more flexible and extensible) than other structured data approaches. More links add value, just as with web pages. Figure 2.4 shows how we add more value by

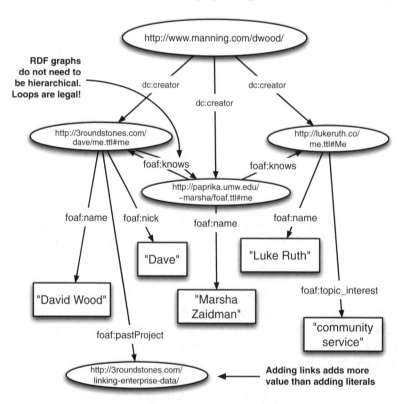

Figure 2.4   More links add value—just like with web pages

including other resolvable URIs in our sample graph. We can arbitrarily extend the information a reader of our graph can access by adding new resolvable URIs. For example, we could add URIs to social media accounts, such as Facebook, LinkedIn, and Twitter, for each of the authors. We could also link to more Linked Data. The URIs you add may be to other data or to the general Web. As with the third principle, RDF doesn't require you to link to other data, but Linked Data does.

Do you remember the Linked Data mug shown in the first chapter? Providing links to other data moves your RDF from 4-Star data to 5-Star data. Creating 5-Star Linked Data should always be your goal.

In this section, you've seen how the Linked Data principles are implemented using RDF as the data model and how the Linked Data principles build on top of RDF. Linked Data encourages you to use HTTP URIs as names, even though RDF allows you to use string literals. Linked Data encourages you to make your URIs resolvable on the Web and for those web pages to say something meaningful. Linked Data encourages you to link to other people's data. Taken together, the Linked Data principles create a Web of Data.

2.2　The RDF data model

Now let's look at RDF in more detail. You've already seen how RDF statements, also called triples, can connect to each other to form graphs and how subjects, predicates, and some objects are named with URIs. We'll now discuss additional details of the data model.

The RDF data model defines what each component of a triple can be, such as a URI or a literal. It also defines other key concepts such as how to restrict literals with data types or in which (human) language they're written. Some components of the data model, named with URIs, can be collected into classes so they may be more easily discovered, searched, or queried. This section describes all of the components of the RDF data model so you become familiar with these terms.

2.2.1　Triples

The RDF triples you've seen so far have been pretty short. There's no restriction in RDF or Linked Data that suggests that you can't have very long literals—sometimes you do. The bonobo example in chapter 1 could easily be extended by pulling in the remainder of the DBpedia data about bonobos. That data includes an abstract and comments in a number of languages, some of which are lengthy. Figure 2.5 shows the addition of an `rdfs:comment` in English to the example graph.

There are practical reasons to avoid very long literal objects in RDF. Most RDF databases (and databases in general) aren't optimized to hold very long objects. In general, you should link to a page holding a lot of data instead of shoving it into a literal object. The definition of "a lot" is up to you.

The bonobo example data all came from Wikipedia, but it isn't necessary to restrict yourself to data from a single source. RDF graphs can be created from many

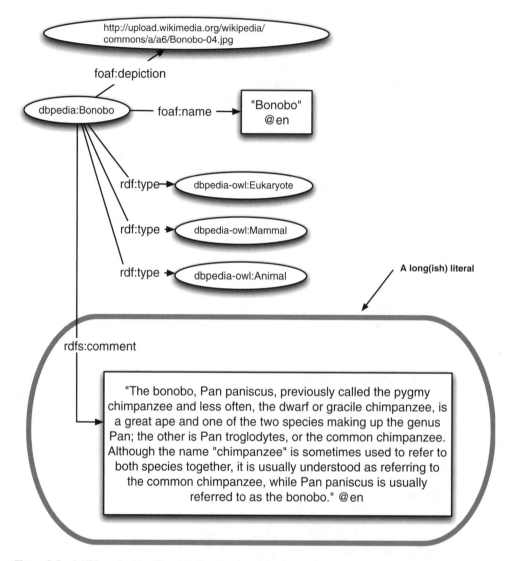

Figure 2.5   Addition of a long literal to the bonobo example graph

sources. For example, you could add a triple to the bonobo example that tells readers to look for more information about bonobos at the Encyclopedia of Life. That is done with the seeAlso relationship from the RDF Schema vocabulary. Figure 2.6 shows you how. Resolving the URI in the object will bring you a nice page about bonobos.

Figure 2.6 Use of `rdfs:seeAlso` to provide links to external resources

2.2.2 *Blank nodes*

Objects of RDF statements can be one more thing other than URIs and literals: blank nodes. A blank node is like a URI without a name and is also sometimes called an anonymous resource. They can be useful when you need to link to a collection of items but don't want to bother making up a URI for it.

You should note that many people avoid using blank nodes. Blank nodes can cause some difficulty when you get them back in query results because you can't query them later. They don't have a name, so you can't resolve them. For this reason, many people just make up URIs whenever they need to and avoid blank nodes altogether. But you need to know about them because other people do use them and you'll see them in data available on the Web.

Figure 2.7 shows the use of a blank node to represent the address of the San Diego Zoo. The zoo has a URI, but the address itself does not. An alternative would be to make up a URI for the address by using the natural keys found in the address information, such as http://example.com/address/usa/california/san_diego (using a DNS domain that you control).

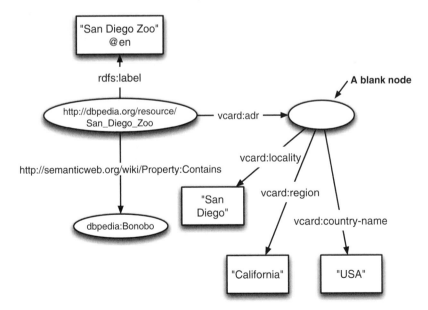

Figure 2.7 Using a blank node to create an address

Some RDF databases and other systems implementing the SPARQL query language for RDF automatically assign URIs to blank nodes so they may be more easily operated upon. This process is known as *skolemization* and is described in RDF 1.1 Concepts and Abstract Syntax (http://www.w3.org/TR/rdf11-concepts/).

2.2.3   *Classes*

RDF resources may be divided into groups called classes using the property `rdf:type` in the RDF Schema (RDFS) standard. RDFS is a vocabulary definition language for RDF and helps to create new RDF vocabularies. The members of a class are known as instances of the class, just as they are in object-oriented programming, although the two concepts are completely different. RDFS classes are themselves RDF resources and are of type `rdfs:Class`. The `rdfs:subClassOf` property may be used to state that one class is a subclass of another. Another vocabulary definition language for RDF is the Web Ontology Language (OWL).[2] OWL has a way to define classes, too.

For example, we could note that bonobos are held in the San Diego Zoo and the Columbus Zoo and Aquarium in the United States. Figure 2.8 demonstrates how we

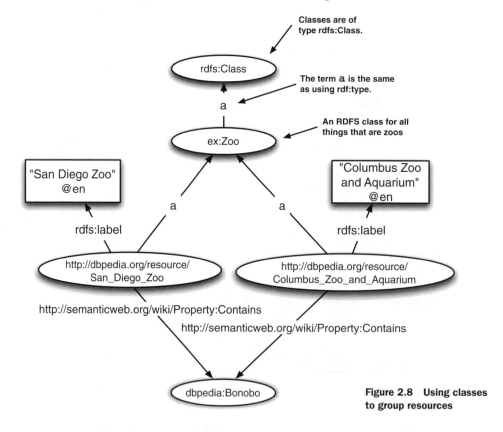

Figure 2.8   Using classes to group resources

---

[2]   OWL's acronym comes from the character Owl in *Winnie the Poo,* who misspelled his name WOL.

can say that both zoos are a type of `ex:Zoo` (short for http://example.com/Zoo, a made-up URI), which is designated an `rdfs:Class`. Many RDF databases are capable of understanding RDFS class relationships, even if they don't implement more complete logical formalisms found in systems like OWL.

2.2.4 Typed literals

So far you've only seen RDF literals that are simple strings, like names for people, zoos, and places. Naturally, you sometimes want to describe numbers, dates, or other data types. RDF allows literals to be marked as being of any data type in the XML Schema Datatype standard. You can also make your own data types, but that's not generally done in Linked Data because it hurts interoperability between existing systems.

Figure 2.9 shows the use of a data type. The San Diego Zoo has an exhibit called Pygmy Chimps at Bonobo Road that opened on April 3, 1993 (in San Diego, which is in the UTC-8 hours time zone). The same figure also shows another use of a blank node.

NOTE The full list of XML Schema data types may be found at http://www.w3.org/TR/xmlschema11-2/.

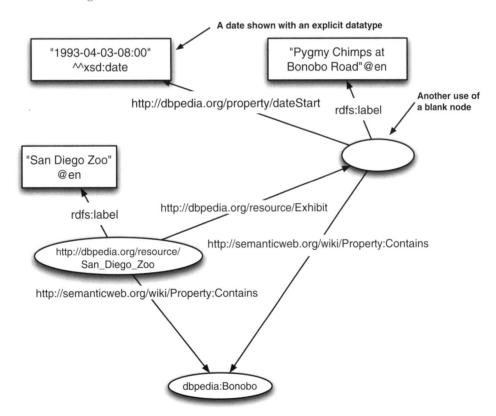

Figure 2.9 Using explicit data type properties

The RDF data model is the foundation of Linked Data. It's used to define data elements, to relate them to one another, and to provide the common framework needed to combine data from various sources. Understanding the RDF data model is the first step toward understanding how Linked Data really works.

You've seen how RDF predicates are used to relate one thing to another thing. You can collect some such predicates into a grouping called a vocabulary. RDF vocabularies serve the same purpose as schemas in a relational database; they describe what the data represents. Linked Data vocabularies are, as you'd expect by now, named using HTTP URIs, and their descriptions are resolvable on the Web. The next section explains how to understand, find, use, and even create your own vocabularies.

2.3   *RDF vocabularies*

You've already seen a number of terms used in Linked Data in the bonobo example, such as foaf:name, rdfs:label, and vcard:locality. It may or may not have been obvious that those terms are grouped together to form RDF vocabularies. For example, the terms rdfs:label, rdfs:comment, and rdfs:seeAlso are all defined in the RDF Schema vocabulary, which has the URI associated with the rdfs: prefix; see http://www.w3.org/2000/01/rdf-schema#. Similarly, the terms vcard:locality, vcard:region, and vcard:country-name all come from the vCard vocabulary associated with the vcard: prefix; see http://www.w3.org/2006/vcard/ns#.

RDF vocabularies provide a schema for the Web of Data. Like a relational database's schema, RDF vocabularies provide definitions of the terms used to make relationships between data elements. Unlike a relational database's schema, however, RDF vocabularies are distributed over the Web, are developed by people all over the world, and only come into common use in Linked Data if a lot of people choose to use them.

Anyone can make an RDF vocabulary, and many people do. This would seem to be a recipe for disaster. How can anyone reuse Linked Data if it contains terms that you've never seen before? There are two ways to make this problem tractable, one technical and the other social: Make certain that the URIs defining Linked Data vocabularies themselves follow the Linked Data principles, and reuse existing vocabularies whenever possible.

RDF vocabularies that use resolvable HTTP URIs and present useful information describing the vocabulary allow anyone to "follow their nose" to the information that's required for learning how a new term is being applied.

Reusing existing vocabularies ensures that for the most common use cases most people will use the most common vocabularies. This is a social contract that should probably be added as an additional Linked Data principle.

Some vocabularies get used over and over in practice. They evolved to become central to what most people do with Linked Data. We'll call these *core vocabularies*. Others are used whenever certain information needs to be represented but are less common than the everyday core vocabularies. We'll call those *authoritative vocabularies*. Both types are described in this section and their URLs are given.

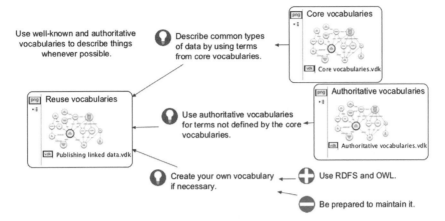

Figure 2.10 Reuse vocabularies whenever possible (credit: Richard Howlett).

Figure 2.10 summarizes the best-practice guidance for reusing existing vocabularies.

2.3.1 Commonly used vocabularies

The kinds of objects often described first in Linked Data are people, projects, web resources, publications, and addresses. You might also want to migrate an existing taxonomy or other classification scheme into an RDF vocabulary. The vocabularies that define these terms are sometimes called the core RDF vocabularies.

Figure 2.11 shows the core RDF vocabularies and suggests how you might use them to model the most common types of Linked Data.

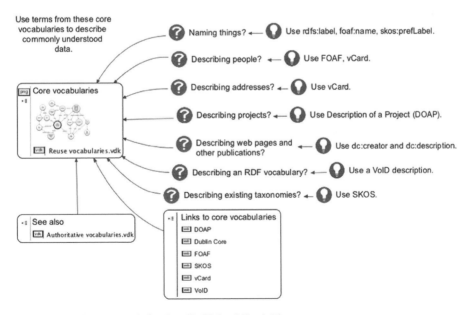

Figure 2.11 Core vocabularies (credit: Richard Howlett)

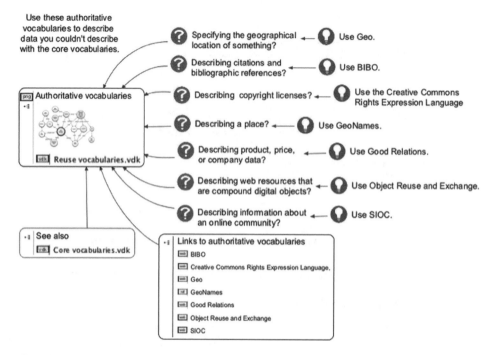

Figure 2.12   Other authoritative vocabularies (credit: Richard Howlett)

Other vocabularies have become authoritative because they model other common objects and have been widely adopted. Figure 2.12 shows examples, including products for sale, geographic locations and place names, bibliographic information, licenses, online communities and social networks, and compound digital objects.

Taken together, figure 2.11 and figure 2.12 allow you to quickly find the most commonly used RDF vocabularies. Look at table 2.2 if you don't see what you need.

Table 2.2 lists some of the most commonly used RDF vocabularies used in Linked Data, along with their preferred short prefix, their namespace URI, and their purpose. These aren't the only vocabularies you'll see, but they'll be enough to get you going and to understand much of what you'll see in Linked Open Data on the public web.

NOTE   The LODStats project generates statistics for the most commonly used vocabularies at http://stats.lod2.eu/vocabularies.

Table 2.2   Core and other commonly used RDF vocabularies

Name	Prefix	Namespace URI	Describes
Airport Ontology	`air:`	http://www.daml.org/2001/10/html/airport-ont#	Nearest airports
BIBO	`bibo:`	http://purl.org/ontology/bibo/	Bibliographies

Table 2.2   **Core and other commonly used RDF vocabularies** *(continued)*

Name	Prefix	Namespace URI	Describes
Bio	`bio:`	http://purl.org/vocab/bio/0.1/	Biographical information
Creative Commons Rights Expression Language	`cc:`	http://creativecommons.org/ns#	Licenses
DOAP	`doap:`	http://usefulinc.com/ns/doap#	Projects
Dublin Core Elements	`dc:`	http://purl.org/dc/elements/1.1/	Publications
Dublin Core Terms	`dct:`	http://purl.org/dc/terms/	Publications
FOAF	`foaf:`	http://xmlns.com/foaf/0.1/	People
Geo	`pos:`	http://www.w3.org/2003/01/geo/wgs84_pos#	Positions
GeoNames	`gn:`	http://www.geonames.org/ontology#	Locations
Good Relations	`gr:`	http://purl.org/goodrelations/v1#	Products
Object Reuse and Exchange	`ore:`	http://www.openarchives.org/ore/terms/	Resource maps
RDF	`rdf:`	http://www.w3.org/1999/02/22-rdf-syntax-ns#	Core framework
RDFS	`rdfs:`	http://www.w3.org/2000/01/rdf-schema#	RDF vocabularies
SIOC	`sioc:`	http://rdfs.org/sioc/ns#	Online communities
SKOS	`skos:`	http://www.w3.org/2004/02/skos/core#	Controlled vocabularies
vCard	`vcard:`	http://www.w3.org/2006/vcard/ns#	Business cards
VoID	`void:`	http://rdfs.org/ns/void#	Vocabularies
Web Ontology Language (OWL)	`owl:`	http://www.w3.org/2002/07/owl#	Ontologies
WordNet	`wn:`	http://xmlns.com/wordnet/1.6/	English words
XML Schema Datatypes	`xsd:`	http://www.w3.org/2001/XMLSchema#	Data types

If you still can't find a vocabulary you need, try searching for relevant terms on Sindice, a Semantic Web search engine (http://sindice.com). You can use Sindice to search for terms and then find vocabularies where those terms are defined. (Sindice is an Italian word and pronounced without a silent *e*, like "sindee'cheh".)

If you *still* can't find a vocabulary that suits your needs, read on!

2.3.2 *Making your own vocabularies*

The goal of RDF and Linked Data is to allow anyone to describe anything. The ability to create your own vocabularies and resolve them on the Web is a critical part of both RDF and Linked Data. It provides an unlimited number of possible terms in order to scale RDF descriptions as the Web scales.

You've seen an example of a custom vocabulary term in the bonobo example: `ex:Zoo`. The `ex:` URI, http://example.com, exists solely for the purpose of allowing people to use it in examples without risking it either going away or, worse, allowing many people to conflict with one another by defining terms in the same namespace without coordination. You're free to use http://example.com in any example but should never publish a real vocabulary using that URI.

You could make the `ex:Zoo` term into a real Linked Data term by searching Sindice. If you try that, you'll see that DBpedia (of course) already defines a term for a zoo: http://dbpedia.org/resource/The_Zoo. You can thus replace all instances of `ex:Zoo` with `dbpedia:The_Zoo` and be done. Putting in placeholders and looking up terms before publishing your vocabulary is often the best way to deal with what you don't immediately have a vocabulary for.

If we couldn't find an existing vocabulary term to replace our placeholder term, we'd need to make a new vocabulary and create the term there. Let's say that we want to create an RDF triple that says that bonobos smell like old socks. It's rather unlikely that an existing vocabulary defines such subjective terms. The RDF triple that we want would be something like `dbpedia:Bonobo ex:smellsLike ex:OldSocks`. Now we need to create real terms for `ex:smellsLike` and `ex:OldSocks`, create a vocabulary document to contain them, and publish the document.

The term `ex:OldSocks` could become an RDFS class, because we might one day wish to have other classes of things that animals can smell like. It could just as easily be an OWL class, and there's nothing to stop us making it both. The term `ex:smellsLike` is used as a predicate and so is probably best as an RDFS property.

We also need to make up a prefix to replace `ex:`. Let's use `odor:` because our vocabulary relates to smells.

As a last step, we need a URI where we'll publish our new vocabulary. We can call it whatever we like as long as we have the right to publish it to the place we define. For the purposes of demonstration only, we'll use http://linkeddatadeveloper.com/ns/odor#.

Listing 2.1 shows our final vocabulary. The only thing left to do is to publish that document at the URI http://linkeddatadeveloper.com/ns/odor#. If you want to publish it for real, change the DNS domain in the HTTP authority (and the path if you want to) and change the URI associated with the `odor:` prefix in the document.

> **Listing 2.1   A custom RDF vocabulary in Turtle format**

```
@prefix rdf: <http://www.w3.org/1999/02/22-rdf-syntax-ns#> .
@prefix rdfs: <http://www.w3.org/2000/01/rdf-schema#> .
@prefix owl: <http://www.w3.org/2002/07/owl#> .
@prefix odor: <http://linkeddatadeveloper.com/ns/odor#> .
```

```
# Classes
odor:OldSocks a rdfs:Class, owl:Class ;
rdfs:label "Old socks" ;
  rdfs:comment "The odor associated with old socks or bonobos." .


# Properties
odor:smellsLike
    rdf:type rdf:Property ;
    rdfs:label "smells like" ;
    rdfs:comment "Relates an arbitrary subject to a class that identifies an
    odor." .
```

NOTE You can generate nice-looking HTML documentation for your vocabularies using SpecGen. See https://github.com/specgen/specgen for details. Alternatives include OWL-Doc, LODE, and Parrot.

Sometimes after a vocabulary is published you find that someone else created a term very similar to, or even identical to, one that you created. It might be difficult for you to change all of your terms, or you might not trust that the other vocabulary publisher will keep their vocabulary published. What do you do now? Fortunately, there's an easy solution: Publish a single RDF triple saying that the two terms mean the same thing. The predicate to use when associating two terms is `owl:sameAs`.

Let's say that our `odor:smellsLike` predicate means exactly the same thing as a term in someone else's vocabulary called `smells:like`. You can publish an RDF triple to the Web that reads `odor:smellsLike owl:sameAs smells:like` and you're finished. Anyone picking up that triple will be able to know that your term means the same thing as `smells:like`.

Many `owl:sameAs` triples have been collected on a website at http://sameAs.org. You should get into the habit of checking that site before you make your own vocabulary or publish new `owl:sameAs` triples.

You should probably work with others if you want to get really good at creating RDF vocabularies. Vocabulary creation expert Richard Cyganiak has published guidelines for working on vocabularies with a group at http://richard.cyganiak.de/blog/2011/03/creating-an-rdf-vocabulary/.

2.4 RDF formats for Linked Data

RDF is a data model, not a format. Many different formats can serialize RDF data and therefore Linked Data. We focus on four here because they're the ones most commonly used.

Why should RDF have different formats at all? Because different systems have different "native" formats you might start from. Also, client systems (for example, phones and browsers) may wish to minimize computation to get into a native format for further processing. For example, web developers often prefer to use JSON because of good library support in JavaScript, and enterprises that have invested heavily in XML technologies might want to use an XML format.

The four formats you will see here are

- *Turtle*—A simple, human-readable format
- *RDF/XML*—The original RDF format in XML
- *RDFa*—RDF embedded in HTML attributes
- *JSON-LD*—A newer format aimed at web developers

It's important to note that all RDF formats represent data in the RDF data model. They're interchangeable. Data in any of these formats may be parsed into RDF, and data from multiple formats may be combined in a single RDF graph. Because of this flexibility, you can work in whatever format is easiest for you to understand and then use tools to convert your data into other forms if you need to.

Let's take two RDF triples from the bonobo example to demonstrate how they're presented in each of the four formats: `<http://dbpedia.org/resource/San_Diego_Zoo>` `rdfs:label "San Diego Zoo"@en` and `dbpedia:Bonobo rdf:type dbpedia-owl:Mammal`. These triples mean "The San Diego Zoo is called the San Diego Zoo in English" and "A bonobo is a mammal."

This section introduces the formats at a high level and helps you learn to read them.

Can you find all the RDF statements from the bonobo example in each of the different formats? Try to find at least a few of them as you read about each format.

2.4.1 *Turtle—human-readable RDF*

Turtle is the easiest of the RDF formats for most people to read, and it's the format most Semantic Web and Linked Data developers choose to use most of the time. The name *Turtle* was derived from Terse RDF Triple Language.

Figure 2.13 shows the two example triples in abstract form and again in Turtle. The subjects, predicates, and objects are shown so you can see how the format works.

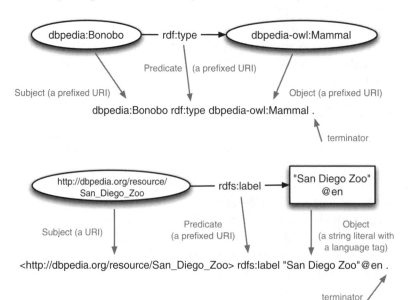

Figure 2.13 RDF triples represented in Turtle format

You can see that Turtle in its simplest form is a direct mapping of subjects, predicates, and objects in order of appearance. Each statement is followed by a period or full stop to mark its end.

If prefixed URIs are used, the prefixes are typically declared at the top of the file but may appear anywhere as long as they're declared before they're used.

The following listing shows the entire bonobo example data in Turtle format. Note the prefix declarations at the top of the listing.

Listing 2.2   Bonobo example data in Turtle format

```
@prefix dbpedia:     <http://dbpedia.org/resource/> .
@prefix dbpedia-owl:     <http://dbpedia.org/ontology/> .
@prefix foaf:     <http://xmlns.com/foaf/0.1/> .
@prefix ex: <http://example.com/> .
@prefix rdf:     <http://www.w3.org/1999/02/22-rdf-syntax-ns#> .
@prefix rdfs: <http://www.w3.org/2000/01/rdf-schema#> .
@prefix vcard: <http://www.w3.org/2006/vcard/ns#> .
@prefix xsd: <http://www.w3.org/2001/XMLSchema#> .

dbpedia:Bonobo
    rdf:type     dbpedia-owl:Eukaryote , dbpedia-owl:Mammal ,
dbpedia-owl:Animal ;
        rdfs:comment "The bonobo, Pan paniscus, previously called the pygmy
          chimpanzee and less often, the dwarf or gracile chimpanzee, is a great
          ape and one of the two species making up the genus Pan; the other is Pan
          troglodytes, or the common chimpanzee. Although the name \"chimpanzee\"
          is sometimes used to refer to both species together, it is usually
          understood as referring to the common chimpanzee, while Pan paniscus is
          usually referred to as the bonobo."@en ;
        foaf:depiction     <http://upload.wikimedia.org/wikipedia/commons/a/a6/
          Bonobo-04.jpg> ;
        foaf:name     "Bonobo"@en ;
        rdfs:seeAlso <http://eol.org/pages/326448/overview>
    .

<http://dbpedia.org/resource/San_Diego_Zoo> rdfs:label "San Diego Zoo"@en ;
        <http://semanticweb.org/wiki/Property:Contains> dbpedia:Bonobo ;
        vcard:adr _:1 ;
        dbpedia:Exhibit _:2 ;
        a ex:Zoo
    .

<http://dbpedia.org/resource/Columbus_Zoo_and_Aquarium> rdfs:label "Columbus
      Zoo and Aquarium"@en ;
        <http://semanticweb.org/wiki/Property:Contains> dbpedia:Bonobo ;
        a ex:Zoo
    .

_:1 vcard:locality "San Diego" ;
        vcard:region "California" ;
        vcard:country-name "USA"
    .
```

Location of the "Bonobos are mammals" triple

Location of the "San Diego Zoo label" triple

```
_:2 rdfs:label "Pygmy Chimps at Bonobo Road"@en ;
    <http://dbpedia.org/property/dateStart> "1993-04-03-08:00"^^xsd:date ;
    <http://semanticweb.org/wiki/Property:Contains> dbpedia:Bonobo
.

ex:Zoo a rdfs:Class .
```

Turtle also includes shortcuts so you don't need to list every component of every triple. The "Bonobos are mammals" triple is `dbpedia:Bonobo rdf:type dbpedia-owl:Mammal`. It could appear just that way in a Turtle document. The components are broken up in listing 2.2 so the subject `dbpedia:Bonobo` can apply to other triples. Triples that differ only in the object can separate objects with commas, as in `dbpedia:Bonobo rdf:type dbpedia-owl:Eukaryote, dbpedia-owl:Mammal, dbpedia-owl:Animal`, for example. Triples that share just the same subject may be separated with semicolons. Can you see where the subject `dbpedia:Bonobo` is shared by all the triples in the first block of statements?

Blank nodes are represented by "temporary" identifiers that start with an underscore and a colon (the same as `_:1` in listing 2.2). These identifiers will be thrown away by whatever software or system parses a Turtle file and replaced with local blank identifiers. Look at the listing to find the two blank nodes used in the example RDF.

URIs may be further abbreviated in Turtle by using the `@base` directive. `@base` defines a base URI. All relative URI references in the document will be appended to that base URI to form complete URIs. For example, you could replace the `ex:` vocabulary namespace in listing 2.2 (`@prefix ex: <http://example.com/> .`) with a base URI (like `@base <http://example.com/> .`). Then you could use relative URIs to replace any references to the `ex:` vocabulary. In that case, `ex:Zoo` would change to the relative URI `<Zoo>`.

NOTE Turtle is fully described at http://www.w3.org/TR/turtle/.

2.4.2   *RDF/XML—RDF for enterprises*

RDF/XML was the original serialization format for RDF. Unfortunately, it caused substantial confusion because of the complexities of its formatting and its standardization prior to XML itself. RDF/XML isn't used as much as it once was, but it still has value as an RDF serialization format that works with many XML tools.

Enterprise users should especially take note of RDF/XML because they're more likely to have an XML-based infrastructure.

Figure 2.14 shows our two example triples in RDF/XML format. The first things you'll probably notice are the presence of XML tags (in angle brackets) and the fact that the components of triples may be split across tags, tag attributes, and content.

You can make sense of the format if you think about RDF/XML as a series of RDF triples that are connected head to tail: subject (in a tag) followed by a predicate (in a tag) followed by an object URI (in a tag) or an object literal (in a tag's content). The pattern can repeat each time an object becomes a subject.

Take a close look at the "Bonobos are mammals" triple. You'll see that it violates the pattern we just described! The subject is given in an XML attribute called `rdf:about`. You'll also see that the predicate is implied and the object URI is given in the tag itself. This confuses a lot of people. The predicate in this triple is the special predicate `rdf:type`, and you've already seen it treated specially in earlier examples when we noted that it could be replaced with just a in the Turtle format.

Prefixed URIs may be used as long as their prefixes are defined as XML namespaces in the opening XML tag. Technically, this form of prefixes is called QNames, and you may hear that term from XML people or read it in the specification. But it serves the same purpose as the prefix naming scheme used in Turtle to shorten URIs for easier reading. A restriction on QNames is that the part after the colon must be a valid XML element (tag) name.

The second triple in figure 2.14 is more representative of the pattern. It includes an extra triple. Can you see it? The first tag is `<ex:Zoo>`, which adds the "extra" triple that says that the San Diego Zoo is an instance of the `ex:Zoo` class. We could have avoided this in the example, but we wanted to make the point more clearly than it might have been without it. A good way to avoid it would have been to have a tag for just the subject, `dbpedia:San_Diego_Zoo`.

Try to find some more triples from the bonobo examples in the RDF/XML shown in listing 2.3. Remember that you can look back at the more easily readable Turtle listing!

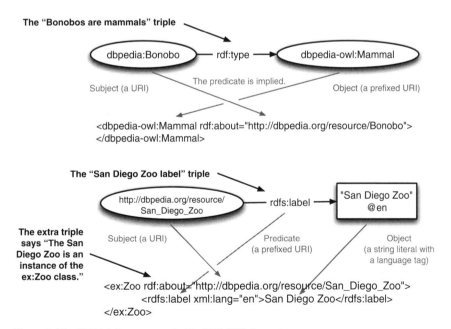

Figure 2.14   RDF triples represented in RDF/XML format

Listing 2.3   Bonobo example data in RDF/XML format

```
<?xml version="1.0"?>
<rdf:RDF xmlns:rdfs="http://www.w3.org/2000/01/rdf-schema#"
    xmlns:dbpedia="http://dbpedia.org/resource/" xmlns:xsd="http://
    www.w3.org/2001/XMLSchema#" xmlns:foaf="http://xmlns.com/foaf/0.1/"
    xmlns:vcard="http://www.w3.org/2006/vcard/ns#" xmlns:ex="http://
    example.com/" xmlns:rdf="http://www.w3.org/1999/02/22-rdf-syntax-ns#"
    xmlns:dbpedia-owl="http://dbpedia.org/ontology/" xmlns:wiki="http://
    semanticweb.org/wiki/" xmlns:property="http://dbpedia.org/property/">
  <dbpedia-owl:Eukaryote rdf:about="http://dbpedia.org/resource/Bonobo">
      <rdf:type rdf:resource="http://dbpedia.org/ontology/Mammal" />
      <rdf:type rdf:resource="http://dbpedia.org/ontology/Animal" />
      <rdfs:comment xml:lang="en">The bonobo, Pan paniscus, previously
   called the pygmy chimpanzee and less often, the dwarf or gracile
   chimpanzee, is a great ape and one of the two species making up the
   genus Pan; the other is Pan troglodytes, or the common chimpanzee.
   Although the name "chimpanzee" is sometimes used to refer to both
   species together, it is usually understood as referring to the common
   chimpanzee, while Pan paniscus is usually referred to as the bonobo.</
   rdfs:comment>
      <foaf:depiction rdf:resource="http://upload.wikimedia.org/wikipedia/
   commons/a/a6/Bonobo-04.jpg" />
      <foaf:name xml:lang="en">Bonobo</foaf:name>
      <rdfs:seeAlso rdf:resource="http://eol.org/pages/326448/overview" />
  </dbpedia-owl:Eukaryote>
  <ex:Zoo rdf:about="http://dbpedia.org/resource/San_Diego_Zoo">
      <rdfs:label xml:lang="en">San Diego Zoo</rdfs:label>
      <wiki:Property:Contains rdf:resource="http://dbpedia.org/resource/
   Bonobo" />
      <vcard:adr vcard:locality="San Diego" vcard:region="California"
   vcard:country-name="USA" />
      <dbpedia:Exhibit>            ⟵──  The exhibit description triples
          <rdf:Description>
              <rdfs:label xml:lang="en">Pygmy Chimps at Bonobo Road</
   rdfs:label>
              <property:dateStart rdf:datatype="http://www.w3.org/2001/
   XMLSchema#date">1993-04-03-08:00</property:dateStart>
              <wiki:Property:Contains rdf:resource="http://dbpedia.org/
   resource/Bonobo" />
          </rdf:Description>
      </dbpedia:Exhibit>
  </ex:Zoo>
  <ex:Zoo rdf:about="http://dbpedia.org/resource/
   Columbus_Zoo_and_Aquarium">
      <rdfs:label xml:lang="en">Columbus Zoo and Aquarium</rdfs:label>
      <wiki:Property:Contains rdf:resource="http://dbpedia.org/resource/
   Bonobo" />
  </ex:Zoo>
  <rdfs:Class rdf:about="http://example.com/Zoo" />
</rdf:RDF>
```

The "Bonobos are mammals" triple ⟶ (points to the rdf:type lines)

The "San Diego Zoo label" triple ⟶ (points to the rdfs:label line)

RDF/XML also has a way to abbreviate URIs by defining a base URI. That's done using the xml:base directive in the rdf:RDF tag, near the namespace declarations. To replace the ex: namespace with a base URI, you'd replace the ex: namespace declaration (`xmlns:ex="http://example.com/"`) with a base declaration (like `xml:base="http://example.com"`).

NOTE RDF/XML is fully described at http://www.w3.org/TR/rdf-syntax-grammar/.

2.4.3 *RDFa—RDF in HTML*

Most of the Web consists of documents, not just structured data in their own files. We tend to include things in unstructured text that are themselves data elements, such as telephone numbers, addresses, people's names, and even product descriptions. Wouldn't it be nice to be able to mark up those elements in our web pages so they could be extracted as the structured data they're supposed to be? Fortunately, there is a way to do so, and it's known as RDFa, for "RDF in (HTML) Attributes."

RDFa documents are simply HTML—with a bit of extra markup. An HTML page's `DOCTYPE` is modified so RDFa parsers can quickly determine that the page is worth parsing, and HTML attributes are used to provide just enough information to create RDF triples when the page is parsed. Table 2.3 provides the `DOCTYPE` declarations used by web pages that can include RDFa.

Table 2.3 RDFa DOCTYPE headers

Document type	HTML DOCTYPE declaration
XHTML1+RDFa 1.0	`<!DOCTYPE html PUBLIC "-//W3C//DTD XHTML+RDFa 1.0//EN"` `"http://www.w3.org/MarkUp/DTD/xhtml-rdfa-1.dtd">`
XHTML1+RDFa 1.1	`<!DOCTYPE html PUBLIC "-//W3C//DTD XHTML+RDFa 1.1//EN"` `"http://www.w3.org/MarkUp/DTD/xhtml-rdfa-2.dtd">`
HTML+RDFa 1.1 or XHTML5+RDFa 1.1	`<!DOCTYPE html>` or any other DOCTYPE found

Figure 2.15 shows our example triples in HTML with RDFa. A web browser that doesn't know what RDFa is will simply ignore any HTML attributes it doesn't understand and so for the first one would see simply `<span>Here are some things we know about Bonobos </span>`. An RDFa-aware system would display exactly the same text but also provide the RDF triple `dbpedia:Bonobo rdf:type dbpedia-owl:Mammal`. The `resource` attribute provides the subject, and the special `typeof` attribute provides the `rdf:type` predicate. The second triple shows how any predicate can be provided using the `property` attribute.

RDFa has a way to shorten URIs, as other formats do. RDFa's way is known as Compact URI Expressions (CURIEs). They are technically an extension to RDF/XML's QNames because they allow the part after the colon to have values that aren't valid XML element names. CURIEs are a superset of QNames.

RDFa may be used for search engine optimization (SEO) and with the schema.org scheme that several large search engines now promote. This is because the search engines use that RDFa to enhance their search results. Have you searched for a movie

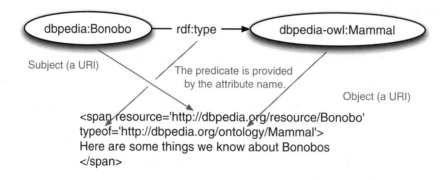

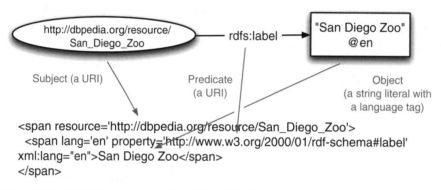

Figure 2.15   RDF triples represented in HTML+RDFa format

and seen that show times and links to reviews are present in the results? Or seen a product that lists its prices? That information may have come from RDFa.

Developers can use http://rdfa.info/tools/ or similar tools to extract RDFa from HTML. For example, try listing 2.4 in http://rdfa.info/play/ to recover the RDF statements from the bonobos example.

Can you find the date the bonobo exhibit opened at the San Diego Zoo in the following listing?

Listing 2.4   Bonobo example data in HTML+RDFa format

```
<?xml version='1.0' encoding='utf-8'?>
<!DOCTYPE html PUBLIC "-//W3C//DTD XHTML+RDFa 1.1//EN" "http://www.w3.org/
    MarkUp/DTD/xhtml-rdfa-2.dtd">
<html xmlns='http://www.w3.org/1999/xhtml'>
    <head>
        <base href='' />
        <title>
            Stuff we know about bonobos
        </title>
    </head>
    <body>
        <p>
```

The "Bonobos are mammals" triple ⊳

```
            <span resource='http://dbpedia.org/resource/Bonobo'
      typeof='http://dbpedia.org/ontology/Eukaryote http://dbpedia.org/
      ontology/Mammal
      http://dbpedia.org/ontology/Animal'><span>Here are some things we know
      about <span lang='en' property='http://xmlns.com/foaf/0.1/name'
      xml:lang="en">Bonobos</span>:</span> <span lang='en' property='http://
      www.w3.org/2000/01/rdf-schema#comment' xml:lang="en">The bonobo, Pan
      paniscus, previously called the pygmy chimpanzee and less often, the
      dwarf or gracile chimpanzee, is a great ape and one of the two species
      making up the genus Pan; the other is Pan troglodytes, or the common
      chimpanzee. Although the name "chimpanzee" is sometimes used to refer to
      both species together, it is usually understood as referring to the
      common chimpanzee, while Pan paniscus is usually referred to as the
      bonobo.</span> <span>Bonobos are mammalian animals and are thus also
      eukaryotes.</span> <span><img src='http://upload.wikimedia.org/
      wikipedia/commons/a/a6/Bonobo-04.jpg' property='http://xmlns.com/foaf/
      0.1/depiction' /></span> <span>More information may be found at <a
      href='http://eol.org/pages/326448/overview' property='http://www.w3.org/
      2000/01/rdf-schema#seeAlso'>the bonobo entry at the Encyclopedia of
      Life</a></span></span>
        </p>
        <p>
            Some zoos that contain bonobos include:
        </p>
        <ul>
            <li>
                <span resource='http://dbpedia.org/resource/
      Columbus_Zoo_and_Aquarium' typeof='http://example.com/Zoo'><span
      lang='en' property='http://www.w3.org/2000/01/rdf-schema#label'
      xml:lang="en">Columbus Zoo and Aquarium</span><span rel='http://
      semanticweb.org/wiki/Property:Contains' resource='http://dbpedia.org/
      resource/Bonobo'> </span></span>
            </li>
            <li>
                <span resource='http://dbpedia.org/resource/San_Diego_Zoo'
      typeof='http://example.com/Zoo'><span lang='en' property='http://
      www.w3.org/2000/01/rdf-schema#label' xml:lang="en">
      San Diego Zoo</span> <span rel='http://www.w3.org/2006/vcard/ns#adr'
      resource='_:1'>which is located in <span property='http://www.w3.org/
      2006/vcard/ns#locality'>San Diego</span>, <span property='http://
      www.w3.org/2006/vcard/ns#region'>California</span>, <span
      property='http://www.w3.org/2006/vcard/ns#country-name'>USA</span>.</
      span><span rel='http://semanticweb.org/wiki/Property:Contains'
      resource='http://dbpedia.org/resource/Bonobo'> </span><span
      rel='http://dbpedia.org/resource/Exhibit' resource='_:2'>The main bonobo
      exhibit is called <span lang='en' property='http://www.w3.org/2000/01/
      rdf-schema#label' xml:lang="en">Pygmy Chimps at Bonobo Road</span>. It
      has been at the San Diego Zoo since <span content='1993-04-03-08:00'
      datatype='http://www.w3.org/2001/XMLSchema#date' property='http://
      dbpedia.org/property/dateStart'>Saturday, 03 April 1993</span>.<span
      rel='http://semanticweb.org/wiki/Property:Contains' resource='http://
      dbpedia.org/resource/Bonobo'> </span></span></span>
            </li>
        </ul>
    </body>
</html>
```

The "San Diego Zoo label" triple ⊳

NOTE   RDFa is fully described at http://www.w3.org/TR/rdfa-primer/ and http://rdfa.info/.

2.4.4   *JSON-LD—RDF for JavaScript Developers*

It seems that every web developer knows JavaScript Object Notation (JSON) and that every major programming language has multiple libraries that can parse it. One frequent comment heard by the Linked Data community goes something like this: "Why not just put data into JSON?"

One answer to date has been that we like RDF because it can so easily be combined with other RDF data from other sources. That is, if we want to combine data, we need to use an RDF serialization format. Now there is JSON-LD, JSON for Linking Data, an RDF serialization format in JSON.

The Linked Data community is hoping that JSON-LD is both accessible to developers used to reading and writing JSON and capable of showing those developers how to combine data on the Web.

Figure 2.16 shows our example triples in JSON-LD. At the top of the figure is the @context object, where prefixes are defined. This allows shortened URIs to be used in the remainder of the document in a manner similar to the other formats.

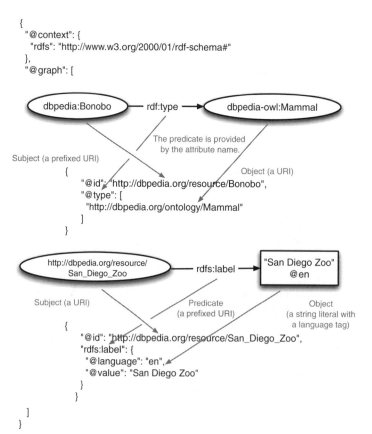

Figure 2.16   RDF triples represented in JSON-LD format

The rest of the document contains the RDF triples in the @graph object. @id identifies RDF subjects and @type identifies the special rdf:type predicate. Other predicates are simply named as a string in quotes, as with rdfs:label in the figure.

A potential source of confusion in any form of JSON is the use of square versus curly brackets. Curly braces ({ and }) surround objects and square brackets ([and]) denote arrays. With that knowledge, you can see that in figure 2.16 @type is an array of only one class, dbpedia-owl:Mammal, but it could hold more. RDF objects are JSON objects that may contain a URI, a literal denoted by @value, and, optionally, data type or language information.

Can you find the image of a bonobo represented in the following listing? Look for the URI ending in .jpg if you get stuck.

Listing 2.5   Bonobo example data in JSON-LD format

```
{
  "@context": {
    "foaf": "http://xmlns.com/foaf/0.1/",
    "rdf": "http://www.w3.org/1999/02/22-rdf-syntax-ns#",
    "rdfs": "http://www.w3.org/2000/01/rdf-schema#",
    "vcard": "http://www.w3.org/2006/vcard/ns#",
    "xsd": "http://www.w3.org/2001/XMLSchema#"
  },
  "@graph": [
    {
      "@id": "_:t0",
      "vcard:country-name": "USA",
      "vcard:locality": "San Diego",
      "vcard:region": "California"
    },
    {
      "@id": "_:t1",
      "http://dbpedia.org/property/dateStart": {
        "@type": "xsd:date",
        "@value": "1993-04-03-08:00"
      },
      "http://semanticweb.org/wiki/Property:Contains": {
        "@id": "http://dbpedia.org/resource/Bonobo"
      },
      "rdfs:label": {
        "@language": "en",
        "@value": "Pygmy Chimps at Bonobo Road"
      }
    },
    {
      "@id": "http://dbpedia.org/resource/Bonobo",
      "@type": [
        "http://dbpedia.org/ontology/Eukaryote",          The "Bonobos are
        "http://dbpedia.org/ontology/Mammal",       ◁──┘  mammals" triple
        "http://dbpedia.org/ontology/Animal"
      ],
      "foaf:depiction": { "@id": "http://upload.wikimedia.org/wikipedia/
  commons/a/a6/Bonobo-04.jpg" },
```

```
    "foaf:name": {
      "@language": "en",
      "@value": "Bonobos"
    },
    "rdfs:comment": {
      "@language": "en",
      "@value": "The bonobo, Pan paniscus, previously called the pygmy
 chimpanzee and less often, the dwarf or gracile chimpanzee, is a great
 ape and one of the two species making up the genus Pan; the other is Pan
 troglodytes, or the common chimpanzee. Although the name \"chimpanzee\"
 is sometimes used to refer to both species together, it is usually
 understood as referring to the common chimpanzee, while Pan paniscus is
 usually referred to as the bonobo."
    },
    "rdfs:seeAlso": {
      "@id": "http://eol.org/pages/326448/overview"
    }
  },
  {
    "@id": "http://dbpedia.org/resource/Columbus_Zoo_and_Aquarium",
    "@type": "http://example.com/Zoo",
    "http://semanticweb.org/wiki/Property:Contains": {
      "@id": "http://dbpedia.org/resource/Bonobo"
    },
    "rdfs:label": {
      "@language": "en",
      "@value": "Columbus Zoo and Aquarium"
    }
  },
  {
    "@id": "http://dbpedia.org/resource/San_Diego_Zoo",
    "@type": "http://example.com/Zoo",
    "http://dbpedia.org/resource/Exhibit": { "@id": "_:t1" },
    "http://semanticweb.org/wiki/Property:Contains": {
      "@id": "http://dbpedia.org/resource/Bonobo"
    },
    "rdfs:label": {
      "@language": "en",                        The "San Diego
      "@value": "San Diego Zoo"            ◁──┘  Zoo label" triple
    },
    "vcard:adr": { "@id": "_:t0" }
  }
  ]
}
```

NOTE   JSON-LD is fully described at http://www.w3.org/TR/json-ld-syntax/ and http://json-ld.org

2.5   *Issues related to web servers and published Linked Data*

Some web browsers need additional support to properly display Linked Data content because we want Linked Data published on the Web to be reused by others. Developers and users both need to be aware of these issues. This section addresses techniques that you would use so web servers can appropriately inform web browsers (or other

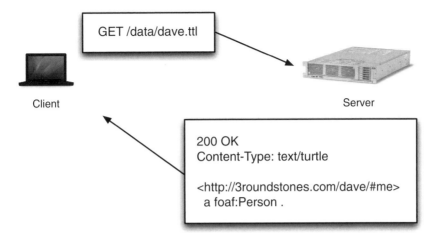

Figure 2.17 A simplified HTTP conversation showing a Content-Type header

types of clients) of the type of Linked Data they are serving and so the clients can decide how to present it. This is accomplished using the HTTP Content-Type header.

Figure 2.17 shows how this works in practice. A web browser requests a URL whose path on the server is /data/dave.ttl. The server finds the file and successfully sends it back (that's what the 200 OK status code means). The Content-Type of text/turtle matches the file extension .ttl by convention; such Content-Types are registered with the Internet Assigned Numbers Authority (IANA). The content of the file follows the headers after a blank line.

The Content-Type header for Linked Data varies with the specific format used. Most of the examples in this book use the readable Turtle format for RDF, which is served with the Content-Type text/turtle. Those producing RDF from XML sources, especially enterprise developers, may use the older RDF/XML format, which is served with the Content-Type application/rdf+xml.

> **NOTE:** HTTP Content-Types are also known as MIME types. MIME stands for Multipurpose Internet Mail Extensions and is the technique used to encode multimedia email attachments (such as images, videos, or office documents) as plain text during email transmission. The Web uses the same mechanism to encode multimedia during HTTP transmission.

Other formats require more detailed explanations. RDFa is a way of embedding Linked Data into web pages. As table 2.4 illustrates, RDFa doesn't have its own Content-Type because the data is buried inside HTML. Instead, an HTML page is served with the Content-Type text/html. A web client is responsible for determining the presence of (or ignoring) any embedded RDFa.

A new way to publish Linked Data in JSON format is JSON-LD. The preferred Content-Type for JSON-LD files is application/ld+json, but it's a form of JSON and thus may also be served as application/json.

Table 2.4   Linked Data Content-Types

RDF Format	Preferred Content-Type	Alternative Content-Type
RDF Turtle file	text/turtle	
RDF/XML file	application/rdf+xml	
RDFa	text/html	
JSON-LD file	application/ld+json	application/json
OWL file	application/owl+xml	application/rdf+xml
N-Triples	application/N-Triples	text/plain

OWL is a related standard of the W3C that's used for knowledge representation. It's a more formal way to represent logical relations between bits of information. OWL is occasionally used on the Linked Data Web and, being written in RDF, plays well with other Linked Data. OWL files are generally written in XML and served using Content-Types application/owl+xml or application/rdf+xml. The choice of one over the other is subtle; serving an OWL file as application/owl+xml suggests a different way of interpreting the data such that some information is inferred. We'll leave it to you to read the OWL specifications (http://www.w3.org/2004/OWL/#specs) if you care about this subtlety. This book won't describe OWL in any detail.

Finally, we have the lowly N-Triples format. N-Triples is the simplest possible format for RDF but is rarely used outside of automated tests or bulk data transfers (data dumps). The new Content-Type for N-Triples is application/N-Triples, although they have historically been served as plain text (text/plain).

NOTE   The preferred Content-Types for JSON-LD and N-Triples haven't been formally adopted as of this writing, but we expect them to be shortly. We encourage their use so your files will match the way others will use Content-Types by the time you read this. You may see the (older) alternative Content-Types in use by many existing services.

2.6   *File types and web servers*

Web servers should automatically serve the appropriate Content-Type headers, and generally they do. You don't need to tell a web server how to serve PNG or JPEG images or HTML pages because web servers generally ship with support for those file types by default. Unfortunately, most web servers don't yet provide default support for RDF Content-Types. You'll often need to configure your web server to support Linked Data Content-Types or ask your systems administrator to do it for you.

If you don't configure your web server appropriately, files will be served with whatever your web server considers to be its default Content-Type, typically text/plain or the catchall application/octet-stream. Web clients won't have the information they need to determine how to handle your Linked Data content. In the case of text/plain, most browsers will simply display the content as a text file. Content treated as binary (application/octet-stream) will generally cause a browser to prompt the user to save the file. In other words, web browsers won't know what to do with files with an inappropriate Content-Type. Configuring your web server to properly handle Linked Data Content-Types will avoid these problems.

2.6.1 When you can configure Apache

The easiest way to ensure that you serve your Linked Data correctly is to configure your web server to serve the appropriate Content-Type headers. This isn't as hard as it sounds. The directives you need to add are shown in the following listing.

> **Listing 2.6 Apache directives for Linked Data Content-Types**

```
# Directives to ensure RDF files are served as the appropriate Content-Type
AddType text/turtle .ttl
AddType application/rdf+xml .rdf
AddType application/ld+json .jsonld
AddType application/N-Triples .nt
```

The directives may be added to your Apache instance's httpd.conf file, vhost (virtual host) configuration files, or .htaccess files.

> **NOTE** The directives map file extensions to Content-Types. This means that you need to use the file extensions listed in order for the correct Content-Type to be used. For example, any filename in Turtle format must end in .ttl, and JSON-LD filenames must end in .jsonld if you use the directives just shown.

You can create multiple file extensions for a given Content-Type if you like, but good practice suggests that you should use a single one consistently.

> **NOTE** The W3C publishes "Best Practice Recipes for Publishing RDF Vocabularies" at http://www.w3.org/TR/swbp-vocab-pub/. That document contains detailed recipes for publishing RDF content using Apache HTTP servers that include advanced considerations, such as how your data URIs are formed, how to publish RDF documents alongside HTML documents on the same URL, and how to use PURLs.

2.7 When you have limited control over Apache

What do you do if you can't configure Apache directly? You might be able to use a .htaccess file, as described previously, but that will work only if the server administrator has allowed you to override the AddType directive. Fortunately, many bulk web-hosting providers do allow some level of Apache configuration, frequently via an administration interface called cpanel. Cpanel is open source software and is used by many hosting services. If you're fortunate enough to have access to a cpanel to configure your web server, you'll probably have the option to associate Apache handlers with file extensions.

One of the Apache handlers installed by default with Apache is mod_asis, used to send a file as is. A file sent that way can contain HTTP headers separated by a blank line. Using that trick, you can force the web server to send any HTTP headers you wish, including a particular Content-Type. To serve the file /data/dave.ttl with a Content-Type of text/turtle, just configure mod_asis to serve files with the .ttl extension as is and add the appropriate HTTP headers to the file itself, as shown in the following listing.

Listing 2.7 HTTP headers added to a file served with Apache's mod_asis

```
Content-Type: text/turtle

@prefix foaf: <http://xmlns.com/foaf/0.1/> .

<http://3Roundstones.com/dave/#me>
  a foaf:Person .
...
```

NOTE The blank lines shown in listing 2.7 are intentional. The HTTP headers given in an as-is file must be separated by a blank line from the document body, just as they are in an email message. Additionally, a blank line is commonly placed in a Turtle file between the prefixes and the remainder of the document (although that isn't strictly required; it only aids readability).

The combination of mod_asis and a file (with a mapped extension) containing custom HTTP headers will result in the remainder of the file being served with the designated headers. In this case, that means that you can return the appropriate Content-Types from any URL you wish using a stock web-hosting service.

2.8   Linked Data platforms

Naturally, you aren't forced to use Apache or any other particular web server. You could use one of the many Linked Data platforms or Semantic Web products to serve your data instead. Linked Data and Semantic Web platforms and products already know about Turtle, RDF/XML, RDFa, JSON-LD, OWL, and N-Triples and serve the correct Content-Type headers for those types of content.

Chapter 9 will demonstrate the use of Callimachus, an Open Source Linked Data management system. Some of the many alternatives may be found at http://semanticweb.org/wiki/Category:Tool and http://www.w3.org/2001/sw/wiki/Tools.

2.9   Summary

This chapter introduced the Resource Description Framework (RDF) and its relationship to Linked Data. We particularly highlighted the areas where the Linked Data principles further restrict RDF to more closely link data into the World Wide Web. The RDF data model was described along with the key concepts that you're likely to use in your own Linked Data.

Four RDF serialization formats were described: Turtle is the simplest and most human-readable serialization format and the one preferred by most Linked Data professionals. RDF/XML was the first RDF format and is still used widely within enterprises and by those with XML tooling at their fingertips. RDFa is the preferred way to embed RDF data into web pages to describe textual content in HTML. JSON-LD is a new format aimed at web developers who already know and love working with structured data in JSON.

This chapter described how to find and use RDF vocabularies, including how to note that a term in one vocabulary is the same as in another and how to make your own vocabularies. The process for determining when you need to find or create a term was presented.

In closing this chapter, we addressed some common issues of file types and web servers and techniques for resolving those issues. Developers and users both need to be aware of these concerns.

Consuming Linked Data

This chapter covers

- Thinking the Web way
- Finding Linked Data on the Web
- Retrieving Linked Data from web pages
- Combining Linked Data from multiple sources
- Displaying basic Linked Data in HTML

The World Wide Web that most of us envision is technically a subset better defined as the Web of Documents (the Classic Web). Another facet of the WWW is the Web of Data. You should think of the Semantic Web as a web of data that can be processed directly and indirectly by machines.

Just as web documents employ hyperlinks to connect to each other, linked datasets establish connections through the use of RDF links between data items in different datasets. Linked Data conforms to a set of principles for publishing structured data on the World Wide Web.

This chapter will facilitate your understanding of the Web of Data by demonstrating how you can be a consumer of its content. We'll demonstrate how Linked Data is distributed and utilized. We'll show how you can use tools to find embedded Linked Data. We'll illustrate how you can develop programs that retrieve Linked

Data from one source and use those results to retrieve additional data from a different source. We expect that you'll gain a better understanding of the Web of Data and how various companies are utilizing Linked Data to better serve their customers.

3.1 *Thinking like the Web*

Thinking like the Web is important because it enables you to make the best use of this resource. Thinking like the Web means recognizing that the Web provides a global information space that flourishes because embedded links establish relationships among published resources. These resources are stored on different servers in different physical locations. People and machines can traverse these hyperlinks and uncover new information. Search engines can index these links and infer relationships between the documents. By using unambiguous URIs, you facilitate the inferring of relationships.

In general, people search the Web of Documents and manually aggregate related information to fulfill their needs. The volume of hits and ambiguity of unstructured data complicate the task of assembling truly relevant information. For example, how would you know that the Marsha Zaidman in Facebook is the same as the Marsha Zaidman in Twitter? After all, names aren't unique identifiers. If both references to Marsha Zaidman use the same URI, then the identification is unique and the association is obvious.

Here's an example of unstructured data. Imagine an HTML document that contains the following text:

> There is a person "Anakin," known as "Darth Vader" and "Anakin Skywalker." Anakin Skywalker has a wife named Padme Amidala.

Here's similar information presented as structured data using the RDF Turtle format:

```
@base <http://rosemary.umw.edu/~marsha/starwars/foaf.ttl#> .
@prefix foaf: <http://xmlns.com/foaf/0.1/> .
@prefix rdf: <http://www.w3.org/1999/02/22-rdf-syntax-ns#> .
@prefix rdfs: <http://www.w3.org/2000/01/rdf-schema#> .
@prefix rel: <http://purl.org/vocab/relationship>.
@prefix stars: <http://www.starwars.com/explore/encyclopedia/characters/> .
 <me> a foaf:Person;
        foaf:family_name "Skywalker";
        foaf:givenname "Anakin";
        foaf:nick "Darth Vader";
        rel:Spouse_Of <stars:padmeamidala/> .
```

Resolvable URIs eliminate ambiguity over references.

In this sample of structured data, the URIs are resolvable and hence eliminate ambiguity over the identity of Anakin Skywalker and Padme Amidala, his wife. The format of the structured data is predictable and lends itself to machine readability and may be used as input to other applications. Unlike unstructured data, these statements are in a predictable format, precise, and unambiguous. Historically, data on the Web was published as unstructured data in disparate, incompatible formats that impaired machine readability and automated aggregation of related data. Although multiple RDF formats are used in Linked Data, they're compatible because they share a common data model. Therefore, within the RDF formats, you can select one that works best for your particular context without sacrificing interoperability with other data.

In thinking like the Web, you're recognizing the distributed and interconnected highway of information. In using structured data, you're enabling machine readability and indexing of this data. In interlinking published data on the Web, you're enabling reuse of your information. In short, you're facilitating the sharing of information on the Web.

3.2   *How to consume Linked Data*

In this example of how to consume Linked Data, we'll raise a single question and show you how numerous data sources are linked. The ultimate benefit is that you'll learn about Linked Data resources and observe how this data is interlinked across the Web. When these links are traversed manually, you're employing the follow-your-nose method of discovery. Suppose you wanted to know: is President Barack Obama a *Star Wars* fan? Prior to reading this book, you'd likely try one of the popular search engines like Google, Yahoo!, or Bing to help you answer this question. But in this section, we're going to attempt to answer this question using Linked Data.

In general, you can start with any web resource that contains links and then follow your nose from one link to the next. One possible starting point is http://data.NYTimes.com, a portal to a Linked Open Data (LOD) site of *New York Times* sources. We selected this starting point because it's a useful and reliable resource. This page provides an interface that facilitates human browsing of individual records. Selecting "O" and then searching on "Obama, Barack" brings you to a unique URI (http://data.nytimes.com/47452218948077706853). Figure 3.1 *The New York Times* LOD for Barack Obama, is a sample of the HTML display of the subject "Obama, Barack." This page contains a link to a topics page, http://topics.nytimes.com/top/reference/timestopics/people/o/barack_obama/index.HTML.

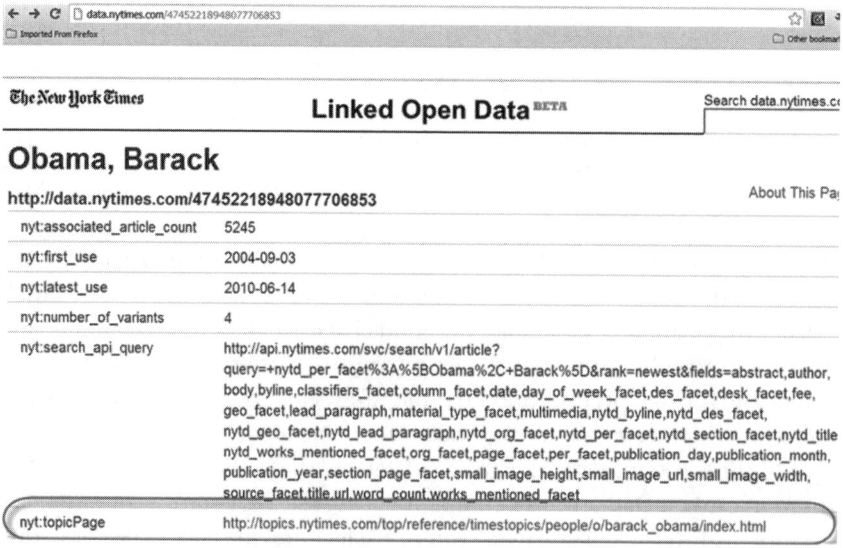

Figure 3.1   *The New York Times* **LOD for Barack Obama**

The topics page contains references and links to a broad variety of information about the subject and other related information. Although this source doesn't provide the answer to our question, it does provide links to other resources that could be useful. Because Obama was a resident of Chicago, perhaps the link to the *Chicago Tribune* would yield further information about Obama and his interest in *Star Wars*. Following these links takes you to the Barack Obama watch maintained by the *Chicago Tribune* (http://www.chicagotribune.com/topic/politics/government/barack-obama-PEPLT007408.topic).

From the *Chicago Tribune* page, you can search for articles related to *Star Wars* and follow the links to http://latimesblogs.latimes.com/washington/2009/09/obama-lightsaber-remix.HTML. This page contains links to http://latimesblogs.latimes.com/washington/2009/09/obi-wan-obama-white-house-olympics.HTML, shown in figure 3.2, and http://www.geeksofdoom.com/2009/09/17/greek-cred-president-obama-with-lightsaber/, shown in figure 3.3. Although we've not yet totally confirmed that Obama is an avid *Star Wars* fan, we've demonstrated the interlinked nature of the Web. We've demonstrated the unintentional reuse of information and benefitted from the unambiguous connections to the RDF data stored in *the New York Times* LOD site. Could you have predicted that you'd navigate from *the New York Times* LOD stores to the *Chicago Tribune*, the *Los Angeles Times*, and the Geeks of Doom website in your quest? Would a Google search have been easier? Maybe, but you wouldn't have been able to automate such a search as you'll learn to do using Linked Data.

Data and documents are distributed over many sites. You navigate from site to site following the links as you might follow the clues in a scavenger hunt. A user or a web spider can follow these links, amassing related data along the way, much like humans follow clues in a scavenger hunt. The next section shows additional examples.

Figure 3.2 Obama using a light saber to defend Chicago as his choice for the Olympics

Figure 3.3 Obama unveiled as a sci-fi fan

3.3   *Tools for finding distributed Linked Data*

Let's assume that you need to find Linked Data for an application that you're developing. Sometimes you may already be aware of a previously published dataset that you can use. More often you need to find such data. Most likely this data is distributed across multiple sources. Numerous tools, such as Sindice, sameas.org, and the Data Hub, that facilitate finding Linked Data are available. You'll find other uses for these tools in chapter 8.

3.3.1   *Sindice*

One useful technology is Sindice (http://sindice.com/main/about), the Semantic Web Index. Sindice does for data what Google does for documents. The objective of Sindice is to provide multiple services: interactive data visualization and validation services, discovery and indexing of data, and search and query services. Sindice describes itself as a platform to build applications on top of semantic data. Sindice collects web data in many ways following existing web standards and updates its holdings frequently. A search using "Star Wars Episode I The Phantom Menace" resulted in identifying more than 2500 documents containing Linked Data that were distributed over 100 sets of Linked Data. Figure 3.4 is a screen shot of these results.

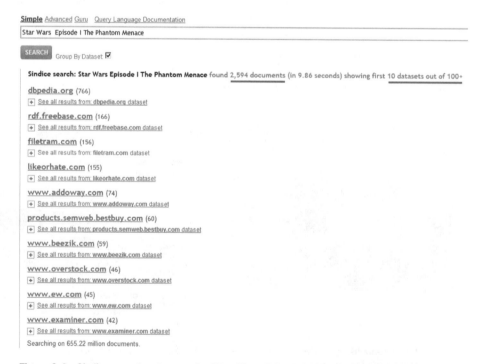

Figure 3.4   Sindice search outcomes for "Star Wars Episode I The Phantom Menace"

```
1.http://dbpedia.org/resource/Ep._1
■ ■ ■
57.http://dbpedia.org/resource/Star_Wars_Episode_I:_The_Phantom_Menace_(comic)
58.http://dbpedialite.org/things/50793#id
■ ■ ■
107.http://dbtropes.org/resource/Main/ThePhantomMenace
108.http://mpii.de/yago/resource/Invasion_of_Naboo
109.http://rdf.freebase.com/ns/m.0ddt_
110.http://rdf.freebase.com/ns/m.0d4dp5
111.http://rdf.freebase.com/ns/m.0f46bd
112.http://rdf.freebase.com/ns/en.star_wars_the_queens_gambit
113.http://rdf.freebase.com/ns/guid.9202a8c04000641f800000000006333f
114.http://rdf.freebase.com/ns/guid.9202a8c04000641f8000000000c232a5
115.http://rdf.freebase.com/ns/guid.9202a8c04000641f8000000000d2194c
116.http://rdf.freebase.com/ns/en.star_wars_episode_i_the_phantom_menace
117.http://sw.opencyc.org/concept/Mx4rvy4d7pwpEbGdrcN5Y29ycA
118.http://sw.opencyc.org/2008/06/10/concept/Mx4rvy4d7pwpEbGdrcN5Y29ycA
119.http://sw.opencyc.org/2009/04/07/concept/Mx4rvy4d7pwpEbGdrcN5Y29ycA
120.http://sw.opencyc.org/2008/06/10/concept/en/StarWarsThePhantomMenace_TheMovie
121.http://sw.opencyc.org/2009/04/07/concept/en/StarWarsThePhantomMenace_TheMovie
122.http://umbel.org/umbel/ne/wikipedia/Invasion_of_Naboo
```

Figure 3.5   Equivalent URIs for dbpedia.org/resource/Star_Wars_Episode_I:_The_Phantom_Menace

3.3.2   SameAs.org

Another avenue for discovery of Linked Data is SameAs.org (http://www.sameas.org). Its objective is to identify equivalent URIs to the Linked Data URI entered and provide an entry point to perform a Sindice search on a general search term.

One such search (see figure 3.5) performed using dbpedia.org/resource/ Star_Wars_Episode_I:_The_Phantom_Menace yielded 122 equivalent URIs for http:// dbpedia.org/resource/Star_Wars_Episode_I:_The_Phantom_Menace. In reviewing those lists of results, you can see that these 122 equivalents are contained in different datasets such as dbpedia.org/resource, dbpedialite.org/things, and rdf.freebase.com/ns.

3.3.3   Data Hub

The Data Hub (http://thedatahub.org) is a community-run catalog of useful sets of Linked Data on the Web. Here you can search and collect links from around the Web. The Data Hub is an openly editable open data catalog, in the style of Wikipedia. Most of the data indexed at the Data Hub is openly licensed, so if you find relevant data, you can use it. Unfortunately, the datasets recovered by our *Star Wars* example aren't relevant. Conducting our search using terms like "Star Wars Episode I" and "Star Wars The Phantom Menace" yielded no results. Trying a more general term yielded useful results. As you can see from figure 3.6, the Internet Movie Database (IMDb) is represented as one of the top three options. Obviously, you'll want to keep this resource in mind for future searches.

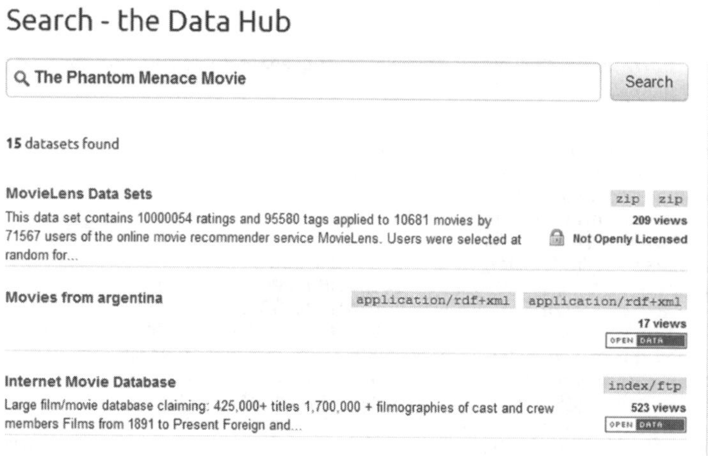

Figure 3.6   Results of searching for datasets on the Data Hub

3.4   Aggregating Linked Data

In section 3.1, we discussed manually finding Linked Data, and we examined tools to facilitate this process. In this section, we'll search published datasets that we're already aware of. You'll become familiar with extracting data from them and learn about the data they contain. We'll use these datasets later in the chapter to illustrate automating the extraction of data that we'll use in a sample application. For this example, we'll use *Star Wars: Episode I* as a sample movie and demonstrate how to find Linked Data about it. In particular, we'll be extracting data from two RDF databases, IMDb and ProductDB.

3.4.1   Aggregating some Linked Data from known datasets

Movies are well represented on the Web and in the Linked Open Data cloud. A good source for movie data is IMDb (http://www.imdb.com). Figure 3.7 is a screenshot of the IMDb listing for *Star Wars: Episode I.*

The IMDb URL associated with *Star Wars: Episode I* can be used as a search term in ProductDB (http://www.productdb.org). You can use this URL as a search key to obtain Linked Data about *Star Wars: Episode I* from ProductDB, an open source Linked Data database about products in general.

As its developer and maintainer Ian Davis says, "ProductDB aims to be the World's most comprehensive and open source of product data." His goal is "to create a page for every product in the world and to connect the underlying structured data together into one huge interlinked dataset." This data is compiled from open sources including ProductWiki (www.productwiki.com/), MusicBrainz (http://musicbrainz.org/), DBpedia (http://dbpedia.org/), Freebase (www.freebase.com/), and OpenLibrary (http://openlibrary.org/). It also is gathered by search engines' crawl sites that publish Good-Relations[1] RDFa or Open Graph protocol (http://opengraphprotocol.org/) data in

---

[1]   GoodRelations, The Web Vocabulary for E-Commerce, http://www.heppnetz.de/projects/goodrelations/.

Figure 3.7   IMDb entry for *Star Wars: Episode I – The Phantom Menace*

their pages; for example, BestBuy, IMDb, and Spotify, (http://www.spotify.com/). This aggregated data is gathered, combined, and analyzed to form linkages and correspondences between resources.

Here's the sequence of steps needed to manually obtain the ProductDB entry for *Star Wars: Episode I.*

Point your browser at http://www.productdb.org, as shown in figure 3.8.

ProductDB has numerous terms available via its pull-down menu that you can use to access the database, including an IMDb URL, as shown in figure 3.9.

We're using the selection IMDb URL. After you input a product code, enter the corresponding URL in the text box below. See figure 3.10 for the completed screen.

Figure 3.8   Homepage for ProductDB

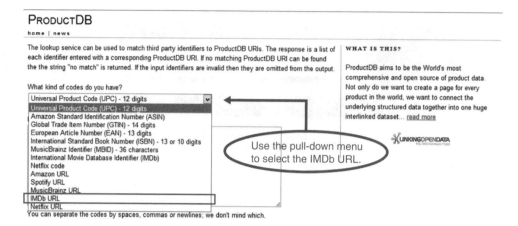

Figure 3.9   **Lookup page for ProductDB**

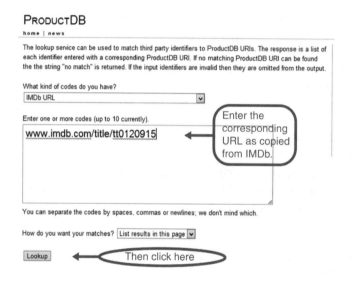

Figure 3.10   **ProductDB lookup page for** *Star Wars: Episode I – The Phantom Menace*

ProductDB accesses its records and displays all matches, as shown in figure 3.11. In this case, there's a single match.

Click the result, and you'll obtain the product information page for the associated item. Note that ProductDB.org leads you to Netflix, Rotten Tomatoes, MOODb, Wikipedia, and other sites.

Figure 3.11   **ProductDB Matches (results) page for** *Star Wars: Episode I – The Phantom Menace*

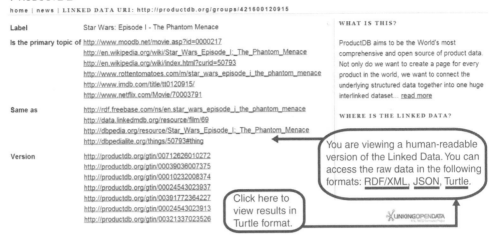

Figure 3.12 ProductDB.org entry for *Star Wars: Episode I – The Phantom Menace*

You can obtain the raw data in Turtle format, as shown in figure 3.12, by clicking the Turtle link on the right-hand side. Those results are shown in listing 3.1.

Listing 3.1 ProductDB.org data for *Star Wars: Episode I* in Turtle format

```
@prefix rdf: <http://www.w3.org/1999/02/22-rdf-syntax-ns#> .
@prefix owl: <http://www.w3.org/2002/07/owl#> .
@prefix ns0: <http://dbpedialite.org/things/50793#> .
@prefix foaf: <http://xmlns.com/foaf/0.1/> .
@prefix ns1: <http://www.rottentomatoes.com/m/> .
@prefix rdfs: <http://www.w3.org/2000/01/rdf-schema#> .
@prefix dct: <http://purl.org/dc/terms/> .
<http://productdb.org/groups/421600120915>
owl:sameAs    <http://data.linkedmdb.org/resource/film/69> ,
<http://rdf.freebase.com/ns/en.star_wars_episode_i_the_phantom_menace> ,
<http://dbpedia.org/resource/Star_Wars_Episode_I:_The_Phantom_Menace> ,

ns0:thing ;
foaf:isPrimaryTopicOf <http://www.imdb.com/title/tt0120915/> ,
<http://www.netflix.com/Movie/70003791> ,
ns1:star_wars_episode_i_the_phantom_menace ,
<http://en.wikipedia.org/wiki/Star_Wars_Episode_I:_The_Phantom_Menace> ,
<http://en.wikipedia.org/wiki/index.HTML?curid=50793> ,
<http://www.moodb.net/movie.asp?id=0000217> ;
rdfs:label "Star Wars: Episode I - The Phantom Menace" .
<http://productdb.org/gtin/00024543023913> dct:isVersionOf  <http://
    productdb.org/groups/421600120915> .
<http://productdb.org/gtin/00010232008374> dct:isVersionOf <http://
    productdb.org/groups/421600120915> .
<http://productdb.org/gtin/00391772364227> dct:isVersionOf <http://
    productdb.org/groups/421600120915> .
<http://productdb.org/gtin/00321337023526> dct:isVersionOf <http://
    productdb.org/groups/421600120915> .
```

Note the use of owl:sameAs to provide additional links.

Note the use of foaf:isPrimaryTopicOf to provide additional links.

```
<http://productdb.org/gtin/00039036007375> dct:isVersionOf <http://
    productdb.org/groups/421600120915> .
<http://productdb.org/gtin/00024543023937> dct:isVersionOf <http://
    productdb.org/groups/421600120915> .
<http://productdb.org/gtin/00712626010272> dct:isVersionOf <http://
    productdb.org/groups/421600120915> .
```

By focusing on the underlying RDFa data compiled by ProductDB, you should see the relationship between *Star Wars: Episode I—The Phantom Menace* and content available from other sources like Netflix (http://www.netflix.com/Movie/70003791), Rotten Tomatoes (http://www.rottentomatoes.com/m/star_wars_episode_i_the_phantom_menace), and MOODb (http://www.moodb.net/movie.asp?id=0000217), among others. This shows how following the data links establishes unanticipated connections. George Lucas would be unlikely to encourage viewers to seek out the description at Rotten Tomatoes. Here episode I is described as "Lucas needs to improve on the plot and character development, but there's plenty of eye candy to behold." Lucas may not approve of this information being tied to his movie, but such data is easily gatherable via Linked Data by referencing the embedded URIs.

3.4.2   Getting Linked Data and RDF from web pages using browser plug-ins

When viewing a web page, the underlying RDFa is generally hidden to the viewer but could be useful when extracted. As an example, the IMDb page contains RDFa, including an image file associated with the movie. One approach to discovering the presence of RDFa data is to install a browser plug-in. We've used a Firefox plug-in called RDFa Developer, but there are many others. The underlying RDFa as discovered by RDFa Developer is displayed in figure 3.13. But you can also automate the finding, extraction, and utilization of RDFa data. We'll demonstrate this technique later in the chapter.

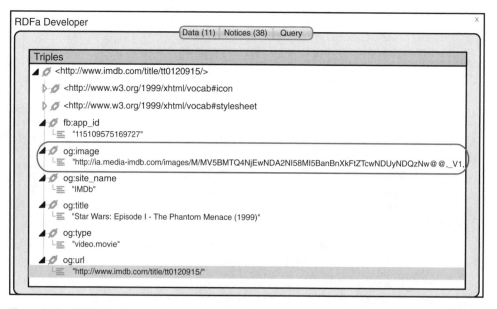

Figure 3.13   IMDb entry for *Star Wars: Episode I – The Phantom Menace* with discovered RDFa displayed

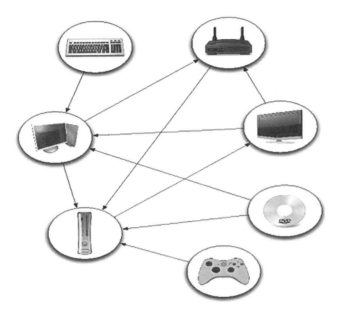

Figure 3.14 Illustration of linked relationships of common products

Jay Myers of Best Buy reports that as many as 100 different criteria could affect the purchase of one product.[2] He expects that the use of semantic data can enhance the Best Buy site, improve the visibility of more than 85% of the products, and help consumers identify more appropriate products. Figure 3.14 demonstrates the semantic relationships between products. Myers expects that "RDFa can ultimately create rich relationships between products, which will in turn 'create a deeper visibility to additional products' when a customer is shopping."[3]

Best Buy's site is a great source of RDFa; see figure 3.15. Myers, lead web development engineer, is a proponent of Linked Data. At the 2010 Semantic Technology Conference, he reported that Best Buy had a 30% increase in search traffic after incorporating RDFa data in its web pages. Myers also reported that the rank of the pages that incorporated Good Relations (a Semantic Web vocabulary) and RDFa rose significantly in Google search results. Myers intends to continue to explore other uses of Linked Data to help consumers discover more relevant products that better meet their needs.

Best Buy's RDFa is linked from ProductDB.org. In addition, you can use SameAs.org to find more data by following links from Best Buy's URIs to other datasets. SameAs.org has 122 related links for *Star Wars: Episode I* given the dbpedia.org URL we retrieved from ProductDB.org. You can use the results from SameAs.org, shown in figure 3.16, to manually discover additional related data.

---

[2] "Better Retailing through Linked Data. Opportunities, perspectives, and vision on Linked Data in retail," http://www.slideshare.net/jaymmyers/better-retailing-through-linked-data.

[3] Richard MacManus, interviewing Jay Myers, "How Best Buy Is Using the Semantic Web," June 30, 2010, http://www.readwriteWeb.com/archives/how_best_buy_is_using_the_semantic_Web.php.

RDFa Developer		X

Data (19)   Notices (15)   Query

Triples	Number of children
◢ 🔗 <http://www.bestbuy.com/site/Star+Wars%3A+Episode+I+-+The+Phant...?id=30545&skuid=4244785&s	9
▷ 🔗 <http://www.w3.org/1999/xhtml/vocab#stylesheet	11
◢ 🔗 fb:app_id	1
└ ☰ "125188000891129"	
◢ 🔗 og:description	1
└ ☰ "Star Wars: Episode I - The Phantom Menace - Widescreen - DVD"	
◢ 🔗 og:image	1
└ ☰ "http://images.bestbuy.com:80/BestBuy_US/images/products/4244/4244785s.jpg"	
◢ 🔗 og:site_name	1
└ ☰ "Best Buy"	
◢ 🔗 og:title	1
└ ☰ "Star Wars: Episode I - The Phantom Menace - Widescreen - DVD"	
◢ 🔗 og:type	1
└ ☰ "product"	
◢ 🔗 og:upc	1
└ ☰ "024543023920"	
◢ 🔗 og:url	1
└ ☰ "http://www.bestbuy.com/site/Star+Wars%3A+Episode+I+-+The+Phant...?id=30545&skuid=4244785&st=star%	

Figure 3.15   Best Buy's RDFa for *Star Wars: Episode I*

You can use the outcome of SameAs.org to help identify a *canonical URL* for a given item. A canonical URL is the best URL among available choices. For example, you may consider www.example.com, example.com/, www.example.com/index.HTML, and example.com/home.asp interchangeable. However similar, each of these URLs may return different content. A canonical URL is the preferred URL and often refers to an item's homepage.

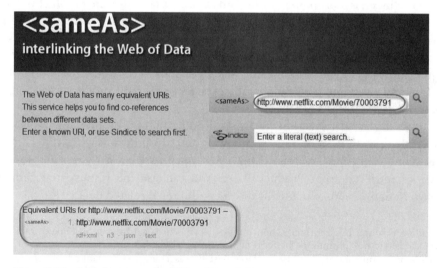

Figure 3.16   SameAs.org results for *Star Wars: Episode I*

3.5 *Crawling the Linked Data Web and aggregating data*

In previous sections we've illustrated how to manually follow your nose and use tools to find data on the Web. As a developer, you may be interested in consuming existing data by combining extracted data and using it in another application. For such purposes, we'd prefer to automate the processing of the aggregation of data. In this section, we'll develop an application that will illustrate such automation. This application will show you how to use the Python scripting language, RDFLib, and html5lib to access the RDFa data available from Best Buy for a sample product, the Darth Vader Alarm Clock Radio. This application also accesses the data stored for the Darth Vader Alarm Clock Radio from the ProductDB database. All of this RDF data is gathered and displayed in a three-column table of subject, predicate, and object.

3.5.1 *Using Python to crawl the Linked Data Web*

We've chosen the Python scripting language because it supports gathering and using aggregated RDF information. The example script (listing 3.2) will gather RDFa Linked Data about the Darth Vader Alarm Clock Radio, shown in figure 3.17, from Best Buy web pages and use that data to obtain more linked information from ProductDB.

In the case of the Darth Vader Alarm Clock Radio, the RDFa Developer plug-in identified a triple that contained the UPC for this product. This UPC is used to search ProductDB. The output (output.html) contains the HTML for a web page that displays these discovered triples as a table of TTL statement components, as shown in figure 3.18.

> **NOTE** The execution of this script requires that a Python interpreter be installed together with RDFlib and html5lib.

You can download a Python interpreter from Python.org (http://python.org). Follow the guidelines at http://wiki.python.org/moin/BeginnersGuide/Download to select the installation package to meet your needs.

Best Buy › Home › Cartoon & Popular Characters › Star Wars Merchandise › Product Info

Star Wars - Darth Vader Alarm Clock Radio - Black

Model: 15200 SKU: 4711825

⭐⭐⭐⭐⭐ 4.0 of 5 (2 reviews)

Shipping: Usually leaves our warehouse in 1 business day

Estimate Arrival Time

Store Pickup:

Check Stores

Learn about Store Pickup Plus

Figure 3.17   Best Buy's Web page for Darth Vader Alarm Clock Radio

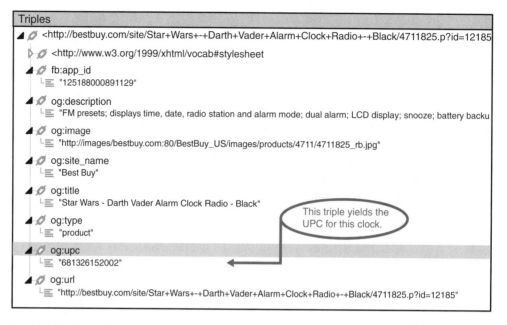

Figure 3.18   RDFa data from Best Buy's web page

To run these scripts successfully, the libraries RDFLib and html5lib *must* be installed. You can obtain RDFLib from https://github.com/RDFLib/rdflib. This library will allow you to successfully pull down the Turtle file from ProductDB. Best Buy utilizes HTML5, which requires html5lib. This library is available from http://code.google.com/p/html5lib/downloads/detail?name=html5lib-0.95.tar.gz&can=2&q=. These downloads should be stored in [PYTHON HOME]/lib. Installing these libraries should take no more than a few minutes and will allow you to run the Python script outlined in the following listing.

Listing 3.2   A Python script for aggregating RDF data for HTML display

```
#! /usr/bin/python

import rdflib
import html5lib

output = open("output.HTML", "w")

productDBGraph = rdflib.Graph()
productDBResult =
    productDBGraph.parse('http://productdb.org/gtin/00681326152002.ttl',
    format='turtle')

bestBuyGraph = rdflib.Graph()
bestBuyResult =
```

Establish the graph from ProductDB using RDFLib to parse it.

Establish the graph from Best Buy using RDFLib and html5lib to parse it.

```
    bestBuyGraph.parse('http://purl.org/net/BestBuyDarthVaderClock',
      format='rdfa')
print >>output, """<HTML>
<head>
    <title>Product Information</title>
</head>
<body>
<table border="1">"""

print >>output,
    "<tr><th>Subject</th><th>Predicate</th><th>Object</th></tr>"

for sub, pred, obj in productDBGraph:
    print >>output, "<tr><td>%s</td><td>%s</td><td>%s</td></tr>" % (sub,
      pred, obj)

for sub, pred, obj in bestBuyGraph:
    print >>output, "<tr><td>%s</td><td>%s</td><td>%s</td></tr>" % (sub,
      pred, obj)

print >>output, """</table>
</body></HTML>"""
```

> Begin printing HTML page that will contain RDF.

> A PURL was used here instead of a very long Best Buy URL.[4] This is a redirect so that the URL is more readable.

> Print subject, predicate, and object of all triples pulled from both ProductDB and Best Buy and place them into an HTML table.

3.5.2   Creating HTML output from your aggregated RDF

In addition to aggregating RDF data from both Best Buy and ProductDB, the Python script in listing 3.2 creates an HTML output file named output.html. We could have retained the aggregated data in a file of triples, but we chose to display it in HTML format so that you could better appreciate the findings. This file should be opened in a browser. The first screen of the HTML file produced should contain the content shown in table 3.1. Each row in the table represents a set of Turtle triples.

Table 3.1   Representative sample output for listing 3.2

Subject	Predicate	Object
http://productdb.org/ gtin/00681326152002	http://purl.org/goodrelations/ v1#hasGTIN-14	00681326152002
http://productdb.org/ gtin/00681326152002	http://purl.org/goodrelations/ v1#hasManufacturer	http://productdb.org/brands/star-wars
http://productdb.org/ gtin/00681326152002	http://schema.org/manufac- turer	http://productdb.org/brands/star-wars
http://productdb.org/ gtin/00681326152002	http://schema.org/image	http://images.bestbuy.com/BestBuy_US/images/ products/4711/4711825_rc.jpg

---

[4] Best Buy URL referenced in listing 3.2, http://www.bestbuy.com/site/Star+Wars+-Darth+Vader+Alarm+Clock +Radio+-+Black/4711825.p?id=1218515225401&skuId=4711825&st=Star%20Wars&cp=1&lp=7

Table 3.1   Representative sample output for listing 3.2 (continued)

Subject	Predicate	Object
http://productdb.org/gtin/00681326152002	http://schema.org/url	http://www.bestbuy.com/site/Star+Wars+-+Darth+Vader+Alarm+Clock+Radio+-+Black/4711825.p?id=1218515225401&skuId=4711825&cmp=RMX&ky=2nBwHqIqwH8HeGDnJH2Cia1DoDKws99jo
http://productdb.org/gtin/00681326152002	http://schema.org/productID	0681326152002
http://productdb.org/gtin/00681326152002	http://schema.org/name	Star Wars - Darth Vader Alarm Clock Radio – Black
http://productdb.org/gtin/00681326152002	http://open.vocab.org/terms/category	http://productdb.org/classifications/bestbuy/pcmcat263000050000
http://productdb.org/gtin/00681326152002	http://www.w3.org/1999/02/22-rdf-syntax-ns#type	http://schema.org/Product
http://productdb.org/gtin/00681326152002	http://www.w3.org/1999/02/22-rdf-syntax-ns#type	http://purl.org/goodrelations/v1#ProductOrService-Model

This application aggregated data and demonstrated how Python can be used together with RDFLib and html5lib to extract RDF data from Best Buy and ProductDB. We then formatted the aggregated data as HTML so that you can examine the output in a browser. In chapters 6, 7, and 9, we'll illustrate how this aggregated data can be retained or piped and reused in other applications.

3.6   *Summary*

The purpose of this chapter was to expose you to the multiple facets of consuming Linked Data from the Web. To this end, we explored what it means to think the Web way. We explored finding Linked Data on the Web by manually following your nose and facilitating the process through the use of special tools. Finally, we illustrated how you could use Python, RDFLib, and html5lib to develop programs that retrieve Linked Data from one source and use those results to retrieve additional data from a different data source. In subsequent chapters, we'll emphasize techniques for developing and publishing your own Linked Data and enhanced search techniques for aggregating such data.

Part 2

Taming Linked Data

What's the Friend of a Friend (FOAF) vocabulary, and how can you use it to publish a FOAF profile about yourself? What are some other related vocabularies, and where do you find them? What is SPARQL, and how can you use it to find desired Linked Data on the Web?

Part 1 focused on understanding and consuming Linked Data. After completing part 2, you'll be able to create and publish your own FOAF profile. You'll be able to use SPARQL to query the Web of Data and aggregate those results for future applications.

Creating Linked Data with FOAF

This chapter covers

- A brief description of the Friend of a Friend (FOAF) project
- Creating a personal description of yourself using FOAF
- Using your FOAF profile and a gift wish list to discover relevant product information
- Updating and extending your FOAF profile

Now that you've had experience discovering published Linked Data, this chapter will guide you in creating and publishing your own data. A simple way to start is by creating a personal Linked Data profile. Such profiles are based on the Friend of a Friend vocabulary.

The FOAF project was started in 2000 to generate a web of machine-readable pages that describe people, thus supporting the Semantic Web goal of creating a machine-accessible Web of Data. The project is popular and has exceeded its expectations. FOAF facilitates a Semantic Web equivalent of a typical HTML homepage. This chapter will familiarize you with FOAF, illustrate how you can create your personal FOAF profile, and show you how to join the FOAF community by publishing your data publicly.

The FOAF project began as an "experimental linked information project." Dan Brickley[1] and Libby Miller[2] are responsible for its inception, and Edd Dumbill (http://radar.oreilly.com/edd) and Leigh Dodds (www.ldodds.com/) notably contributed to its success. FOAF enables you to describe people, their interests, their achievements, their activities, and their relationship with other people. Because it produces RDF data files, that information can be easily machine harvested and aggregated. Like all RDF vocabularies, FOAF descriptions can be easily combined with other RDF vocabularies. Hence, FOAF documents can be linked together. Such aggregations enrich the Web of Data.

This chapter will guide you in developing such a profile by demonstrating the process using Anakin Skywalker and his alter ego, Darth Vader. We'll demonstrate two methods for developing a FOAF profile: (1) by manually developing Anakin's profile using a simple editor and several verification tools, and (2) by having the user enter the desired information into an HTML form that automatically produces a FOAF profile. We selected this sequence so that you'd be familiar with the contents of a FOAF profile and be able to appreciate the ease with which you can create a basic profile using an online tool we developed.

Regardless of the method that you choose to follow, you'd publish this profile and related documents on the Web. We'll then develop and demonstrate a Python program that extracts data from a FOAF profile and a personal gift wish list (RDF/Turtle format) and discovers other related information. In the process, we'll demonstrate how additional vocabularies can be used to expand a basic FOAF profile.

4.1   Creating a personal FOAF profile

This section will introduce the FOAF vocabulary and illustrate how you can use it to create a personal FOAF profile document, the equivalent of a personal HTML homepage. Anakin Skywalker (Darth Vader) will be the subject of our FOAF profile. The schema and descriptions of the FOAF vocabulary are accessible from http://xmlns.com/foaf/0.1/. FOAF contains the classes and properties listed in table 4.1.

Table 4.1   FOAF classes and properties[a]

Classes		
Agent	OnlineAccount	Person
Document	OnlineChatAccount	PersonalProfileDocument
Group	OnlineEcommerceAccount	Project
Image	OnlineGamingAccount	
LabelProperty	Organization	

[1]   Resume of Dan Brickley, http://danbri.org/cv/DanBrickley2012ResumePub.pdf.
[2]   Resume of Dr. Libby Miller, http://www.bris.ac.uk/ilrt/people/libby-m-miller/overview.html.

Table 4.1 FOAF classes and properties[a] *(continued)*

Properties		
account	homepage	pastProject
accountName	icqChatID	phone
accountServiceHomepage	img	plan
age	interest	primaryTopic
aimChatID	isPrimaryTopicOf	publications
based_near	jabbered	schoolHomepage
birthday	knows	sha1
currentProject	lastName	skypeID
depiction	logo	status
depicts	made	surname
dnaChecksum	maker	theme
familyName	mbox	thumbnail
family_name	mbox_sha1sum	tipjar
firstName	member	title
focus	membershipClass	topic
fundedby	msnchatID	topic_interest
geekcode	myersBriggs	weblog
gender	name	workInfoHomepage
givenName	nick	workplaceHomepage
givenname	openid	yahooChatID
holdsAccount	page	

a. "FOAF Vocabulary Specification 0.98," Namespace Document, 9 August 2010, http://xmlns.com/foaf/spec/#term_Person.

NOTE http://xmlns.com/foaf/0.1/ is a PURL (Persistent URL) for http://xmlns.com/foaf/spec/. PURLs are web addresses that act as permanent identifiers.[3] If the underlying web address is relocated, then the PURL will ensure that the proper redirection will automatically occur. Thus, PURLs provide continuity of references to network resources that may migrate from machine to machine. In this case, the use of the PURL ensures permanent access to the FOAF vocabulary.

4.1.1 Introducing the FOAF vocabulary

As table 4.1 illustrates, the FOAF vocabulary has many classes and properties. Rather than expanding on all of these, we'll restrict our discussion to the Person class. The Person class could be viewed as a key component of the FOAF vocabulary and is actually a subclass of Agent. We'll illustrate its properties and basic usage in composing

---

[3] Purl administrator interface, http://purl.oclc.org/docs/index.html.

our FOAF profile for Anakin Skywalker. The `Person` class is the core of the FOAF vocabulary. Its purpose is to describe people. They can be alive, dead, real, or fictitious. The `Person` class contains the properties listed in table 4.2.

Table 4.2   Properties of FOAF `Person` class

myersBriggs	familyName	publications	lastName
family_name	plan	firstName	currentProject
surname	knows	workInfoHomepage	pastProject
geekcode	schoolHomepage	workplaceHomepage	img

The meanings of most of these terms are easily inferred from their names. You may also notice that some properties appear redundant, like `familyName`, `family_name`, and `Surname`. These overlapping terms were included to recognize worldwide cultural diversity in common usage. A detailed explanation and description of the significance of each term are available at http://xmlns.com/foaf/spec/#term_Person.

NOTE   Keep in mind that a FOAF profile is like a personal homepage and is meant to be a public profile, so be careful only to say things on the Web that you want to be public.

4.1.2   *Method I: manual creation of a basic FOAF profile*

Using our editor and our knowledge of Anakin Skywalker, we've drafted a basic FOAF profile that Anakin might publish. Listing 4.1, the basic FOAF profile for Anakin Skywalker, contains statements that apply many of the FOAF classes and properties, especially from the `Person` class. Like a personal homepage, this document conveys "My name is Anakin Skywalker; I'm a Jedi; my nickname is The Chosen One; for more information see Darth_Vader's profile." Once published, FOAF profiles can be linked to form a Web of Data. The advantage over an HTML homepage description is that the vocabulary is well defined and unambiguous. This FOAF profile applies 14 of the properties from the FOAF vocabulary listed in table 4.1 and table 4.2.

Listing 4.1   Sample FOAF profile for Anakin Skywalker, aka Darth Vader

```
@base <http://rosemary.umw.edu/~marsha/starwars/foaf.ttl#>.
@prefix foaf: <http://xmlns.com/foaf/0.1/> .
@prefix rdf: <http://www.w3.org/1999/02/22-rdf-syntax-ns#> .          Prefix abbreviations
@prefix rdfs: <http://www.w3.org/2000/01/rdf-schema#> .               for web references
@prefix stars: <http://www.starwars.com/explore/encyclopedia/characters/>.

    <me> a foaf:Person;
        foaf:family_name "Skywalker";
        foaf:givenname "Anakin";
        foaf:gender "Male";
        foaf:title "Mr.";
        foaf:homepage <http://www.imdb.com/character/ch0000005/bio>;
```

```
Encoded       ┌─▷   foaf:mbox_sha1sum "d37a210cadc241b0f7aeb76069e58843bd8940a0";
shalsum             foaf:name "Anakin Skywalker";
mailbox             foaf:nick "The Chosen One";
address             foaf:phone <tel:8665550100>;                    ◁─   The tel: notation
                    foaf:title "Jedi";                                    isn't a namespace;
                    foaf:workplaceHomepage <stars:anakinskywalker/> .     it's a URI scheme
              <me> a foaf:PersonalProfileDocument;                        the same as http:.⁴
                    foaf:primaryTopic  <me>;
                    rdfs:seeAlso <http://live.dbpedia.org/page/Darth_Vader> .
```

You'll notice that the email address (darthvader@example.com) isn't published as plain text but is encoded using an algorithm. Discussions and descriptions of the sha1sum algorithm are accessible from http://xmlns.com/foaf/spec/#term_mbox_sha1sum and www.gnu.org/software/coreutils/manual/html_node/Summarizing-files.html #Summarizing-files.

Publishing a plain-text email address is an invitation to trouble. Another important point about `foaf:mbox_sha1sum` is that this property as well as `foaf:mbox` and `foaf:homepage` are inverse functional properties. This means that an aggregator that finds two resources with the same values for an inverse functional property may safely merge the descriptions and relations as belonging to the same person. This process is referred to as *smushing*. Some controversy about the appropriateness of such smushing exists within the Linked Data community. Some developers prefer that such inferences be drawn by other means. Although some of the properties illustrated are from the FOAF vocabulary but outside the `Person` class, these properties were included because they're self-explanatory and help us provide a richer description of Anakin Skywalker, aka Darth Vader.

4.1.3   *Enhancing a basic FOAF profile*

Now that we've illustrated a FOAF profile (listing 4.1) with basic metadata about Anakin Skywalker, we'll take this a step further and describe, in listing 4.2, his relationship with another person. The `foaf:knows` property simply asserts that there is some relationship between two people. It deliberately doesn't imply that this relationship is reciprocal. Other vocabularies and other communities can further define the different types of relationships. The URI for one such vocabulary is http://purl.org/vocab/ relationship. When abbreviating terms, the suggested prefix is `rel`.

Each class or property in the vocabulary has a URI constructed by appending a term name to the vocabulary URI, for example, http://purl.org/vocab/relationship/ friendOf.

Listing 4.2   Enhanced FOAF profile modeling the `foaf:knows` relationship

```
@base <http://rosemary.umw.edu/~marsha/starwars/foaf.ttl#>.
@prefix foaf: <http://xmlns.com/foaf/0.1/> .
@prefix rdf: <http://www.w3.org/1999/02/22-rdf-syntax-ns#> .
```

---

⁴ The tel: URI scheme is defined in RDF 3966, http://tools.ietf.org/html/rfc3966.

```
@prefix rdfs: <http://www.w3.org/2000/01/rdf-schema#> .
@prefix stars:
   <http://www.starwars.com/explore/encyclopedia/characters/>.

<me> a foaf:Person;
    foaf:family_name "Skywalker";
    foaf:givenname "Anakin";
    foaf:gender "Male";
    foaf:title "Mr.";
    foaf:knows   [
        a foaf:Person;
        foaf:mbox_sha1sum
            "aadfbacb9de289977d85974fda32baff4b60ca86";
        foaf:name "Obi-Wan Kenobi";
        rdfs:seeAlso <http://live.dbpedia.org/page/Obi-
            Wan_Kenobi>
        ];
    foaf:homepage
        <http://www.imdb.com/character/ch0000005/bio>;
    foaf:mbox_sha1sum
        "d37a210cadc241b0f7aeb76069e58843bd8940a0";
    foaf:name "Anakin Skywalker";
    foaf:nick "The Chosen One";
    foaf:phone <tel:8665550100>;
    foaf:title "Jedi";
    foaf:workplaceHomepage <stars:anakinskywalker/> .
    <me> a foaf:PersonalProfileDocument;
    foaf:primaryTopic  <me> .
```

Example of foaf:knows

The next listing illustrates the Relationship vocabulary and smushing. Not only does Anakin Skywalker "know" Obi-Wan Kenobi, but the `rel:enemyOf` property implies that Anakin is unlikely to invite Obi-Wan to dinner. Certainly this is a more precise relationship than the broader and imprecise `foaf:knows`.

Listing 4.3   An enhanced FOAF profile using additional `rdfs` and `rel` properties

```
@base <http://rosemary.umw.edu/~marsha/starwars/foaf.ttl#>.
@prefix foaf: <http://xmlns.com/foaf/0.1/> .
@prefix rdf: <http://www.w3.org/1999/02/22-rdf-syntax-ns#> .
@prefix rdfs: <http://www.w3.org/2000/01/rdf-schema#> .
@prefix rel: <http://purl.org/vocab/relationship>.
@prefix stars:
    <http://www.starwars.com/explore/encyclopedia/characters/>.
<me> a foaf:Person;
    foaf:family_name "Skywalker";
    foaf:givenname "Anakin";
    foaf:gender "Male";
    foaf:title "Mr.";

    foaf:knows   [
        a foaf:Person;
        foaf:mbox_sha1sum "d37a210cadc241b0f7aeb76069e58843bd8940a0";
        foaf:name "Darth Vader";
        rel:enemyOf <http://live.dbpedia.org/page/Obi-Wan_Kenobi>;
```

Examples of rel:enemyOf

```
        ];
                                                                Examples of
        foaf:knows  [                                           rel:enemyOf
            a foaf:Person;
            foaf:mbox_sha1sum "aadfbacb9de289977d85974fda32baff4b60ca86";
            foaf:name "Obi-Wan Kenobi";
            rdfs:seeAlso <http://live.dbpedia.org/page/Obi-Wan_Kenobi>;
            rel:enemyOf <me>;
            ];
        foaf:homepage <http://www.imdb.com/character/ch0000005/bio>;
        foaf:mbox_sha1sum "d37a210cadc241b0f7aeb76069e58843bd8940a0";
        foaf:name "Anakin Skywalker";
        foaf:nick "The Chosen One";
        foaf:phone <tel:8665550100>;
        foaf:title "Jedi";
        foaf:workplaceHomepage <stars:anakinskywalker/> .
    <me> a foaf:PersonalProfileDocument;
        foaf:primaryTopic  <me> .
```

You'll notice that the foaf:mbox_sha1sum properties are identical for Anakin Sky-walker and Darth Vader. Within the Linked Data community, these two are recognized as the same person.

Now that we have a FOAF profile, we need to publish it to the Web and link this new information into the existing web of FOAF data. To publish a profile on the Web, store it in a publicly accessible web space.

In our case, we've published Anakin's FOAF profile at http://rosemary.umw.edu/~marsha/starwars/foaf.ttl. As we've done, you should title your file foaf.ttl. You're now in a position to join the FOAF community by publishing your own FOAF profile and applying one or both of the following methods. Use the HTML link tag to point to FOAF descriptions. Here's how it should look:

```
<link rel="alternate" type="text/turtle" href="http://
    yourPublicWebSpace/FOAF.ttl" title="My FOAF" />
```

- Include references to the FOAF files of your friends by including links to those files in your FOAF profile. For example, you can reference Marsha's FOAF description by adding

```
rdfs:seeAlso <http://rosemary.umw.edu/~marsha/foaf.ttl>
```

- You could also use seeAlso to provide a link to a Facebook, LinkedIn, or Pinter-est account of yourself or a friend.

4.1.4 *Method II: automated generation of a FOAF profile*

The purpose of creating a FOAF profile manually was to acquaint you with the FOAF vocabulary. But a simpler way to generate a FOAF profile document is to use an application like the 3 Round Stones FOAF profile generator we developed, which you can access from http://purl.org/net/LinkedData/FoafGenerator. This application will guide you through entering your personal data and will produce a FOAF profile in Turtle format. Note that none of the information you enter in this page is used or

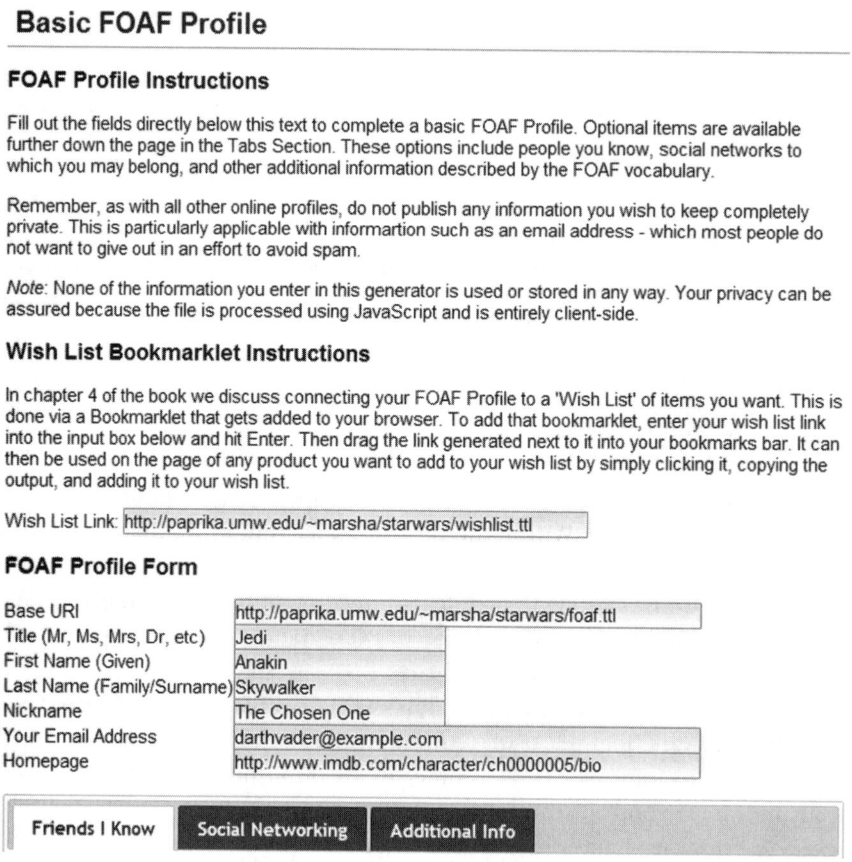

Basic FOAF Profile

FOAF Profile Instructions

Fill out the fields directly below this text to complete a basic FOAF Profile. Optional items are available further down the page in the Tabs Section. These options include people you know, social networks to which you may belong, and other additional information described by the FOAF vocabulary.

Remember, as with all other online profiles, do not publish any information you wish to keep completely private. This is particularly applicable with informartion such as an email address - which most people do not want to give out in an effort to avoid spam.

Note: None of the information you enter in this generator is used or stored in any way. Your privacy can be assured because the file is processed using JavaScript and is entirely client-side.

Wish List Bookmarklet Instructions

In chapter 4 of the book we discuss connecting your FOAF Profile to a 'Wish List' of items you want. This is done via a Bookmarklet that gets added to your browser. To add that bookmarklet, enter your wish list link into the input box below and hit Enter. Then drag the link generated next to it into your bookmarks bar. It can then be used on the page of any product you want to add to your wish list by simply clicking it, copying the output, and adding it to your wish list.

Wish List Link: http://paprika.umw.edu/~marsha/starwars/wishlist.ttl

FOAF Profile Form

Base URI	http://paprika.umw.edu/~marsha/starwars/foaf.ttl
Title (Mr, Ms, Mrs, Dr, etc)	Jedi
First Name (Given)	Anakin
Last Name (Family/Surname)	Skywalker
Nickname	The Chosen One
Your Email Address	darthvader@example.com
Homepage	http://www.imdb.com/character/ch0000005/bio

Friends I Know   Social Networking   Additional Info

Figure 4.1   FOAF profile generator—opening screen

automatically stored in any way. Figure 4.1 is the opening screen for this application. The user completes the basic information as desired. You may omit any field as needed. After completing the basic information, you should select each of the tabs at the bottom of the page and submit the requested information.

The top section of figure 4.1 refers to personal metadata. When you click the Friends I Know tab you'll see data about people you know. Entering links to their email addresses and/or FOAF profiles will enable your FOAF profile to link to others on the Web of Data. The Social Networking tab requests data about your links to other social networking sites and connects your FOAF profile to other related data on the Web. The Additional Info tab refers to additional personal information like your most recent publication(s). When you've entered all of the desired data, follow the instructions displayed. Your FOAF profile document in Turtle format will be displayed in the text box at the center of the screen shown in figure 4.2. You'll need to save this and publish it on the Web.

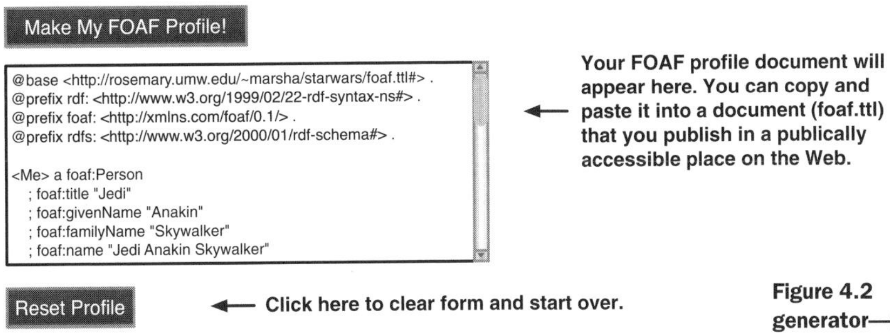

Make My FOAF Profile!

```
@base <http://rosemary.umw.edu/~marsha/starwars/foaf.ttl#> .
@prefix rdf: <http://www.w3.org/1999/02/22-rdf-syntax-ns#> .
@prefix foaf: <http://xmlns.com/foaf/0.1/> .
@prefix rdfs: <http://www.w3.org/2000/01/rdf-schema#> .

<Me> a foaf:Person
  ; foaf:title "Jedi"
  ; foaf:givenName "Anakin"
  ; foaf:familyName "Skywalker"
  ; foaf:name "Jedi Anakin Skywalker"
```

◄— **Your FOAF profile document will appear here. You can copy and paste it into a document (foaf.ttl) that you publish in a publically accessible place on the Web.**

Reset Profile ◄— **Click here to clear form and start over.**

Figure 4.2 FOAF profile generator—final screen

Most of the requested data in this section of the generator is self-explanatory. But the Base URI refers to the URI of where this FOAF profile will ultimately be stored for web accessibility. The Homepage refers to the URI of your HTML homepage. Although you're entering your email address in human-readable form, that address will be encrypted using a sha1sum algorithm, which we discussed in section 4.1.2, creating a personal FOAF profile

You may submit information for as many friends as you'd like; just click Add Friend for each friend more than the first three. Again, their email addresses will be encrypted in the final FOAF profile generated. When you finish entering information for your friends, click another tab (Social Networking or Additional Info). You can go back to any of the tabbed sections to review and edit your information as needed.

The Social Networking tab is intended to help establish connections to typical social media sites. This information is often included on a personal HTML homepage, and because a FOAF profile is similar to that, you'd expect to see these links included here as well.

The FOAF profile in Turtle format is complete and ready to be published. Listing 4.4 is the FOAF profile produced by the 3 Round Stones FOAF profile generator. You can see many similarities to the FOAF profiles that we generated manually earlier in this chapter.

The output from the 3 Round Stones FOAF profile generator is formatted a little differently from listings 4.1, 4.2, and 4.3. In listing 4.4, the semicolons and periods that terminate Turtle statements are found at the start of subsequent statements rather than the end of the previous line. This is a preferred style because all the punctuation is vertically aligned. The use of prefixes is limited to common vocabulary prefixes. Logically, the FOAF profile generated automatically is equivalent to those we wrote manually in this chapter.

Listing 4.4 FOAF profile as generated by 3 Round Stones FOAF profile generator

```
@base <http://rosemary.umw.edu/~marsha/starwars/foaf.ttl#> .
@prefix rdf: <http://www.w3.org/1999/02/22-rdf-syntax-ns#> .
@prefix foaf: <http://xmlns.com/foaf/0.1/> .
@prefix rdfs: <http://www.w3.org/2000/01/rdf-schema#> .

<Me> a foaf:Person
```
Common vocabularies and their prefixes

```
; foaf:title "Jedi"
; foaf:givenName "Anakin"
; foaf:familyName "Skywalker"
; foaf:name "Jedi Anakin Skywalker"
; foaf:nick "The Chosen One"
; foaf:mbox_sha1sum "d37a210cadc241b0f7aeb76069e58843bd8940a0"
; foaf:homepage <http://www.imdb.com/character/ch0000005/bio>
; foaf:account <https://www.facebook.com/pages/Darth-Vader/10959490906484>

; foaf:age "100"
; foaf:img <http://www.starwars.com/img/explore/encyclopedia/characters/
  darthvader_detail.png>
.


<http://rosemary.umw.edu/~marsha/starwars/foaf.ttl#Me>
  foaf:knows <d37a210cadc241b0f7aeb76069e58843bd8940a0> .

<d37a210cadc241b0f7aeb76069e58843bd8940a0> a foaf:Person
  ; foaf:name "Darth Vader"
.


<http://rosemary.umw.edu/~marsha/starwars/foaf.ttl#Me>
  foaf:knows <548a58890349e5af34cee097c31c8c16591cd58f> .

<548a58890349e5af34cee097c31c8c16591cd58f> a foaf:Person
  ; foaf:name "Obi-Wan Kenobi"
.
```

This section introduced you to the FOAF vocabulary and demonstrated its use in creating a personal FOAF profile. The FOAF profile produced in this section closely resembles the content you'd expect in your homepage. You can create this profile manually using an editor or you can use our automated 3 Round Stones FOAF profile generator, http://purl.org/net/LinkedData/FoafGenerator. In either case, you can retain and later optionally edit this profile to include additional data.

4.2   *Adding more content to a FOAF profile*

You can customize your foaf.ttl document further by adding statements with additional information about yourself. There are numerous vocabularies in widespread use that cover common types of data and that should be used wherever possible. One of these vocabularies, the Basic Geo (WGS84 lat/long) vocabulary at http://www.w3.org/2003/01/geo/, defines terms such as *lat* and *long* for describing geographically located things. The following listing illustrates the use of the WGS84 vocabulary.

Listing 4.5   Example of using the WGS84 Basic Geo vocabulary

Defining geo as the prefix to the Geo vocabulary

```
@base <http://rosemary.umw.edu/~marsha/foaf.ttl> .
@prefix foaf: <http://xmlns.com/foaf/0.1/> .
@prefix dc: <http://purl.org/dc/elements/1.1/> .
@prefix geo: <http://www.w3.org/2003/01/geo/wgs84_pos#> .
```

Defining dc as the prefix to the Dublin Core vocabulary

```
<me> a foaf:person;
    foaf:based_near  [
            geo:lat "38.301304";
            geo:long "-77.47447" ];
    foaf:homepage [
            dc:title "Marsha's home page" ],
            <http://rosemary.umw.edu/~marsha/index.html>;
    foaf:name "Marsha Zaidman" .
```

Use of the geo:lat and geo:long properties

You can further enhance your FOAF profile by including statements that utilize additional properties from the FOAF (http://xmlns.com/foaf/0.1/) and Relationship vocabularies (http://vocab.org/relationship/.html). Terms from the Relationship vocabulary created by Eric Vitiello are listed in table 4.3. The following example will apply the property foaf:img as well as other properties from the Relationship vocabulary.

NOTE foaf:img should have been called foaf:mug_shot because it's intended to relate a person to an image. It's inappropriate to use it in the context of an image of an animal or other object. This img property doesn't have any restrictions on the dimensions or color depth of the image to which it relates.

Table 4.3 Terms from the Relationship vocabulary

acquaintanceOf	enemyOf	lostContactWith
ambivalentOf	engagedTo	mentorOf
ancestorOf	friendOf	neighborOf
antagonistOf	grandchildOf	parentOf
apprenticeTo	grandparentOf	Participant
childOf	hasMet	participantIn
closeFriendOf	influencedBy	Relationship
collaboratesWith	knowsByReputation	siblingOf
colleagueOf	knowsInpassing	spouseOf
descendantOf	knowsOf	worksWith
employedBy	lifePartnerof	wouldLikeToKnow
employerOf	livesWith	

The terms in the Relationship vocabulary provide a rich context within which you could establish contacts and go well beyond foaf:knows in describing these relationships. The next listing is a simple example applying the spouseOf relationship. You'd use similar statements when you use other terms from table 4.3.

Listing 4.6 Enhanced FOAF profile applying foaf:img and rel:spouseOf

```
@base <http://rosemary.umw.edu/~marsha/starwars/foaf.ttl#>.
@prefix foaf: <http://xmlns.com/foaf/0.1/> .

@prefix rdf: <http://www.w3.org/1999/02/22-rdf-syntax-ns#> .
```

```
@prefix rdfs: <http://www.w3.org/2000/01/rdf-schema#> .
@prefix rel: <http://purl.org/vocab/relationship>.
@prefix stars: <http://www.starwars.com/explore/encyclopedia/characters/>.

<me> a foaf:Person;
          foaf:family_name "Skywalker";
          foaf:givenname "Anakin";
          foaf:gender "Male";
          foaf:title "Mr.";
          foaf:img <stars:anakinskywalker_detail.png>;
          rel:spouseOf <stars:padmeamidala/>;

          foaf:knows  [
              a foaf:Person;
              foaf:mbox_sha1sum
      "d37a210cadc241b0f7aeb76069e58843bd8940a0";
              foaf:name "Darth Vader";
              foaf:img  <stars:darthvader_detail.png>;
              rel:enemyOf <http://live.dbpedia.org/page/Obi-
      Wan_Kenobi>;
                    ];

          foaf:knows  [
              a foaf:Person;
              foaf:mbox_sha1sum
      "aadfbacb9de289977d85974fda32baff4b60ca86";
              foaf:name "Obi-Wan Kenobi";
              rdfs:seeAlso <http://live.dbpedia.org/page/Obi-
      Wan_Kenobi>;
              rel:enemyOf <me>;
                    ];
        foaf:homepage <http://www.imdb.com/character/ch0000005/bio>;
        foaf:mbox_sha1sum "d37a210cadc241b0f7aeb76069e58843bd8940a0";
        foaf:name "Anakin Skywalker";
        foaf:nick "The Chosen One";
        foaf:phone <tel:8665550100>;
        foaf:title "Jedi";
        foaf:workplaceHomepage <stars:anakinskywalker/> .
<me>  a foaf:PersonalProfileDocument;
        foaf:primaryTopic  <me> .
```

Applying rel:spouseOf

Applying foaf:img

There are many RDF vocabularies, and these standardized vocabularies should be used as much as possible to facilitate inclusion and expansion of the Web of Data. This practice is consistent with thinking like the Web and reinforces Tim Berners-Lee's four principles of Linked Data. Common choices for vocabularies were presented in chapter 2; see table 2.2 for that list.

4.3   *Publishing your FOAF profile*

After you've incorporated the desired content into your FOAF profile, verify the correctness of your document by uploading the statements to an RDF validator. We recommend Joshua Tauberer's RDF Validator and Converter, which also covers RDF/XML and Turtle, at http://www.rdfabout.com/demo/validator/. Now you can publish your error-free file (foaf.ttl) in a web space accessible by the public.

Here's a summary of the steps you should follow to create and publish a syntactically correct FOAF profile for yourself:

- Use a FOAF profile generator to create a basic FOAF profile. We recommend the one available at http://purl.org/net/LinkedData/FoafGenerator.
- Enter all of the desired information into the form provided.
- Click Submit to generate the Turtle version of your FOAF information.
- Highlight and copy the output from the FOAF profile generator and paste it into a text editor.
- Save your file as foaf.ttl.
- Optionally, enhance your profile by inserting additional statements using additional FOAF classes and properties (`foaf`), relationships from the Relationship vocabulary (`rel`), or any other appropriate schema.
- Save your modified file.
- Verify the syntactic correctness of this modified profile by accessing an RDF validator such as the one developed by Joshua Tauberer at http://www.rdfabout.com/demo/validator/.
- Save the validated file.
- Publish this validated file in a publically accessible file space on the Web.

Congratulations! You've now created Linked Data and published it on the Web of Data. You've also joined the FOAF community. Welcome!

4.4 Visualization of a FOAF profile

You can see an HTML visualization of your FOAF profile using Morten Frederiksen's (http://www.wasab.dk/morten/en/) FoaF Explorer. You can access this application at http://xml.mfd-consult.dk/foaf/explorer/. This tool will generate an HTML view of FOAF data, complete with referenced images and links to other data. For example, figure 4.3 is a view of Anakin Skywalker's FOAF profile, as created in listing 4.3. Tools like this facilitate your visualization of RDF data.

In sections 4.2 and 4.3 we discussed two methods for creating a FOAF profile, customizing this profile, and publishing a FOAF profile that should contain content similar to what you'd expect in a personal homepage. Using a validator ensures that your FOAF profile is syntactically correct. But seeing an HTML visualization of this content is helpful in ensuring that you've entered the content correctly.

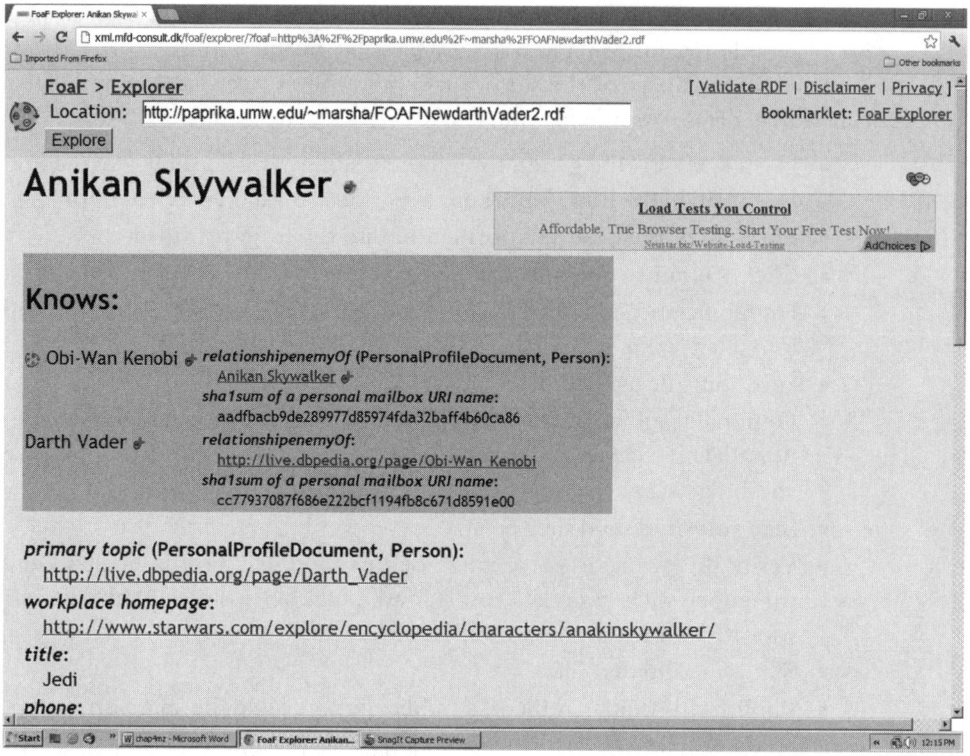

FoaF > Explorer   [Validate RDF | Disclaimer | Privacy]

Location: http://paprika.umw.edu/~marsha/FOAFNewdarthVader2.rdf   Bookmarklet: FoaF Explorer

Explore

Anikan Skywalker ◦

Load Tests You Control
Affordable, True Browser Testing. Start Your Free Test Now!
Neustar Inc/Website-Load-Testing   AdChoices ▷

Knows:

Obi-Wan Kenobi ◦ *relationshipenemyOf* (PersonalProfileDocument, Person):
　　　　　　Anikan Skywalker ◦
　　　　sha1sum of a personal mailbox URI name:
　　　　　　aadfbacb9de289977d85974fda32baff4b60ca86

Darth Vader ◦　*relationshipenemyOf*:
　　　　　　http://live.dbpedia.org/page/Obi-Wan_Kenobi
　　　　sha1sum of a personal mailbox URI name:
　　　　　　cc77937087f686e222bcf1194fb8c671d8591e00

primary topic (PersonalProfileDocument, Person):
　http://live.dbpedia.org/page/Darth_Vader
workplace homepage:
　http://www.starwars.com/explore/encyclopedia/characters/anakinskywalker/
title:
　Jedi
phone:

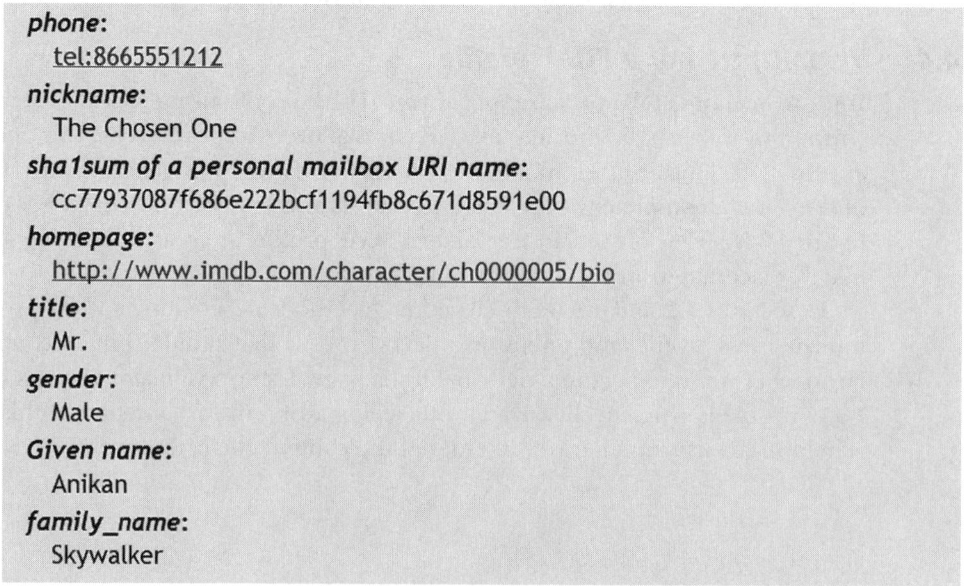

Start ▦ ◎ ◯ " W chap4nz - Microsoft Word | FoaF Explorer: Anikan... | SnagIt Capture Preview　　　« 🔊 ◉ 12:15 PM

---

phone:
　tel:8665551212
nickname:
　The Chosen One
sha1sum of a personal mailbox URI name:
　cc77937087f686e222bcf1194fb8c671d8591e00
homepage:
　http://www.imdb.com/character/ch0000005/bio
title:
　Mr.
gender:
　Male
Given name:
　Anikan
family_name:
　Skywalker

Figure 4.3　FoaF Explorer rendition of Darth Vader FOAF profile

4.5 *Application: linking RDF documents using a custom vocabulary*

You may be wondering if a FOAF profile is useful beyond using it to join the FOAF community. Actually, a FOAF profile is an RDF document that contains personal information. Like any RDF document, it contains links to other RDF data. In this application, we're going to show how you can link two RDF documents to each other. We're going to create a customized vocabulary and apply it to our RDF documents. Then we'll use data found in these RDF documents to find related data on the Web. The techniques utilized in this application aren't limited to FOAF profiles and wish lists but can be used in general to select content from multiple documents and use that data to retrieve data from other sources. Chapter 5 contains another application that uses a FOAF profile.

This application extends Anakin's profile by connecting it to a web-based RDF wish list. This wish list will be linked directly to his FOAF profile and can in turn contain products from anywhere on the Web. To reinforce the techniques and concepts we've covered, you should try this for yourself and create a personal wish list to link to your personal FOAF profile.

4.5.1 *Creating a wish list vocabulary*

Creating the document is as simple as writing another Turtle file. The only thing that you need to include in this document (prior to adding desired items to the stored wish list) is the prefix that will be used to connect your FOAF profile to your wish list and your wish list to your items. But we needed a vocabulary to support our wish list. This is a perfect example of the process discussed in chapter 2 regarding the creation of vocabularies and their terms. We wanted to describe the relationship of a person to a wish list and the wish list to the items on it, but a vocabulary didn't yet exist for that. After searching and not finding those relationships, we defined them ourselves and proceeded to use them in our data. In this case, the appropriate vocabulary and associated schema, shown in the following listing, has been created for you and published at http://purl.org/net/WishListSchema.

> **Listing 4.7   Source code for defining a wish list vocabulary**

```
# Vocabulary for Linked Data wish list App
# Luke Ruth (luke @ http://3Roundstones.com)
# 13 September 2012

@prefix wish: <http://purl.org/net/WishListSchema> .

# Properties
wish:wish_list
  rdf:type rdf:Property ;
  rdfs:isDefinedBy <http://purl.org/net/WishListSchema>;
  rdfs:label "has a wish list" ;
rdfs:comment "Indicates the entire wish list a person is related to." .
```

```
wish:wish_list_item
  rdf:type rdf:Property ;
  rdfs:isDefinedBy <http://purl.org/net/WishListSchema>;
  rdfs:label "has an item" ;
rdfs:comment "Indicates a single item that is listed on a wish list." .
```

4.5.2   Creating, publishing, and linking the wish list document

Using our custom vocabulary, you can complete the creation and publication of the wish list document. You'll do the following:

- Create a wish list document.
- Publish it to the Web (most likely in the same location as your FOAF profile).
- Link this wish list document to your FOAF profile.

Using an editor, begin to create a wish list document containing this single line:

```
@prefix wish: http://purl.org/net/WishListSchema  .
```

This statement establishes the URI of the wish list vocabulary and the use of wish as the associated prefix. Next, publish this document in the same manner, and in the same location, as you did your FOAF profile earlier in the chapter. Once you've done this and the document is live on the Web, you can create the link to it from your FOAF profile by adding a single statement to the end of the FOAF profile file, an example of which is shown in listing 4.8. That statement is

```
<http://yourDomain/yourFoafProfile.ttl>  wish:wishlist  <http://yourDomain/
    yourWishList.ttl> .
```

Obviously, you need to replace the values for yourDomain and yourWishList with the appropriate URIs, but once you've done that, your FOAF profile will be linked to your wish list.

Listing 4.8   FOAF profile with link to wish list

```
@base <http://rosemary.umw.edu/~marsha/starwars/foaf.ttl#> .
@prefix rdf: <http://www.w3.org/1999/02/22-rdf-syntax-ns#> .
@prefix foaf: <http://xmlns.com/foaf/0.1/> .
@prefix rdfs: <http://www.w3.org/2000/01/rdf-schema#> .

@prefix wish: <http://purl.org/net/WishListSchema> .        ⟵  Prefix that
                                                                makes the wish
                                                                list vocabulary
                                                                available

<Me> a foaf:Person
  ; foaf:title "Jedi"
  ; foaf:givenName "Anakin"
  ; foaf:familyName "Skywalker"
  ; foaf:name "Jedi Anakin Skywalker"
  ; foaf:nick "The Chosen One"
  ; foaf:mbox_sha1sum "d37a210cadc241b0f7aeb76069e58843bd8940a0"
  ; foaf:homepage <http://www.imdb.com/character/ch0000005/bio>
  ; foaf:account <https://www.facebook.com/pages/Darth-
➡   Vader/10959490906484>
```

```
    ; foaf:age "100"
    ; foaf:img <http://www.starwars.com/img/explore/encyclopedia/characters/
    darthvader_detail.png>
.


<http://rosemary.umw.edu/~marsha/starwars/foaf.ttl>  wish:wish_list
    <http://rosemary.umw.edu/~marsha/starwars/wishList.ttl>
.

<http://rosemary.umw.edu/~marsha/starwars/foaf.ttl#Me>
    foaf:knows <d37a210cadc241b0f7aeb76069e58843bd8940a0> .

<d37a210cadc241b0f7aeb76069e58843bd8940a0> a foaf:Person
    ; foaf:name "Darth Vader"
.


<http://rosemary.umw.edu/~marsha/starwars/foaf.ttl#Me>
    foaf:knows <548a58890349e5af34cee097c31c8c16591cd58f> .

<548a58890349e5af34cee097c31c8c16591cd58f> a foaf:Person
    ; foaf:name "Obi-Wan Kenobi"
.
```

> Statement that
> links FOAF profile
> document to wish
> list document

Listing 4.8 is an example of a completed FOAF profile containing the link to the wish list document. We published this document at http://rosemary.umw.edu/~marsha/starwars/foafWishList.ttl.

4.5.3 Adding wish list items to our wish list document

At the moment, our wish list document doesn't contain references to any products.

You can begin adding items to your wish list by using an editor to manually insert these triples. Each triple contains

```
<URI of associated wishlist.ttl>  wish:wish_list_item  <URI of desired item>
```

You can also generate these triples by locating the desired item with your browser, then using a tool we've developed called the "wish list bookmarklet." You can obtain this tool at http://purl.org/net/LinkedData/FoafGenerator and add it to your browser simply by dragging the link into your Bookmarks toolbar, as illustrated in figure 4.4.

Using the bookmarklet is simple. Browse to the item that you want to add to your wish list. Click the Create Bookmarklet application on your Bookmarks toolbar. The bookmarklet will generate a wishlistItem triple and display that triple in a pop-up window. Figure 4.5 shows a screen shot of this bookmarklet in action.

You need to copy the displayed text and paste it into your wish list document. You can do this repeatedly for as many items as you desire in your wish list.

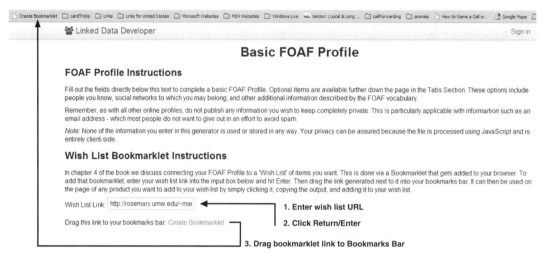

Figure 4.4   Obtaining the wish list bookmarklet

1. Browse to desired item
2. Click Create Bookmarklet on toolbar
3. Copy text from pop-up window to wish list

Figure 4.5   Using the wish list bookmarklet

Listing 4.9 is a representative wish list. We published it at http://rosemary.umw.edu/ ~marsha/starwars/wishlist.ttl. You'll notice the `prefix` statement at the head of the document. This document contains two triples that refer to Best Buy items selected by the user. Each triple has the wish list document as its subject, the `wish_list_item` from the Wish List Schema as the predicate, and the URL of the desired object as found in the URL associated with the product as the object. This wish list contains the two items.

Listing 4.9   Sample wish list document

```
@prefix wish: <http://purl.org/net/WishListSchema> .
<http://rosemary.umw.edu/~marsha/starwars/wishlist.ttl>
    wish:wish_list_item  <http://www.bestbuy.com/site/Sony+-+Cyber-
    shot+DSC-WX100+18.2-Megapixel+Digital+Camera+-
```

```
➥   +Black/5430135.p?id=1218645197434&skuId=5430135&st=DSCWX100/B&cp=1&lp=
➥   1> .
<http://rosemary.umw.edu/~marsha/starwars/wishlist.ttl>
➥   wish:wish_list_item  <http://www.bestbuy.com/site/Pro-Form+-
➥   +710+E+Elliptical/4876004.p?id=1218562659510&skuId=4876004> .
```

This application has demonstrated how you link two RDF documents together. We demonstrated the creation of a custom vocabulary and used that vocabulary to link the FOAF profile to the wish list and to create the wish list triples. We incorporated these triples into the wish list document. This application illustrates the interlinking of RDF data files and the creation of a custom vocabulary. We'll use our wish list again in chapter 6.

4.5.4   Explanation of our bookmarklet tool

Here's a brief explanation of a JavaScript bookmarklet, in case you're unfamiliar with it. A *bookmarklet* is JavaScript embedded in a bookmark so that it can be run independently of the page where it was first gathered. Bookmarklets can range in size from very small snippets of JavaScript to pages of complex and intricate code. Our code is relatively short, because the goal is straightforward. We want to automate the process of writing a single triple relating your wish list to the URL of the page you currently have open in your browser.

Luckily, JavaScript and jQuery have all the tools you need to do this. If you think about the problem before writing a single line of code, the design is straightforward. You need only two pieces of information: the URL for your wish list and the URL for the product you're interested in adding to your wish list. After that it's all about formatting and presentation. The following listing is the JavaScript application that implements our wish list application.

Listing 4.10   JavaScript bookmarklet to construct Turtle wish list items

```javascript
<script type="text/javascript">
   $(document).ready(function() {
   $("#wishForm").submit(function() {

   //Create bookmarklet variable as series of strings to avoid multiline
   //parsing issues
   var bookmarklet = "javascript:(function() {";
   bookmarklet += "var url = self.location.href;"
   bookmarklet += "var myWindow = window.open(\"\",\"Wish List Link\",
   \"width=600,height=300,status=1,resizable=1,left=420,top=260,
   screenX=420,screenY=260\");";
   bookmarklet += "myWindow.document.write(\"&lt;textarea rows=\'20\'
   cols=\'80\' id=\'output\'>&lt;/textarea>\");";
   bookmarklet += "myWindow.document.getElementById('output').value =
   '&lt;WISHLISTLINK> \n  wish:wish_list_item \n &lt;' + url + '> .';";
   bookmarklet += "myWindow.focus();";
   bookmarklet += "})();";

   var wishList = $("#userWishListLink").val();
```

Get the value of the wish list URL and place it into a variable.

```
    bookmarklet = bookmarklet.replace(/WISHLISTLINK/, wishList);   ◁─┐

    $("#results").show();                                ◁───────┐
    $("#bookmarkletLink").attr("href", bookmarklet);
    return false;
    }); // Close wishForm.submit
    }); // Close document.ready
</script>
```

Display bookmarklet link and assign the bookmarklet link as an href attribute

Build up the bookmarklet as a string, then assign the entire string as an href

The first piece of information you need is the URL where you've published your wish list. The best way to accomplish this is by pulling it out of a text field using jQuery, like this:

```
var wishList = $("#userWishListLink").val();
```

The second piece of information you need is the URL of the current page containing your wish list item. This is obtained using

```
bookmarklet += "var url = self.location.href;"
```

The critical part about this process is that you're building up the bookmarklet as a string and then assigning the entire string as an `href` in the line

```
$("#bookmarkletLink").attr("href", bookmarklet);
```

In just those few lines you already have all the data you need to create the triple to add to your wish list. The rest of the JavaScript in listing 4.10 is related to creating another window, formatting the output, and placing it into that window for you to copy and paste into your wish list document. As you can see, this bookmarklet could be extended to include other information or write more complex statements.

4.6 *Summary*

The purpose of this chapter was to introduce you to methods of creating and publishing Linked Data on the Web. We developed a FOAF profile manually and through the use of an automated tool. We enhanced this profile using non-FOAF vocabularies. We published this profile and discussed joining the FOAF community. We demonstrated how you can link a FOAF profile to other Linked Data documents.

Now we turn from discovering Linked Data and publishing your own Linked Data to chapter 5, which will focus on techniques for searching published Linked Data with SPARQL.

SPARQL—querying
the Linked Data Web

This chapter covers

- An introduction to the SPARQL query language for RDF
- Sample SPARQL queries
- An overview of SPARQL query types
- SPARQL results formats

Every database needs a query language. SPARQL is to RDF data as SQL is to a relational database. SPARQL is the query language for structured data on the Web, specifically data accessible in RDF formats or representable as such. SPARQL is therefore the query language for Linked Data. The primary purpose of SPARQL is to provide a formal language in which meaningful questions can be phrased.

This chapter discusses how to query the Web of Data as if it were a database—a big, highly distributed database on the internet. A query language for the Web of Data needs to be able to query files containing RDF data, RDF files accessible on the Web, local databases, and databases exposed to the Web. Further, it needs to be able to query multiple data sources at once and thus be able to dynamically build a large, virtual RDF graph from those multiple data sources. SPARQL is best used when you want to query RDF graphs, as if one or more (possibly distributed) RDF graphs formed a database. We're going to show you how you can do just that.

Because many people are already familiar with SQL, it would be handy for our new query language to look and act as much like SQL as possible. That's a good idea for acceptance, even though the traditional relational data model differs significantly from the graph data model of RDF. SPARQL has an SQL-like syntax that's appropriate for RDF and Linked Data.

Like SQL, SPARQL is based on a widely implemented standard, but various vendors have extended the language to suit themselves or show off particular features of their products. This chapter focuses on the standard language components, which are generally appropriate in any case: SPARQL implementations haven't fragmented as much as SQL implementations.

SPARQL's name looks like an acronym, but the truth is the acronym was reverse engineered after the fact. The SPARQL Protocol and RDF Query Language is a recursive acronym in the tradition of the GNU (GNU's Not Unix) Project. SPARQL's name is nicely pronounceable and sounds interesting and fresh. SPARQL *is* interesting and fresh. We hope this chapter shows you why.

SPARQL is defined by a family of W3C Recommendations and related Working Group Notes. The W3C SPARQL logo is shown in figure 5.1

Figure 5.1   W3C's SPARQL logo

5.1   *An overview of a typical SPARQL query*

SPARQL queries can take a number of different forms. The most common is a select query, which selects information based on constraints. It's very similar in form to SQL select queries.

Listing 5.1 contains a representative SPARQL query. Don't worry about understanding this query yet; it's shown here to provide an overview of the organization of a typical SPARQL SELECT query.

Each SPARQL SELECT query is organized as follows:

1 PREFIX (Namespace prefixes.)
2 SELECT (Define what you wish to retrieve.)
3 FROM (Specify the dataset from which to draw the results.)
4 WHERE {
   (Describe the criteria on which to base the selection. This description is in the form of a query triple pattern.)

   }
5 ORDER BY, LIMIT, and the like (Modifiers that affect the desired result.)

Listing 5.1   SPARQL query to find people's locations

```
prefix foaf: <http://xmlns.com/foaf/0.1/>                      Namespace
prefix pos: <http://www.w3.org/2003/01/geo/wgs84_pos#>         prefixes.

select ?name ?latitude ?longitude      ◁── Requesting three fields be retrieved.
from <http://3roundstones.com/dave/me.rdf>                                Results
from <http://semanticweb.org/wiki/Special:ExportRDF/Michael_Hausenblas>  will be
where {                                                                   retrieved
  ?person foaf:name ?name ;                                               from two
          foaf:based_near ?near .   ◁──  Criteria described  Items preceded  sources.¹
  ?near pos:lat ?latitude ;               in the form of a   by ? represent
        pos:long ?longitude .             triple pattern.    variables in the
}                                                            results.
LIMIT 10                           ◁──  Only the first 10 results
                                        will be returned.
```

The query is asking that no more than 10 names and associated locations (latitude and longitude) be retrieved from the RDF contents stored in the URLs in footnote 1. The names will be identified as the object of a triple where the predicate is foaf:name. The latitude and longitude will be identified as the object of pos:lat and pos:long.

A *triple pattern* is a description of desired RDF statements that match our criteria. They're intentionally similar to RDF statements and are meant to constrain which RDF statements we're interested in. Entities that are variable and not an explicit value are represented by a leading ? such as ?person. Therefore, ?s ?p ?o would be a pattern that would match every RDF statement.

The following query

```
select ?o ?x ?y
from <http://3roundstones.com/dave/me.rdf>
from <http://semanticweb.org/wiki/Special:ExportRDF/Michael_Hausenblas>
where {
  ?s foaf:name ?o ;
        foaf:based_near ?z .
  ?z pos:lat ?x ;
       pos:long ?y .
}
LIMIT 10
```

would retrieve exactly the same results as the query in listing 5.1, but it's less readable. This section provided a brief overview of SPARQL. The remainder of the chapter will familiarize you with different types of queries and help you better understand how to form meaningful queries.

5.2   *Querying flat RDF files with SPARQL*

SPARQL is best used when you want to query RDF graphs, as if one or more (possibly distributed) RDF graphs formed a database. Note that there are many native RDF databases,

---

¹ The results will be retrieved from http://3roundstones.com/dave/me.rdf and http://semanticweb.org/wiki/Special:ExportRDF/Michael_Hausenblas.

but you don't need to use one in order to query RDF using SPARQL. This chapter begins by showing you how to query local flat files of RDF, then moves on to querying RDF files and databases on the Web. Because we use URIs to identify both, you may not even notice the difference. We like it that way because RDF and Linked Data are meant to work the way the Web works.

5.2.1   Querying a single RDF data file

The sample query in the following listing looks for people that the owner of a FOAF document knows. We can query a real-world FOAF document, like the one created in chapter 4, to get that information. We'll build this query to show you how to perform distributed queries in SPARQL.

Listing 5.2   SPARQL query to find FOAF friends

Names information to return in the results

Triple patterns used to match RDF statements

Namespace declarations

Defines patterns to match and filters to perform on the data

```
prefix rdfs: <http://www.w3.org/2000/01/rdf-schema#>
prefix foaf: <http://xmlns.com/foaf/0.1/>

select ?name ?url
where {
    ?person rdfs:seeAlso ?url ;
            foaf:name ?name .
}
```

The name space declarations are analogous to those used in the Turtle or RDF/XML syntaxes. Look at the query in listing 5.2 and the RDF graph diagram in figure 5.2 at the same time. The query's WHERE clause defines triple patterns, ways of matching patterns within an RDF graph. We'd like to query the graph in figure 5.2 (which represents the FOAF document for one of the authors).

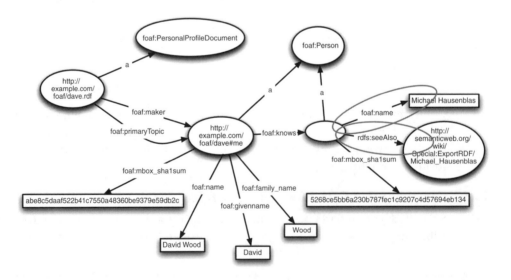

Figure 5.2   Sample FOAF data showing the triple patterns matched by the SPARQL query in listing 5.2

The use of triple patterns in the WHERE clause is one of the primary syntactic differences between SPARQL and SQL. Another is the prefixes at the top of the query. Because RDF and Linked Data sometimes use quite long URIs as universal identifiers, we need a way to make our queries readable. Prefixes do that by mapping a short placeholder to a long URI that may then be used interchangeably in the rest of the query.

In figure 5.2 the triple patterns matched by the query are circled. We wanted to find any resource (that we called ?person) that has a foaf:name property and an rdfs:seeAlso property. We expect the query to return the variables listed in the SELECT clause, which are the two variables ?name and ?url, the objects of the RDF statements that were identified in the query's WHERE clause.

You can see that query in action using the ARQ utility from the Apache Jena Project. ARQ is a SPARQL processor that can be used from a command-line interface.

> **NOTE** You'll really want to download and install ARQ. It's both handy to have a local SPARQL query processor and difficult to find public SPARQL endpoints that will allow you to run arbitrary queries.

ARQ can be downloaded from http://apache.org/dist/jena/. You'll need to download and install ARQ in order to follow along with the examples. Setting up ARQ is straightforward. A single environment variable is used to tell ARQ where its installation directory is located. The next listing shows how that's done on various OSes.

Listing 5.3 Setting up ARQ

```
                # For Unix-like systems, including Linux and OS X:
                $ export ARQROOT='/Applications/ARQ-2.8.8'       ◁──┐
                $ /Applications/ARQ-2.8.8/bin/arq -h                │
Getting help                                                       │ Setting up the ARQ
  for ARQ                                                          │ environment
                # For Windows:                                     │
                set ARQROOT=c:\MyProjects\ARQ                   ◁──┘
                c:\MyProjects\ARQ\bat\arq.bat /h
```

Put the SPARQL query from listing 5.2 into a file called foaf.rq (.rq is the standard file extension for SPARQL queries). Next, get some real FOAF data from (for example) http://3roundstones.com/dave/me.rdf and save it to a file called foaf.rdf. You can query those two files using ARQ. Listing 5.4 shows the relevant command line.

Executing ARQ as shown will result in the output in figure 5.3. ARQ will output its own textual representation of query results when run in a terminal. But there are other result formats. The standard result formats are discussed in section 5.6 and the details provided in appendix B. ARQ's other output options can be found in the ARQ help.

Listing 5.4 Running a SPARQL query from the command line

```
$ /Applications/ARQ-2.8.8/bin/arq --query foaf.rq --data foaf.rdf     ◁──┐
```

Make sure foaf.rdf includes your correct file
path, for example, /Home/Desktop/foaf.rdf.

```
-------------------------------------------------------------------------------------
| name              | url       |
=====================================================================================
| "Michael Hausenblas" | <http://semanticweb.org/wiki/Special:ExportRDF/Michael_Hausenblas> |
-------------------------------------------------------------------------------------
```

Figure 5.3   Partial query results for the FOAF query

This query will return some number of people and their URLs. The exact number may change depending on when you make the query (because the file on the Web may change). Anyone listed in the FOAF file with an `rdfs:seeAlso` URL and a `foaf:name` will be returned. To see how changes will impact your query results, edit the file foaf.rdf and either add more people with those parameters or change some of the existing data; then execute the ARQ again.

Here SPARQL is acting as a query language for RDF when the RDF data is in files. Later we'll show how to use SPARQL to query RDF data on the internet. First, though, we'll demonstrate how to query an RDF graph that's built from multiple data sources.

5.2.2   *Querying multiple RDF files*

Unlike SQL, SPARQL isn't limited to querying a single data source. You can use SPARQL to query multiple files, web resources, databases, or a combination thereof. A simple example will make it clearer.

The personal information in a FOAF profile may be extended with, say, address information. A common way to represent address information in RDF is via the vCard vocabulary (as briefly discussed in chapter 2). vCard files are like virtual business cards. A minimal vCard address file that augments the sample FOAF data we've been working with is available at http://3roundstones.com/dave/vcard.ttl in Turtle format.

Take the vCard data from http://3roundstones.com/dave/vcard.ttl and put it into a file called vcard.ttl. Now you can run ARQ again with both the FOAF and vCard data acting as input, as shown in listing 5.5 and figure 5.4. Note the additional `--data` parameter. Make sure to have the right path to the ARQ utility and put the contents of listing 5.6 into a file called foafvcard.rq.

This shows that RDF files may be combined, just like any other RDF graphs. Graphs of information combine well (unlike tables and trees). The magic is in the reuse of identifiers. Both files refer to the same URI identifying a person.

> **NOTE**   One of the primary assumptions of Linked Data is that two people using the same identifier are talking about the same thing. Reusing identifiers for resources allows data to be combined.

Listing 5.5   Running a SPARQL query from a command line with multiple data files

```
$ arq --query foafvcard.rq --data foaf.rdf --data vcard.ttl
```
   The vCard example
   RDF data is in the
   file vcard.ttl.

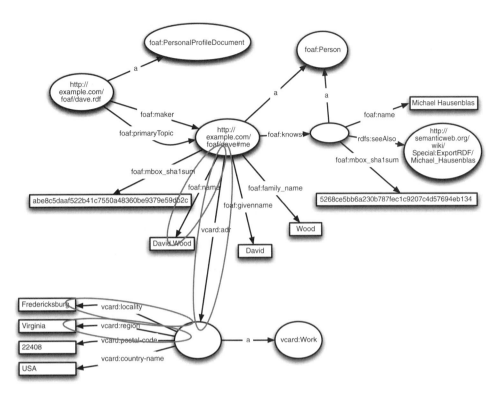

Figure 5.4   Sample combined FOAF/vCard data showing the triple patterns matched by the SPARQL query in listing 5.6

Figure 5.4 shows a query against the combined FOAF and vCard graph. We wish to find the names of people and address information associated with each person. The name comes from the sample FOAF data and the address information comes from the sample vCard data.

Referring to listing 5.6, note how the ?address variable is used: the first constraint in the WHERE clause matches a person with a foaf:name. The next statement (vcard:adr ?address .) matches the same person (that is, triples with the same subject) with a vcard:adr address. The address is a blank node. It doesn't have an identifier. But we can get a handle to it by referring to it as a variable called ?address. The ?address variable can then be used in the next two lines

```
?address vcard:locality ?city ;
         vcard:region ?state .
```

to find the city and state associated with that address. We don't care about the address per se. We're just "walking the graph" to ensure that the address we use is the same one that's associated with the person's name.

Listing 5.6 A SPARQL query that combines FOAF and vCard data

```
prefix foaf: <http://xmlns.com/foaf/0.1/>
prefix vcard: <http://www.w3.org/2006/vcard/ns#>

SELECT ?name ?city ?state
where {
  ?person foaf:name ?name ;
          vcard:adr ?address .
  ?address vcard:locality ?city ;
           vcard:region ?state .
}
```

The SELECT clause, showing three variable bindings to be returned in the results

A triple pattern to find the blank node representing an address

Triple patterns mapping the address to a city and state

The result of running the command in listing 5.5 (with the query in listing 5.6) is shown in figure 5.5. The name comes from the FOAF data, and the city and state come from the vCard data.

```
-------------------------------------------------
| name          | city            | state       |
=================================================
| "David Wood"  | "Fredericksburg" | "Virginia" |
-------------------------------------------------
```

Figure 5.5 Query results for the combined FOAF and vCard query

Developers used to SQL might note that variable names in SPARQL's SELECT clause don't name variables to query from the database; they determine which variables used in the WHERE clause's triple patterns get returned in the output. That's confusing for some new users, but it makes sense once you wrap your mind around the concept of matching triple patterns against an RDF graph. The approach works even if the RDF graph is temporarily created for the purposes of satisfying the query!

5.2.3 Querying an RDF file on the Web

It's possible to use SPARQL to query RDF on the internet, too. Try modifying the query in listing 5.2 by adding a FROM clause after the SELECT clause. Add this line after the select line:

```
FROM <http://3roundstones.com/dave/me.rdf>
```

If you save the modified query into a file called livefoaf.rq (.rq is the file extension for SPARQL queries), you can run the query as shown in the following listing.

Listing 5.7 Running a remote SPARQL query from the command line

```
$ /Applications/ARQ-2.8.8/bin/arq --query livefoaf.rq
```

The command to run arq using a remote query with a FROM clause. Note the lack of a defined data file; the data comes from a URL provided in the query.

The URL in the FROM clause points to David Wood's live FOAF file on the internet. The query will return a larger number of people's names and rdfs:seeAlso URLs than the results shown in figure 5.3. If you want to see an example of a larger FOAF file, you can resolve and save David's or Michael's FOAF files for further study using the URLs given previously.

One of the things that makes structured data on the Web interesting is that it's distributed, unlike a relational database where the data exists in a single system. SPARQL allows you to have multiple FROM clauses in a single query. Try it by adding another FROM clause with a URL to another FOAF file to the previous query (for example, Michael's FOAF URL is given in figure 5.3). Now you'll see a listing of people's names and rdfs:seeAlso URLs from both David's and Michael's FOAF files. Try that with a relational database!

5.3 Querying SPARQL endpoints

So far we've shown how to query RDF data in local files, both singly and using multiple files, and how to query RDF data on the internet using SPARQL's FROM clause. Each time we've used a query stored in a local file. But is there a way to bypass local files altogether and query the internet more like you would a relational database? Of course!

Linked Data sites on the Web often expose a SPARQL endpoint. A SPARQL endpoint is a web-accessible query service that accepts the SPARQL query language. An HTTP GET on a SPARQL endpoint generally returns an HTML query form. The query form for DBpedia is shown in figure 5.6.

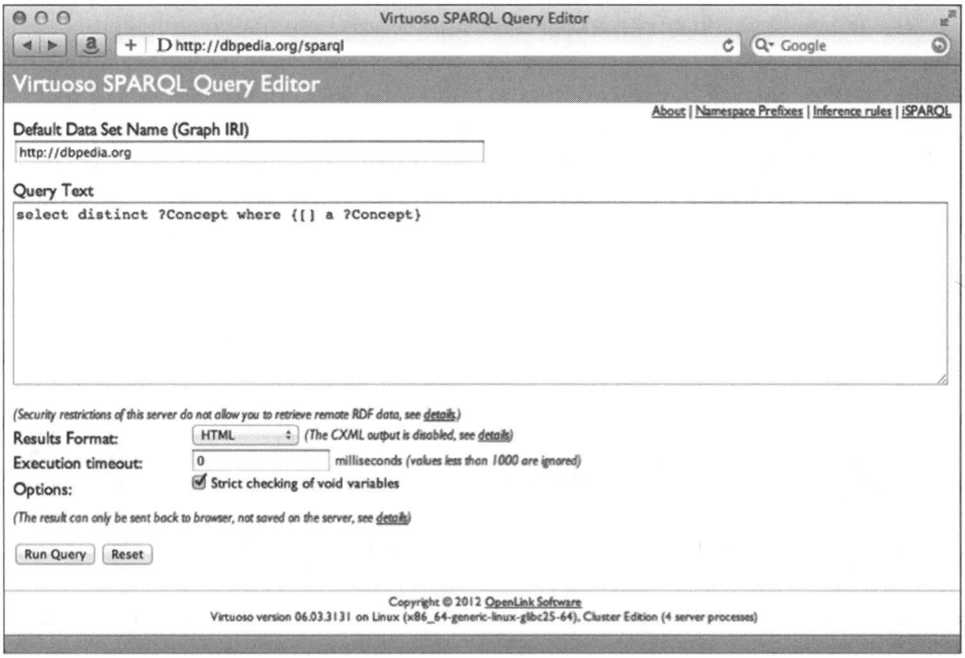

Figure 5.6   DBpedia's SPARQL endpoint's query form and default query

NOTE As is true in Turtle, the syntactical convenience a, when used as a property, is the same as saying rdf:type, which is used to say that an RDF resource is an instance of a particular RDF class. The term [] is a blank node and will therefore match any subject.

The growing convention used by datasets on the Linked Open Data cloud is exposing SPARQL endpoints on the path /sparql. You can generally determine whether a given Linked Data site has a SPARQL endpoint by constructing a URL like http://{hostname here}/sparql. This is just a convention, but it's a useful one. Of course, you can put a SPARQL endpoint on any URL.

DBpedia's default query gives a hint to new users on how they can discover what information the service holds. You can rewrite DBpedia's default query with more whitespace to make it more readable, as shown in the following listing.

Listing 5.8 Query the rdf:types a server holds

```
select DISTINCT ?Concept
WHERE {
  [] a ?Concept
}
```

◁──┐ **The DISTINCT keyword ensures that duplicate results are filtered out; only unique matching results are returned.**

At the time this book was written, DBpedia reported holding information about 20,152,062 unique concepts. That number will change over time, but it's worth noting just how much information is available on DBpedia alone. Each "concept" is an RDF class. RDF classes are often used to categorize information in Linked Data, in much the same way that data is collected into records in a relational database.

The WHERE clause in listing 5.8 contains a single triple pattern that matches any RDF class URIs and places them into the variable ?Concept.

Linked Data isn't meant to be used only by humans; automated processes should also be able to make SPARQL queries. When SPARQL is used over HTTP, we're using the *P* in SPARQL, the SPARQL Protocol. SPARQL endpoints accept a SPARQL query in the parameters of an HTTP GET or POST request. The query is URL encoded to escape special characters and then put in the query string as the value of a variable called query. DBpedia's default query could just as easily be called, as shown in the following listing. Note that DBpedia's SPARQL endpoint also uses a second parameter called default-graph-uri. The parameters are defined in the SPARQL Protocol specification (http://www.w3.org/TR/rdf-sparql-protocol/).

Listing 5.9 An example of a URL-encoded SPARQL query

```
http://dbpedia.org/sparql?default-graph-
    uri=http%3A%2F%2Fdbpedia.org&query=select+distinct+%3FConcept+where+
    %7B%5B%5D+a+%3FConcept%7D&format=text%2Fhtml&timeout=0
```

Now that you've seen some of SPARQL's most common use cases, it's time to look at more technical details of the query language. SPARQL can perform a number of different types of queries. They're described in the next section.

5.4 Types of SPARQL queries

There are several types of SPARQL queries. SELECT queries data in the way we're familiar with in SQL. The DESCRIBE query gives us a quick way to ask, "What is known about a particular resource?" The ASK query allows us to determine whether a particular query would return results, and the CONSTRUCT query allows us to construct new RDF graphs from SPARQL query results. The addition of SPARQL UPDATE in SPARQL 1.1 gives us the ability to add, remove, or otherwise update data accessible via SPARQL endpoints. The following sections introduce each type of query.

5.4.1 The SELECT query

You've already seen the SELECT query in action, which is used much as it is in SQL. The SELECT query type has a number of other options, including the ability to perform subqueries, combine (UNION) graphs, and find the difference between (MINUS) graphs.

One of the most useful additional features is the OPTIONAL block that extends the functionality of the WHERE clause. An OPTIONAL block makes any triple patterns within it optional. That is, they're not required to match but will be returned if they do. The OPTIONAL block is equivalent to a left join, whereas the period-separated triple patterns represent conjunctions; all the patterns are joined to create a result.

Let's look at the query in listing 5.2 again but modify it so that we can return all the names and return any rdfs:seeAlso URLs that might also be there. In other words, a resource that has a foaf:name but not an rdfs:seeAlso URL will still match and still return the name. The record for such a resource will not have an entry for an rdfs:seeAlso URL. The next listing shows the modified query. Take care to note that the order of the WHERE clause constraints has been inverted for readability.

Listing 5.10 Introducing OPTIONAL

```
prefix rdfs: <http://www.w3.org/2000/01/rdf-schema#>
prefix foaf: <http://xmlns.com/foaf/0.1/>

select ?name ?url
where {
  ?person foaf:name ?name .
  OPTIONAL { ?person rdfs:seeAlso ?url }
}
```

Wrap the rdfs:seeAlso triple pattern with an OPTIONAL{} block.

Complete the foaf:name triple pattern and end it with a period. (Mandatory)

The ORDER BY and LIMIT functions work in SPARQL as they do in SQL. If you have a lot of records, you may wish to order them by a particular variable, either numerically or alphabetically as appropriate. You may also wish to limit the number of records that are returned. Execute the query shown in listing 5.11 on DBpedia's SPARQL endpoint, and you'll see a large list of unordered results without the ORDER BY and LIMIT and a short list of ordered results with them. Try it yourself.

There are other query modifiers besides ORDER BY and LIMIT. SQL users will immediately recognize GROUP BY, HAVING, and OFFSET. Those and others are covered in the SPARQL specification.

The COUNT function counts the number of times a variable is matched in a query result. This handy function may be used to determine how many of something there are in a dataset.

Listing 5.11   Introducing ORDER BY and LIMIT

```
select ?link
where {
  <http://dbpedia.org/resource/Linked_Data>
            <http://dbpedia.org/ontology/wikiPageExternalLink> ?link .
} ORDER BY ?link LIMIT 10
```

Orders the results by the variable given. In this case, the URLs will be ordered alphabetically.

Limits the results to 10 records.

Listing 5.12 counts the number of abstracts for DBpedia's Linked_Data resource. Note that the COUNT function is surrounded by parentheses and a new variable (?count) is established to hold the resulting number. The result for such a query will have count as the variable name in the result header (from the ?count variable name).

Features like COUNT are called aggregate functions (or set functions in the SPARQL specification) because they aggregate information already present in a query and calculate something new from it. Other aggregate functions include summation (SUM), average (AVG), minimum (MIN), and maximum (MAX). The GROUP BY and HAVING clauses familiar from SQL also operate on aggregate information. COUNT and other aggregates are only available as of SPARQL 1.1.

COUNT in listing 5.12 calculates the number of times the variable ?abstract is bound and puts that number into ?count. The query would return the number of abstracts for the Linked_Data resource when executed on DBpedia's SPARQL endpoint. That number was 6 when this book was written.

Listing 5.12   Introducing COUNT

```
select (COUNT(?abstract) as ?count)
where {
  <http://dbpedia.org/resource/Linked_Data> dbpedia-owl:abstract ?abstract .
}
```

In many cases, you'd like to match data with more granularity. A classic example from the early days of relational databases is the need to find employees with salaries greater than a certain amount or those with ages between two numbers. These kinds of limits are imposed using FILTERs.

FILTERs in SPARQL can take many forms. FILTERs can operate on numbers, strings, dates, URIs, or other data types. For example, the filter FILTER regex(?name, "Capadisli") would remove any match from the ?name variable whose value was not "Capadisli". The term regex is intentional; many features of standard regular expressions may be used in regex filters. Filters may also be negated: FILTER NOT EXISTS { ?person foaf:name ?name } tests for the absence (instead of the presence) of a pattern.

In this case, the filter ensures that the resource ?person does not have a foaf:name of the value of ?name.

The query in the next listing would return a single abstract in English when executed on DBpedia's SPARQL endpoint. Removing the FILTER would return all abstracts associated with the Linked_Data resource regardless of language.

Listing 5.13 Introducing FILTERs

```
select ?abstract
where {
  <http://dbpedia.org/resource/Linked_Data> dbpedia-owl:abstract ?abstract .
  FILTER (lang(?abstract) = "en")        ◁── The FILTER restricts the
}                                            ?abstract variable to only those
                                             with an English language tag.
```

5.4.2 *The ASK query*

ASK queries give you a way to find out whether some triple patterns would match an answer. The result of an ASK query is always a Boolean (true or false). The syntax of an ASK query uses the same WHERE clause as a SELECT query.

There's no point in using any postprocessing actions on an ASK query because the result is only a Boolean. Therefore, the ORDER BY, LIMIT, and OFFSET operations aren't allowed.

The point of an ASK query is to test whether the triple patterns in the WHERE clause would return an answer. WHERE clauses can become large and complicated, so testing large queries may be very useful. It's often better to test large queries before hammering a database only to determine that no results are returned. Also, as with SQL, it's always possible to construct queries that require a very long time to execute. ASK queries will almost always return faster than the equivalent SELECT query.

The following listing shows an example ASK query. The ASK query type returns a Boolean (true or false) indicating whether the query would return results. This query would return "true" when executed on DBpedia's SPARQL endpoint, indicating that the Linked_Data resource does, in fact, have at least one abstract.

Listing 5.14 An ASK query

```
ASK
where {
  <http://dbpedia.org/resource/Linked_Data> dbpedia-owl:abstract ?abstract .
}
```

5.4.3 *The DESCRIBE query*

It may seem odd that the results of SELECT or ASK queries are not in themselves RDF statements. This is because SPARQL is intended to be SQL-like in its operations. There are times, however, when you might want to retain or make an RDF graph from a SPARQL query. The DESCRIBE and CONSTRUCT query types allow just that.

The DESCRIBE query requires a single URI as a parameter and returns an RDF graph that describes the named resource. An optional WHERE clause may be added.

The SPARQL specification says that the results of a DESCRIBE query are "determined by the SPARQL query processor." In practice, most if not all SPARQL processors return all RDF triples for which the DESCRIBE's URI parameter is the subject, as shown in listing 5.15. This has advantages and disadvantages. An advantage is that the result is easy to determine and to implement. A disadvantage is that indirect relationships (those RDF statements for which a blank node or URI is the object and that act as subjects to successive statements) are not returned. A DESCRIBE result can be, and often is, parsed to form the basis for subsequent queries to gather whatever information is ultimately desired.

The following listing shows a DESCRIBE query. It will return the RDF statements from DBpedia for which the Linked_Data resource is the subject. Unlike SELECT, ASK, or CONSTRUCT queries, DESCRIBE queries can't get any more complicated. The word DESCRIBE and a URI form the entirety of the query.

Listing 5.15   A DESCRIBE query

```
describe <http://dbpedia.org/resource/Linked_Data>
```

5.4.4   *The CONSTRUCT query*

Like the DESCRIBE query type, a CONSTRUCT query returns an RDF graph. Unlike DESCRIBE, however, CONSTRUCT can make any RDF graph you like, based on the information you query in a WHERE clause.

The CONSTRUCT query in listing 5.16 queries all the information in DBpedia about the Linked_Data resource and then filters it to just the parts that are explicitly language-encoded in English. The CONSTRUCT clause then creates a new RDF graph from that information. The result is a subset of the DBpedia information on the Linked_Data resource that's only in English. Of course, any information that's not directly connected to the Linked_Data resource or is not language-encoded in English will be lost. It's possible to make the WHERE clause more complicated to account for any other information you may wish to add to your new graph. Any variables listed in the WHERE clause may be reused in the CONSTRUCT clause, as may literal values that you write into the CONSTRUCT clause by hand.

Listing 5.16   A CONSTRUCT query

CONSTRUCT clause components use variables that are bound in the WHERE clause.

```
CONSTRUCT {
  <http://dbpedia.org/resource/Linked_Data> ?p ?o
}
WHERE {
  <http://dbpedia.org/resource/Linked_Data> ?p ?o .
  filter langMatches( lang(?title), "EN" )
}
```

The CONSTRUCT query makes a new RDF graph using variables from the WHERE clause.

The WHERE clause determines which variables may be used in the CONSTRUCT clause.

5.4.5 *SPARQL 1.1 Update*

For years, the SPARQL standard didn't specify a way to add or remove data from a repository, only ways to query it. This odd situation was one of the growing pains of the Semantic Web standards. That obvious lack has been repaired with SPARQL 1.1. SPARQL 1.1 Update (http://www.w3.org/TR/sparql11-update/) provides standard syntax for updating RDF data using SPARQL.

The next listing shows how SPARQL Update's `INSERT` function may be used to insert RDF triples into a compliant repository.

> **Listing 5.17 A SPARQL `INSERT`**

```
PREFIX dc: <http://purl.org/dc/elements/1.1/>
INSERT DATA
{
  <http://www.linkeddatadeveloper.com/> dc:title "Linked Data" ;
                       dc:creator "David Wood" ;
                       dc:creator "Marsha Zaidman" ;
                       dc:creator "Luke Ruth" ;
                       dc:creator "Michael Hausenblas" .

}
```

An update such as an INSERT operation may only be used on a SPARQL I.I endpoint that you have write permission to.

Other operations under SPARQL Update include the ability to delete triples from a graph (`DELETE`), load the contents of a URL into a graph (`LOAD`), and remove all the triples from a graph (`CLEAR`). Graphs may be created (`CREATE`) or removed (`DROP`). All of the data from one graph may be copied to another (`COPY`), which will first remove any existing data from the destination graph. Similarly, a `MOVE` operation will move all data from one graph to another, thus emptying the source graph. A variation on `COPY` is `ADD`; the `ADD` operation copies data from a source graph to a destination graph without removing any existing information from either graph.

> **NOTE**   A SPARQL Update request may only be used on a SPARQL 1.1 endpoint *that you have write permission to.* You're unlikely to find many public SPARQL endpoints that allow strangers to write data to them! You're more likely to use SPARQL Update to manipulate RDF databases under your control.

5.5 *SPARQL result formats (XML, JSON)*

So far you've seen SPARQL results in a text format, as created by the ARQ utility. The SPARQL standard defines an XML format for SPARQL results. There's also a widely used JSON syntax for SPARQL results, primarily used by web developers working in JavaScript. The details of these formats are provided in appendix B, but an overview is presented here.

The XML format is, as the name suggests, an XML representation of a SPARQL result set. It's a W3C Recommendation and thus implemented by all SPARQL endpoints. Listing 5.18 provides an example of the results for the query in listing 5.2 in XML format. Note that the `<head>` tag contains a list of all the variables named in the

SELECT clause of the query. This facilitates parsing, even though the variable names may also be found in the <results> tag content. The <results> tag contains zero or more <result> tags, each of which contains a result.

A <binding> tag appears for each variable in a result. The name attribute indicates the variable's name and the enclosed tag indicates the binding's data type (for example, literal or uri as shown here; other data types are date, integer, and so on).

Listing 5.18   SPARQL results in XML format for the query in listing 5.2

```
<?xml version="1.0"?>
<sparql xmlns="http://www.w3.org/2005/sparql-results#">
   <head>
      <variable name="name"/>
      <variable name="url"/>
   </head>
   <results>
      <result>
         <binding name="name">
            <literal>Michael Hausenblas</literal>
         </binding>
         <binding name="url">
            <uri>
http://semanticweb.org/wiki/Special:ExportRDF/Michael_Hausenblas</uri>
         </binding>
      </result>
   </results>
</sparql>
```

A SPARQL results document. The <sparql> tag provides the SPARQL results namespace.

The <results> tag contains zero or more <result> tags.

An XML document starts with an XML header.

The <head> tag contains a list of variables from the SELECT clause of the preceding query.

A <binding> tag appears for each variable in a result. The name attribute indicates the variable's name and the enclosed tag indicates the binding's data type.

The JSON format is not a W3C Recommendation, but it is a W3C Working Group Note, which is as good as a standard in the absence of other guidance. Nevertheless, the JSON format is also widely implemented because of its usefulness to web developers.

The JSON format is a JSON object and so is wrapped in curly braces, as shown in the following listing. The header is represented as a key-value member called head with a value of another object. The inner object contains another member whose name is vars and whose content is a JSON array. The array contains the variables from the SELECT clause of the preceding query as strings.

Listing 5.19   SPARQL results in JSON format for the query in listing 5.2

```
{
   "head": {
      "vars": [ "name" , "url" ]
   } ,
   "results": {
      "bindings": [
         {
            "name": { "type": "literal" , "value": "Michael Hausenblas" } ,
            "url": { "type": "uri" , "value":
"http://semanticweb.org/wiki/Special:ExportRDF/Michael_Hausenblas" }
         }
```

A JSON object.

The head member contains a vars member that contains an array of the variables from the SELECT clause of the preceding query.

The results member contains a bindings member, which contains zero or more records, each of which contains a record.

```
      ]
    }
}
```

The results are held in another member with a name of results and a value of an object. The inner object contains a member whose name is bindings and whose value is zero or more objects, each representing a record. There is a record object for each bound variable with the name as the variable string and the value of an object containing a JSON array. The record array contains type and value members, as shown in listing 5.2.

5.6   *Creating web pages from SPARQL queries*

FOAF files often contain approximate locations for people using the foaf:based_near property. Latitude and longitude of the nearest city or another convenient but approximate landmark are used to give a general idea of where someone lives without exposing the exact position of someone's home on the public internet. We can use this property to demonstrate how a SPARQL query of Linked Open Data can be used to dynamically create web pages. You may find the process quite similar to working with a relational data source.

We'll start by creating a SPARQL query for names and foaf:based_near information from David Wood's and Michael Hausenblas's FOAF profiles on the Web. Once we have that information, we can plot the locations we find on a map and also write the textual information into an HTML table. Figure 5.7 shows the final result. This is a simple version of many real-world applications that draw on data sources to create user interfaces. The main difference is that our data sources are published Linked Data.

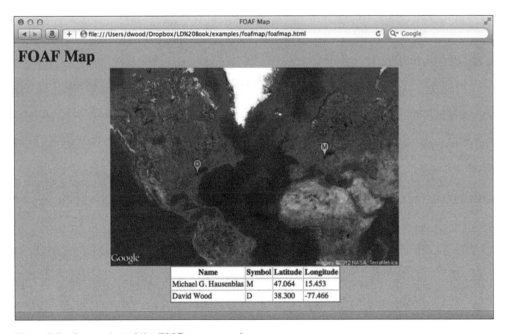

Figure 5.7   Screenshot of the FOAF map example

The process looks like this:

1 Create a SPARQL query to gather the data you want.
2 Execute the SPARQL query and get the results as JSON.
3 Create an HTML page.
4 Write JavaScript that uses the JSON data to display onto the HTML.

5.6.1   Creating the SPARQL query

The query to find someone's "near" location is shown in the following listing.

Listing 5.20   SPARQL query to find people's locations

pos: prefix refers to the WGS84 Position vocabulary,[2] used to encode latitudes and longitudes.

```
prefix foaf: <http://xmlns.com/foaf/0.1/>
prefix pos: <http://www.w3.org/2003/01/geo/wgs84_pos#>

select ?name ?latitude ?longitude
from <http://3roundstones.com/dave/me.rdf>
from <http://semanticweb.org/wiki/Special:ExportRDF/Michael_Hausenblas>
where {
  ?person foaf:name ?name ;
          foaf:based_near ?near .
  ?near pos:lat ?latitude ;
        pos:long ?longitude .
}
```

We want each person's name and position.

Queries David's and Michael's FOAF files.

The foaf:based_near resource is selected, which is a blank node.

The latitude and longitude are acquired from the foaf:based_near resource.

Execute the query and save it as JSON. You can do that with ARQ, as you've already seen. Listing 5.21 shows the command line. In a real application the JSON would probably be created dynamically in real time via a server-side process. Doing it this way allows this example to consist of standalone files and avoids the cross-site scripting constraints of current web browsers.

Listing 5.21   Execute the FOAF map query and save as JSON

```
$ /Applications/ARQ-2.8.8/bin/arq --query foafmap.rq --results JSON
  > foafmap.js
```

Execute the query and request the results in JSON format.

Save the results to a file.

Save the results of the query to a file called foafmap.js and change the first line by adding `var results =` to the beginning of the line (in front of the opening curly brace). This will assign the `results` object to a variable and allow you to use the file immediately in your HTML page with no more coding. This is a convenience for the purposes of this example application. In a real application you may choose to handle your JSON the way you prefer.

The query results are shown in figure 5.8, modified on the first line to add the variable assignment. Note the subtle differences between the query results in the two FOAF

---

[2] For "World Geodetic System," 1984 version.

```
var results = {                          ◄─── A variable assignment has
  "head": {                                   been added to the query
    "vars": [ "name" , "latitude" , "longitude" ]   results for convenience.
  } ,
  "results": {
    "bindings": [
      {
        "name": { "type": "literal" , "xml:lang": "en" ,
"value": "Michael G. Hausenblas" } ,
        "latitude": { "type": "literal" , "xml:lang": "en" ,
"value": "47.064" } ,
        "longitude": { "type": "literal" , "xml:lang": "en" ,
"value": "15.453" }
      } ,
      {
        "name": { "type": "literal" , "value": "David Wood" } ,
        "latitude": { "type": "literal" , "value": "38.300" } ,
        "longitude": { "type": "literal" , "value": "-77.466" }
      }
    ]
  }
}
```

Figure 5.8   Modified JSON query results showing variable assignment

files. One uses explicit language tags for English; the other does not. The aphorism "Real data is dirty" applies to Linked Data as it does to any other type of data. Variations in interpretation or formatting or simple typos often can skew query results.

5.6.2   Creating the HTML page

Next, we need to create an HTML page to hold our map and table. A simple HTML template is shown in the next listing. The page has a title and a heading and only two divisions in the body. These two divisions are where we will (via JavaScript) place the map and table.

Listing 5.22   The FOAF map HTML structure

```
<!DOCTYPE html PUBLIC "-//W3C//DTD HTML 4.01 Transitional//EN"
    "http://www.w3.org/TR/html4/loose.dtd">        ◄─── HTML 4.01 Transitional is used here,
<html lang="en">                                          but any form of HTML will do.
<head>
    <meta http-equiv="Content-Type" content="text/html; charset=utf-8">
    <title>FOAF Map</title>
    <link rel="stylesheet" href="main.css">       ◄─── A CSS stylesheet
...                                                      makes the results
</head>                                                  look nicer.
<body>                              The JavaScript
  <h1>FOAF Map</h1>                 functions will go
  <div id="resultsmap"></div>      into the header.
  <div id="resultstable"></div>   ◄─── The division
</body>                                 used to hold
</html>          The division used      the map.
                 to hold the table.
```

Notice that we've included a link to a CSS stylesheet. This is optional but will typically be present in any real-world application. We can use that stylesheet to make the presentation look nicer.

5.6.3   *Creating the JavaScript for the table*

Three JavaScript components are added to the HTML page's header. They are shown in listing 5.23. The first is JQuery, a popular library to make writing JavaScript easier. JQuery is optional, of course, but used by millions of developers.

The second JavaScript referenced is the file containing the query results, foaf-map.js. The contents of that file are the same as figure 5.8.

Finally, we need JavaScript to use the query results to draw the map and table. We use JQuery's `$(document).ready()` function to call the two functions that will do that, `drawTable()` and `drawMap()`. The `$(document).ready()` function executes when the HTML page and its dependencies (such as JavaScript libraries) are fully loaded by the browser. That prevents JavaScript errors from occurring if execution happened before the dependencies were available.

Listing 5.23   JavaScript libraries for the FOAF map web page

The JQuery library makes scripting easier and neater.

Calls the functions that do the work.

```
<script src="jquery-1.7.1.min.js"></script>
<script src="foafmap.js"></script>
<script type="text/javascript">
<!--
$(document).ready(function(){
    drawTable();
    drawMap();
});
-->
</script>
```

The external file foafmap.js holds the results of the SPARQL query from listing 5.20.[3]

The custom JavaScript functions are created inline on the HTML page.

The `drawTable()` function shown in listing 5.24 creates an HTML table containing the name, latitude, and longitude for each person whose FOAF file was queried. Additionally, we want to be able to use the table as a key for the map, so we add a "symbol" column to the table with the first letter of each person's name as the symbol. You'll use these symbols in map markers to identify each person's position. The symbol is generated by

```
symbol = name.substring(0,1);
```

The name, latitude, and longitude for each person are extracted from the JSON results object via a JavaScript `forEach()` iterator. When completed, the table is inserted into the division with id `resultstable`.

Listing 5.24   JavaScript function to draw the table on the FOAF map web page

```
function drawTable() {
    var table = "<table><tr><th>Name</th><th>Symbol</th>" +
                "<th>Latitude</th><th>Longitude</th></tr>";
```

Creates an HTML table holding data from the SPARQL query results.

---

[3]   In a real application this file could be generated dynamically from a server-side process.

The name, latitude, and longitude
values are extracted from the
current record.

A JavaScript
forEach
function
iterates
through the
result's
records.

```
results.results.bindings.forEach( function(record, idx) {
    name = record.name.value;
    symbol = name.substring(0,1);
    latitude = record.latitude.value;
    longitude = record.longitude.value;
    table += "<tr><td>" + name + "</td><td>" + symbol +
             "</td><td>" + latitude + "</td><td>" + longitude +
             "</td>";
});
table += "</table>";
$("#resultstable").html(table);
}
```

The first character of each
person's name used to create a
symbol to use in a map icon.

An HTML table row is
created for each record.

The HTML table is inserted into
the division with id resultstable.

5.6.4 Creating JavaScript for the map

To draw the map we used the Google Static Maps API 2 which allows developers to construct a URL that calls the Google service and returns a static image in one of several common image formats (PNG, GIF, or JPEG). You can place markers on the map images, control the same type of map face used as Google Maps (roadmap, satellite, terrain, or hybrid), and set the zoom levels and centering. The service is very similar to Google Maps in functionality except that the returned image is static. This allows developers to embed a simple image in a web page without requiring an end user's browser to download, parse, and execute as much JavaScript as the Google Maps API requires. The Static Maps API is described at http://code.google.com/apis/maps/documentation/staticmaps/.

The function drawMap() shown in the next listing does the work of creating a Google Static Maps URL and placing it within an HTML image tag. The image is then fetched and displayed by the rendering browser.

Listing 5.25 JavaScript function to draw the map on the FOAF map web page

The drawMap() function creates
an HTML table holding data from
the SPARQL query results.

A JavaScript forEach
function iterates
through the result's
records.

A color is
randomly
assigned
to each
map
marker.

The name,
latitude, and
longitude values
are extracted
from the current
record.

```
function drawMap() {
var image = "<img src='http://maps.googleapis.com/maps/api/
    staticmap?center=43.0,-
    35&zoom=2&size=600x400&&maptype=satellite&format=png&sensor=false";
    results.results.bindings.forEach( function(record, idx) {
    color = chooseColor();
    sep = "%7C";
    name = record.name.value;
    symbol = name.substring(0,1);
    latitude = record.latitude.value;
```

Map marker's parameters
are separated by pipe
characters (|), which are
represented as a Hex escape
value %7C.

The first character of each
person's name is used to create a
symbol to use in a map icon.

```
        longitude = record.longitude.value;
        image += "&markers=color:" + color + sep + "label:" + symbol
➡  + sep + latitude + "," + longitude;                    ◁┐
        });                                                    │
        image += "'>";                                         │
        $("#resultsmap").html(image);        ◁─┐              │
}                                               │              │
```

A marker parameter list is built up for each record to allow them to use different colors and symbols.

The image is inserted into the division with id resultsmap.

The image URL is based on the Google Static Maps base URL (http://maps.googlea-pis.com/maps/api/staticmap) with a series of query string parameters. The center, zoom, size, maptype, format, and sensor parameters are described in detail in the API's documentation but are reasonably self-explanatory. The center is the latitude and longitude at which the map image is centered. The zoom is an integer from 0 to 21 where 0 is the entire Earth and 21 is at the level of individual buildings. We used a zoom level of 2 centered on the North Atlantic Ocean for this exercise. You'll want to change both the zoom level and the center point if you modify the exercise to plot data on parts of the planet's surface that are not currently shown (such as China, Australia, or Alaska).

The size parameter provides horizontal and vertical pixel dimensions for the image size. We chose to use the satellite map face, which is given in the maptype parameter. The rather arcane sensor parameter controls whether a mobile device's GPS sensor is being used to automatically plot the user's position. That parameter is set to false for most web pages.

The bulk of the work in drawMap() goes into the creation of two sets of map markers. Each marker plots the location of a person found in the SPARQL query. The query in listing 5.20 uses two FOAF files, so one marker is created for each person. If you modify the query to use more FOAF files, you'll want the JavaScript to handle that without modification. Each set of marker parameters assigns a randomly generated color to a marker and uses the first letter of each person's name as a symbol on the marker. This is the same symbol that was used in the HTML table, so the table can serve as a key to the map.

The marker parameters are separated by a pipe symbol (|). URL-encoding a pipe symbol into its hexadecimal notation gives you %7C, which is used in the JavaScript as the separation characters.

The name, latitude, and longitude are extracted from the JSON query results in exactly the same way as was done for the creation of the HTML table. As a final step, the image tag is placed within the division with the id resultsmap.

The color functions are given in listing 5.26. They're not germane to this example, per se, but allow the code to adapt to changes in the SPARQL query in a nicer way. They're presented for completeness. Modify them if you want to change the way colors are generated. Changing the frequency and randomnumber definitions will generate colors from different parts of the spectrum and control the granularity of the pattern's variations. If you don't want the map markers to change colors, replace `color = chooseColor();` in listing 5.25 with a single color assignment.

Listing 5.26   JavaScript to generate random color markers on the FOAF map web page

```
// Thanks to Jim Bumgardner's color tutorial:          Returns a random color for
// http://krazydad.com/tutorials/makecolors.php        use as a marker parameter
function chooseColor () {                               in a Google Static Map.
var frequency = .3;
var randomNumber = Math.floor(Math.random() * 32)
red   = Math.sin(frequency * randomNumber + 0) * 127 + 128;
green = Math.sin(frequency * randomNumber + 2) * 127 + 128;
blue  = Math.sin(frequency * randomNumber + 4) * 127 + 128;
return RGB2Color(red,green,blue);                       Assembles a 24-bit
}                                                       color from red, green,
function RGB2Color (r,g,b) {                            and blue components.
return '0x' + byte2Hex(r) + byte2Hex(g) + byte2Hex(b);
}
function byte2Hex (n) {                                 Returns a hex
    var nybHexString = "0123456789ABCDEF";             string given a byte
    return String(nybHexString.substr((n >> 4) & 0x0F,1)) +   representation.
        nybHexString.substr(n & 0x0F,1);
}
```

Figure 5.7 shows the final result. The HTML has some minor styling that comes from the CSS file referenced in the HTML header. All the files used to create this example can be found on the book's companion site.

The map is a static image, not a live Google Map. The example is easily modifiable to change the static image to a dynamic map by using the Google Maps JavaScript API 3. (See http://code.google.com/apis/maps/documentation/javascript/ for instructions on creating Google Maps using JavaScript.)

Try extending the example application to include other information from the FOAF files. Some good candidates are workplaces, schools, or other friends. That information should probably be OPTIONAL in case it doesn't exist in all FOAF files you query. See listing 5.10 to get the OPTIONAL syntax right. You might group friends into categories and colorize them or use the Google Maps or Google Static Maps APIs to draw arcs showing which people claim to be friends. You might also add additional FROM clauses to the SPARQL query to reference other FOAF files on the internet or even add your own. There's a lot of data on the Web to pull from, so give it a try.

The FOAF map is a simple, straightforward example of using a SPARQL query to dynamically generate a web page from Linked Open Data, but the concepts involved translate almost directly to real-world situations. The only major difference is the dynamic generation of SPARQL results in JSON syntax when the data source URL is requested. That may be accomplished using ARQ, as shown, called from a Java servlet, CGI script, or other server-side process or using one of the many SPARQL libraries available for various programming languages.

5.7   *Summary*

This chapter has introduced the SPARQL query language for RDF. SPARQL allows you to query the Web of Data as if were a database, albeit a very large one with many distributed datasets.

We've shown how simple SPARQL queries work and introduced concepts that should have whetted your appetite. SPARQL's ability to perform distributed queries, pull together disparate datasets, dynamically federate data, and then process it using modern query language constructs gives developers amazing new skills.

SPARQL is *much* more powerful than has been described in this chapter. It's a full query language with many features and extensions. Readers are encouraged to read the official SPARQL specifications to get a full understanding of the language.

NOTE   The SPARQL Query Language for RDF is a rich language and far too complicated to describe in a single book chapter. We highly recommend Bob DuCharme's *Learning SPARQL* (O'Reilly Media, 2011). All the details may be found in the W3C Recommendation that describes SPARQL in detail, at http://www.w3.org/TR/sparql11-query/.

Part 3

Linked Data in the wild

What is RDFa? How can you use it to enhance your HTML web pages and improve search engine optimization? What's the Good Relations vocabulary, and how can you use it to improve click-through rates? What is schema.org, and how can you use its vocabularies with RDFa to enhance web pages for your business? What are the benefits of RDF databases? What techniques should you use to optimize sharing your data and projects on the Web? What are sitemaps, and why should you use them?

Now that you understand how to consume and publish Linked Data, chapters 6-8 will show you more complex applications of Linked Data. We'll demonstrate how to enhance your web pages and improve search engine optimization. We'll demonstrate how RDF facilitates the aggregation of diverse data sources in diverse formats including non-RDF data. We'll walk you through applications where we aggregate diverse data including EPA and NOAA sources, store it in an RDF database, and query that content using SPARQL.

You'll be able to optimize the inclusion of your projects and datasets in Semantic Web search results by publishing DOAP files of your projects and VoID files for your datasets along with a semantic sitemap. You'll be able to publish your qualified datasets on the LOD cloud for others to use.

Enhancing results
from search engines

6

This chapter covers

- Adding Resource Description Framework in Attributes (RDFa) to HTML
- Using RDFa and the GoodRelations vocabulary to enhance HTML
- Using RDFa with schema.org
- Applying SPARQL to extracted RDFa

Previous chapters covered discovering Linked Data on the Web. This chapter will guide you in enhancing your own web pages with RDFa. We'll start with a typical HTML web page designed for human readability and demonstrate how to embed RDFa content that will enable your page to be both human- and machine-consumable. The presence of this Linked Data will improve search engine optimization (SEO) and the likelihood that your web content will be discovered.

We'll then convert a web page designed to showcase a consumer product and embed RDFa that uses the GoodRelations vocabulary. These improvements will improve the discovery of this product by common search engines like Google,

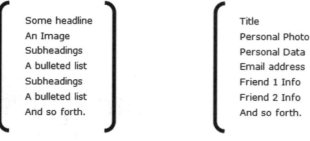

Document A--Without RDFa   Document B--With RDFa

Some headline
An Image
Subheadings
A bulleted list
Subheadings
A bulleted list
And so forth.

Title
Personal Photo
Personal Data
Email address
Friend 1 Info
Friend 2 Info
And so forth.

Figure 6.1   Machine interpretation of HTML documents versus human interpretation

Microsoft, Yandex, and Yahoo!. Finally, we'll demonstrate a similar outcome with the schema.org vocabularies. The embedded RDFa can be extracted and we'll illustrate searching the extracted RDFa using a SPARQL query.

Overall, our goal is to provide semantic meaning to your web content and enable the extraction of Linked Data. We use the FOAF vocabulary because it will be familiar from chapter 4. We use the GoodRelations vocabulary because of its significance to e-commerce, and we use schema.org because it's supported by a collaboration of three major search engines (Yahoo!, Bing, and Google). By embedding RDFa in your HTML documents, you enable search engines to provide more relevant search results and also allow for the incorporation of the content as Linked Data on the Web.

6.1   *Enhancing HTML by embedding RDFa*

Being digitally accessible isn't synonymous with being machine comprehendible. For instance, the cover of a publication may have a digitally accessible photo, but the significance of that photo is not machine understandable. But a barcode on that cover is machine consumable in that it enables a program to identify the object and likely to access its cost and track its purchase. Using RDFa on a web page serves an equivalent purpose to the barcode. It enables a search engine to identify the meaning of the digital data, making it structured data.

RDF provides a mechanism for expressing data and relationships. RDF in Attributes (RDFa) is a language that allows you to express RDF data within an HTML document. This enables your website to be both machine- and human-readable. HTML is a means of describing the desired visual appearance of your content. HTML doesn't differentiate between a book title and a job title. It can only differentiate the font displayed according to the author's direction. The human reader needs to interpret the information based on the context of the page and identify a book title as opposed to a job title. RDFa enables the author to embed structured data that will identify this differentiation. Authors can mark up human-consumable information for interpretation by browsers, search engines, and other programs. The RDFa-specific attributes don't affect the visual display of the HTML content and are ignored by the browser as it would any other attribute not recognizable as HTML.

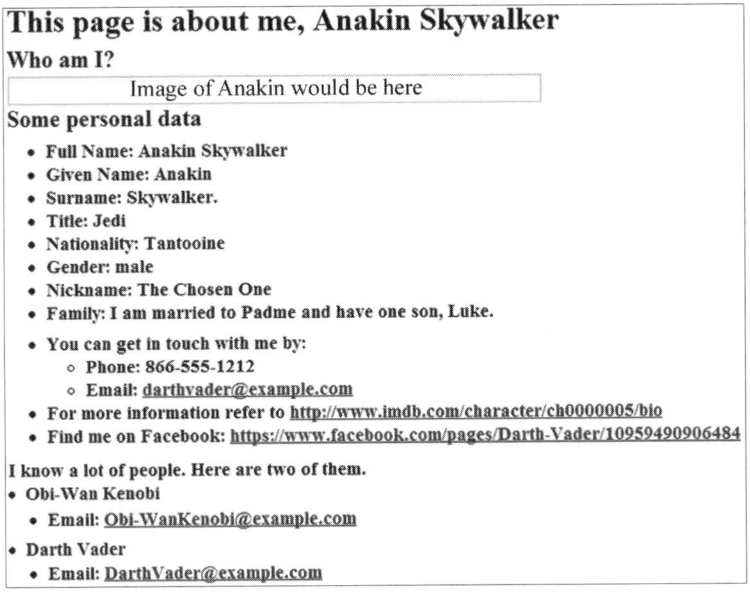

This page is about me, Anakin Skywalker

Who am I?

Image of Anakin would be here

Some personal data

- Full Name: Anakin Skywalker
- Given Name: Anakin
- Surname: Skywalker.
- Title: Jedi
- Nationality: Tantooine
- Gender: male
- Nickname: The Chosen One
- Family: I am married to Padme and have one son, Luke.

- You can get in touch with me by:
  - Phone: 866-555-1212
  - Email: darthvader@example.com
- For more information refer to http://www.imdb.com/character/ch0000005/bio
- Find me on Facebook: https://www.facebook.com/pages/Darth-Vader/10959490906484

I know a lot of people. Here are two of them.
- Obi-Wan Kenobi
  - Email: Obi-WanKenobi@example.com
- Darth Vader
  - Email: DarthVader@example.com

Figure 6.2   Web page produced by listing 6.1

We'll begin our application with a traditional basic HTML document about Anakin Skywalker, shown in listing 6.1. We'll mark up the HTML by embedding RDFa and explain what we're doing as we proceed. As an HTML page without RDFa, the browser interprets the content without regard to its semantic meaning. The page as displayed could contain any content, and the HTML elements affect its visual appearance. Hence, the content is simply as illustrated in Document A of figure 6.1.

As human readers (illustrated as Document B of figure 6.1), we recognize that the web page in figure 6.2 is about Anakin Skywalker. We recognize that it contains an image of Anakin, some of his personal information, and brief information about the people he knows. Our goal is to embed RDFa properties that would enable an automated interpretation of this page as a human reader would. The following listing contains the fundamental HTML description without any embedded RDFa.

Listing 6.1   An HTML description without embedded RDFa

```
<html>
<head>
<title>Anakin Skywalker</title>
<meta content="text/html; charset=UTF-8" http-equiv="Content-Type"
   />
</head>

<body>
<h1> This page is about me, Anakin Skywalker </h1>
<h2>Who am I?</h2>
<img
   src="http://www.starwars.com/img/explore/encyclopedia/
```

⇒   characters/anakinskywalker_detail.png"
⇒   alt="http://www.starwars.com/img/explore/encyclopedia/
⇒   characters/anakinskywalker_detail.png">

```
<h2>
<p>I was born on the planet Tatooine.  I like to invent.
I invented my own droid, C-3PO, from salvaged parts.
My mother is Shmi and she says that I do not have a father.
I was trained as a Jedi knight by Obi-Wan Kenobi.
I am an excellent knight but I don't like authority figures.

While I was assigned to guard Padme, I fell in love with her.
She knew that I loved her and that I distrusted the
political process. I wished we had one strong leader. </p>

<p>As a Jedi Knight, I fought many battles for the Republic
and I rescued many captives. However, after a series
of such episodes, I was injured and succumbed to the
Dark Side.</p>
</h2>
<h2>

Some personal data
</h2>
<ul>
<h3>
<li>Full Name: Anakin Skywalker </li>

<li>Given Name: Anakin </li>

<li>Surname: Skywalker.</li>

<li>Title: Jedi </li>

<li>Nationality: Tatooine </li>

<li>Gender: male</li>

<li>Nickname:  The Chosen One </li>

<li>Family: I am married to Padme and have one son, Luke.</li>
</h3>
</ul>

<h3>
<ul>
<li> You can get in touch with me by: </li>
    <ul>
    <li>Phone:   866-555-1212</li>
    <li>Email:
```
⇒   <a href="mailto:darthvader@example.com">
⇒   darthvader@example.com</a></li>
```
    </ul>
<li> For more information refer to
```
⇒   <a href= "http://www.imdb.com/character/ch0000005/bio">

```
➡    http://www.imdb.com/character/ch0000005/bio    </a> </li>
<li> Find me on Facebook:
➡    <a href= "https://www.facebook.com/pages/Darth-
➡    Vader/10959490906484">
➡    https://www.facebook.com/pages/Darth-Vader/10959490906484    </a> </li>
</ul>
</h3>


<h3>
I know a lot of people.  Here are two of them.
<li> Obi-Wan Kenobi</li>
    <ul>
    <li>Email: <a href="mailto:obiwankenobi@example.com">
➡   Obi-WanKenobi@example.com</a></li>
    </ul>
<li> Darth Vader</li>
    <ul>
    <li>Email:<a href="mailto:darthvader@example.com">
➡   DarthVader@example.com</a></li>
    </ul>
</h3>
</body>
</html>
```

6.1.1   *RDFa markup using FOAF vocabulary*

Now let's embed some RDFa into the HTML of listing 6.1. Our fully enhanced HTML document is contained in listing 6.2. Let's break down the additions to the basic HTML document from listing 6.1. As you enhance your HTML document with RDFa, you should periodically validate your efforts. You'll find an easy-to-use tool at http://www.w3.org/2012/pyRdfa/.

At the beginning of listing 6.2, you'll notice two statements that you need to support both HTML5 and RDFa:

```
<!DOCTYPE HTML>
<html version="HTML+RDFa 1.1" lang="en" >
```

In the remainder of the document, you embed the RDFa elements by applying them in conjunction with HTML tags. RDFa attributes allowed on all elements in the HTML5 content model are

- vocab
- typeof
- property
- resource
- prefix
- content
- about
- rel
- rev
- datatype
- inlist

All other attributes that RDFa may process, like href and src, are only allowed on the elements defined in the HTML5 specification.[1]

---

[1] HTML+RDFa 1.1, Support for RDFa in HTML4 and HTML5, W3C working draft, Sept. 11, 2012, http://www.w3.org/TR/2012/WD-rdfa-in-html-20120911/#extensions-to-the-html5-syntax.

The HTML body tag shown in the following snippet, extracted from listing 6.2, contains a `prefix` attribute. The `prefix` attribute serves the same purpose here as it does in Turtle documents. The various vocabularies listed in the `prefix` attribute of the body tag can be conveniently referred to throughout the body of the document using the associated shorthand prefixes defined.

```
<body id=me
prefix = "
rdf: http://www.w3.org/1999/02/22-rdf-syntax-ns#
rdfs: http://www.w3.org/2000/01/rdf-schema#
xsd: http://www.w3.org/2001/XMLSchema#
dc: http://purl.org/dc/elements/1.1/
foaf: http://xmlns.com/foaf/0.1/
rel: http://purl.org/vocab/relationship/
stars: http://www.starwars.com/explore/encyclopedia/characters/ "
>
```

As you further examine listing 6.2, you'll notice extensive use of the HTML `div` and span tags. These tags don't affect the visual appearance of the document and are primarily used as grouping indicators. The `span` and `div` elements are similar to `<div>a contained block</div>` that starts on a new line. `<span>some text</span>` is an inline separator that identifies the enclosed text as a single entity. The `typeof` attribute defines the enclosed entity as being an object of type `foaf:Person`.

Listing 6.2   HTML sample with RDFa markup from the FOAF vocabulary

```
<!DOCTYPE html>
<html version="HTML+RDFa 1.1" lang="en">        ◁─┐ Statements alerting
<head>                                             │  browser to RDFa
<title>Anakin Skywalker</title>                    │  and use of HTML5
<meta http-equiv="Content-Type" content="text/html; charset=UTF-8"/>
<base href= "http://rosemary.umw.edu/~marsha/starwars/foaf.ttl#" >

</head>


<body id=me
prefix = "
rdf: http://www.w3.org/1999/02/22-rdf-syntax-ns#        ◁─ Prefix
rdfs: http://www.w3.org/2000/01/rdf-schema#                statement
xsd: http://www.w3.org/2001/XMLSchema#
dc: http://purl.org/dc/elements/1.1/
foaf: http://xmlns.com/foaf/0.1/               Defines the start of a
rel: http://purl.org/vocab/relationship/       block named container
stars: http://www.starwars.com/explore/encyclopedia/characters/ "
>
<div id="container"                                    ◁─ Defines the
about="http://rosemary.umw.edu/~marsha/starwars/foaf.ttl#me"  enclosed entity as
typeof="foaf:Person">                                    being an object of
<h1> This page is about me, Anakin Skywalker </h1>       type foaf:Person

<h2>Who am I?</h2>                              Identifies the image to display and
<img property="foaf:img" class="flr"          identifies this object as being a
                                               ◁─ foaf:img property
```

```
src="http://www.starwars.com/img/explore/encyclopedia/characters/
   anakinskywalker_detail.png" alt="http://www.starwars.com/img/explore/
   encyclopedia/characters/anakinskywalker_detail.png">

<h2>
<p>I was born on the planet Tatooine. I like to invent. I invented my own
      droid, C-3PO, from salvaged parts. My mother is Shmi and she says that I
      do not have a father.
I was trained as a Jedi knight by Obi-Wan Kenobi. I am an excellent knight
      but I don't like authority figures.

While I was assigned to guard Padme, I fell in love with her. She knew that I
      loved her and that I distrusted the political process. I wished we had
      one strong leader. </p>

<p>As a Jedi Knight, I fought many battles for the Republic and I rescued
      many captives. However, after a series of such episodes, I was injured
      and succumbed to the Dark Side.</p>
</h2>
<h2>

Some personal data
</h2>
<ul>
<h3>
<li>Full Name: <span property="foaf:name">Anakin Skywalker</span> </li>
<li>Given Name: <span property="foaf:givenname">Anakin</span> </li>
<li>Surname: <span property="foaf:family_name">Skywalker</span></li>
<li>Title: <span property="foaf:title">Jedi</span> </li>
<li>Nationality: Tatooine </li>
<li>Gender: <span property="foaf:gender">male</span></li>
<li>Nickname:  <span property="foaf:nick">The Chosen One</span></li>
<li>Family: I am married to <span property="foaf:knows rel:spouseOf">Padme</
      span> and have one son, <span property="foaf:knows">Luke Skywalker</
      span>.</li>
</h3>
</ul>

<h3>
<ul>
<li> You can get in touch with me by: </li>
      <ul>
      <div vocab="http://xmlns.com/foaf/0.1/">
      <li>Phone:  <span property="phone">866-555-1212</span></li>
      <li>Email: <span property="mbox_sha1sum"
         content="cc77937087f686e222bcf1194fb8c671d8591e00">
      <a href="mailto:darthvader@example.com">AnakinSkywalker</a>
         </span></li>
      </div>
      </ul>

<li> For more information refer to <a property="foaf:homepage" href= "http://
      www.imdb.com/character/ch0000005/bio">http://www.imdb.com/character/
      ch0000005/bio    </a> </li>
```

Defines Padme as someone known to Anakin Skywalker and clarifies that relationship as one of spouse using the Relationship vocabulary[2]

---

[2] "Relationship: A vocabulary for describing relationships between people," created by Ian Davis and Eric Vitiello Jr., http://purl.org/vocab/relationship.

```
<li> Find me on Facebook:   <a typeof="foaf:account" href= "https://
     www.facebook.com/pages/Darth-Vader/10959490906484"> https://
     www.facebook.com/pages/Darth-Vader/10959490906484    </a> </li>
</ul>
I know a lot of people.  Here are two of them.
<div rel="foaf:knows" typeof="foaf:Person">
<ul>
    <li>
    <a property="foaf:homepage" href="http://live.dbpedia.org/page/
        Obi-Wan_Kenobi" />
    <span property="foaf:name">Obi-Wan Kenobi</span>
    <ul>
       <li>
       Email: <span property="foaf:mbox_sha1sum"
           content="aadfbacb9de289977d85974fda32baff4b60ca86">
           <a href="mailto:obiwankenobi@example.com">Obi-Wan Kenobi</a>
           </li>
       </ul>
       </li>
</ul>
</div>

<div rel="foaf:knows" typeof="foaf:Person">
<ul>
    <li>
    <a property="foaf:homepage"
        href="http://www.imdb.com/character/ch0000005/bio" />
    <span property="foaf:name">Darth Vader</span>
    <ul>
       <li>
       Email: <span property="foaf:mbox_sha1sum"
           content="cc77937087f686e222bcf1194fb8c671d8591e00">
           <a href="mailto:darthvader@example.com">DarthVader</a>
           </li>
       </ul>
       </li>
</ul>
</div>
</h3>
</div>
</body>
</html>
```

6.1.2   *Using the HTML span attribute with RDFa*

The first use of the <span></span> tag in conjunction with the RDFa property attribute is in the bulleted items excerpted in listing 6.3. The property attribute identifies which class property is being defined. In the case of

```
<li>Full Name: <span property="foaf:name">Anakin Skywalker</span> </li>
```

it's defining Anakin Skywalker as a foaf:name. Hence the characters "Anakin Skywalker" are now more than just some text to be displayed but are associated with the meaning defined by a foaf:name.

Listing 6.3   Bulleted list excerpt

```
<li>Full Name: <span property="foaf:name">Anakin Skywalker</span> </li>
<li>Given Name: <span property="foaf:givenname">Anakin</span> </li>
<li>Surname: <span property="foaf:family_name">Skywalker</span></li>
<li>Title: <span property="foaf:title">Jedi</span> </li>
<li>Nationality: Tatooine </li>
<li>Gender: <span property="foaf:gender">male</span></li>
<li>Nickname:  <span property="foaf:nick">The Chosen One</span></li>
<li>Family: I am married to <span property="foaf:knows rel:spouseOf">Padme</
    span> and have
    one son, <span property="foaf:knows">Luke Skywalker</span>.</li>
```

NOTE   The full RDFa 1.1 specification is at http://www.w3.org/TR/rdfa-core/.

6.1.3   *Extracting Linked Data from a FOAF-enhanced HTML document*

Entering the HTML document shown in listing 6.2 into the validator and RDFa 1.1 distiller (http://www.w3.org/2012/pyRdfa/) generates the Turtle content shown in the next listing. Although this isn't a necessary step in using RDFa, it illustrates two important points:

- The RDFa enhancements are extractable as Linked Data.
- The extracted RDF data can be saved in a separate file, published, and used as input to other applications, as illustrated in section 6.4.

Listing 6.4   Turtle generated from listing 6.2 RDFa-enhanced HTML

```
@prefix foaf: <http://xmlns.com/foaf/0.1/> .
@prefix rdfa: <http://www.w3.org/ns/rdfa#> .
@prefix rel: <http://purl.org/vocab/relationship/> .

<http://rosemary.umw.edu/~marsha/starwars/foaf.ttl> rdfa:usesVocabulary foaf: .

<http://rosemary.umw.edu/~marsha/starwars/foaf.ttl#me> a foaf:Person;
    rel:spouseOf "Padme";
    foaf:family_name "Skywalker";
    foaf:gender "male";
    foaf:givenname "Anakin";
    foaf:homepage <http://www.imdb.com/character/ch0000005/bio>;
    foaf:img <http://www.starwars.com/img/explore/encyclopedia/characters/
    anakinskywalker_detail.png>;
    foaf:knows [ a foaf:Person;
            foaf:homepage <http://live.dbpedia.org/page/Obi-Wan_Kenobi>;
            foaf:mbox_sha1sum "aadfbacb9de289977d85974fda32baff4b60ca86";
            foaf:name "Obi-Wan Kenobi" ],
        "Padme",
        [ a foaf:Person;
            foaf:homepage <http://www.imdb.com/character/ch0000005/bio>;
            foaf:mbox_sha1sum "cc77937087f686e222bcf1194fb8c671d8591e00";
            foaf:name "Darth Vader" ],
        "Luke Skywalker";
    foaf:mbox_sha1sum "cc77937087f686e222bcf1194fb8c671d8591e00";
    foaf:name "Anakin Skywalker";
```

```
        foaf:nick "The Chosen One";
        foaf:phone "866-555-1212";
        foaf:title "Jedi" .
```

```
<https://www.facebook.com/pages/Darth-Vader/10959490906484> a foaf:account .
```

You'll notice that this output in the previous listing bears a close resemblance to the FOAF profiles that we developed in chapter 4.

You can use the Google Structured Data Testing Tool (http://www.google.com/webmasters/tools/richsnippets) to see the result of your efforts. Unfortunately, you're limited to 1500 characters.

This section illustrated how to use RDFa to enhance a typical HTML homepage to provide meaningful structure to the content that enables machine interpretation of the content. In general, RDFa enhancements improve SEO. In the following section we'll further illustrate how RDFa can be used to enhance business websites.

6.2 *Embedding RDFa using the GoodRelations vocabulary*

GoodRelations is the most widely used RDF vocabulary for e-commerce. It enables you to publish details of your products and services in a way that search engines, mobile applications, and browser extensions can utilize the information and improve your click-through rates. In this section, we use the GoodRelations vocabulary to enhance a web page that describes a product, the Sony Cyber-shot DSC-WX100 camera, thus giving that description more meaning and improving its SEO.

Search engines like Google and Yahoo! recognize GoodRelations data in web pages provided by more than 10,000 product vendors like Sears, Kmart, and Best Buy.

Martin Hepp,[3] professor of e-commerce at University of Bundeswehr München and inventor of the GoodRelations ontology, says that preliminary evidence shows that enhancing your web pages with RDFa will improve your click-through rate by 30%. This is consistent with the results reported by Jay Myers, lead web development engineer at bestbuy.com.[4]

6.2.1 *An overview of the GoodRelations vocabulary*

The GoodRelations website at http://www.heppnetz.de/projects/goodrelations/ contains complete information on the vocabulary and its use. The goals and an overview of the conceptual model of this vocabulary are published at http://wiki.goodrelations-vocabulary.org/Documentation/Conceptual_model. As described there, the purpose of GoodRelations is to enable you to define an object for e-commerce that's industry neutral, valid from raw materials through retail to after-sales services, and syntax neutral.

This is achieved by using just four entities for representing e-commerce scenarios:

- An agent (for example, a person or an organization)
- An object (for example, a camera, a house, a bicycle) or service (for example, a manicure)

---

[3] Personal homepage of Martin Hepp, professor at the chair of General Management and E-Business at Universität der Bundeswehr Munich, http://www.heppnetz.de/.

[4] Paul Miller, "SemTechBiz Keynote: Jay Myers discusses Linked Data at Best Buy," June 6, 2012, http://semanticweb.com/semtechbiz-keynote-jay-myers-discusses-linked-data-at-best-buy_b29622

- A promise (offer) to transfer some rights (ownership, temporary usage, a certain license) on the object or to provide the service for a certain compensation (for example, an amount of money), made by the agent and related to the object or service
- A location from which this offer is available

This Agent-Promise-Object Principle can be found across most industries and is the foundation of the generic power of GoodRelations. It allows you to use the same vocabulary for offering a camera as for a manicure service or for the disposal of used motorcycles.

The respective classes in GoodRelations are:

- `gr:BusinessEntity` for the agent; that is, the company or individual
- `gr:Offering` for an offer to sell, repair, or lease something or to express interest in such an offer
- `gr:ProductOrService` for the object or service
- `gr:Location` for a store or location from which the offer is available

In table 6.1, the first column lists the characteristics that you'd want to specify about a product. The second column has the GoodRelations term associated with each characteristic. Some properties are new to GoodRelations and others are reused from other vocabularies (for example, FOAF and RDF-data vocabularies). You'll see many of these applied in the Sony camera HTML page that we enhance with RDFa. We're including these tables here for your ready reference and to give you an idea of the kind of data that we'd want to enhance in support of e-commerce.

Table 6.1   Google-supported GoodRelations properties associated with products or services[a]

Product characteristic	GoodRelations property
name	`gr:name`
image	`foaf:depiction`
brand	`gr:hasManufacturer` (for the brand link) and `gr:BusinessEntity` for the manufacturer name
description	`gr:description`
review information	`v:hasReview` (from http://rdf.data-vocabulary.org/#)
review format	`v:Review-aggregate` (from http://rdf.data-vocabulary.org/#)

identifier	`gr:hasStockKeepingUnit`
	`gr:hasEAN_UCC-13`
	`gr:hasMPN`
	`gr:hasGTN`

a. Google Webmaster Tools, "Produce properties: GoodRelations and hProduct," May 27, 2013, http://support.google.com/webmasters/bin/answer.py?hl=en&answer=186036

Table 6.2 lists the characteristics of an offer and the associated terms in the GoodRelations vocabulary that you'd use in modeling these characteristics. The second column lists the associated term in GoodRelations and offers guidance on how to apply it. `foaf:page` is the only term not contained in the GoodRelations vocabulary.

Table 6.2   Google-supported GoodRelations properties associated with an offer[a]

Offer characteristic	GoodRelations property
price	Price information is enclosed in the `gr:hasPriceSpecification` tag. Use the `content` attribute of the child `gr:hasCurrencyValue` to specify the actual price (use only a decimal point as a separator).
priceRangeLow	Price information is enclosed in the `gr:hasPriceSpecification` tag. Use the `content` attribute of the child `gr:hasMinCurrencyValue` to specify the lowest price of the available range (use only a decimal point as a separator).
priceRangeHigh	Price information is enclosed in the `gr:hasPriceSpecification` tag. Use the `content` attribute of the child `gr:hasMaxCurrencyValue` to specify the highest price of the available range (use only a decimal point as a separator).
priceValidUntil	`gr:validThrough`
currency	Price information is enclosed in the `gr:hasPriceSpecification` tag. Use the child `gr:hasCurrency` to specify the actual currency.
seller	`gr:BusinessEntity`
condition	`gr:condition`
availability	Inventory level is enclosed in the `gr:hasInventoryLevel` tag. Use the child tag `gr:QuantitativeValue` to specify the quantity in stock. For example, an item is in stock if the value of the content attribute of the enclosed tag `gr:hasMinValue` is greater than 0. Listing 6.6 applies this property.
offerURI	`foaf:page`

identifier	`gr:hasStockKeepingUnit`
	`gr:hasEAN_UCC-13`
	`gr:hasMPN`
	`gr:hasGTN`

a. Google Webmaster Tools, "Product properties: GoodRelations and hProduct," May 27, 2013, http://support.google.com/webmasters/bin/answer.py?hl=en&answer=186036.

When a single product that has different offers (for example, the same pair of running shoes is offered by different merchants), an aggregate offer can be used. These properties and associated GoodRelations terms are listed in table 6.3. As you'd expect, many of these terms are also associated with an offer.

Table 6.3 Google-supported GoodRelations properties associated with an offer-aggregate[a]

Offer-aggregate characteristics	GoodRelations property
priceRangeLow	Price information is enclosed in the `gr:hasPriceSpecification` tag. Use the `content` attribute of the child `gr:hasMinCurrencyValue` to specify the lowest price of the available range.
priceRangeHigh	Price information is enclosed in the `gr:hasPriceSpecification` tag. Use the `content` attribute of the child `gr:hasMaxCurrencyValue` to specify the highest price of the available range.
currency	Price information is enclosed in the `gr:hasPriceSpecification` tag. Use the child `gr:hasCurrency` to specify the actual currency.
seller	`gr:BusinessEntity`
condition	`gr:condition`
availability	Inventory level is enclosed in the `gr:hasInventoryLevel` tag. Use the child tag `gr:QuantitativeValue` to specify the quantity in stock. For example, an item is in stock if the value of the content attribute of the enclosed tag `gr:hasMinValue` is greater than 0. See listing 6.6 for more details.
offerURI	`foaf:page`
identifier	`gr:hasStockKeepingUnit` `gr:hasEAN_UCC-13` `gr:hasMPN` `gr:hasGTN`

a. Google Webmaster Tools, "Product properties: GoodRelations and hProduct," May 27, 2013, http://support.google.com/webmasters/bin/answer.py?hl=en&answer=186036.

6.2.2 Enhancing HTML with RDFa using GoodRelations

As we did in section 6.1, we'll start with a basic HTML file, marking it up using RDFa and the GoodRelations vocabulary. As we mentioned earlier in this chapter, GoodRelations is an important vocabulary for e-commerce. A basic HTML version of a web page for the camera was previously added to our wish list in chapter 4. This HTML document is shown in the next listing. This description will be annotated with many of the properties described in tables 6.1 and 6.2 shortly.

Listing 6.5 Basic HTML without GoodRelations markup

```
<html>
<head>
<title>SONY Camera</title>
<meta content="text/html; charset=UTF-8" http-equiv="Content-Type" />
</head>

<body>

<h2> Sony - Cyber-shot DSC-WX100 <BR>
  18.2-Megapixel Digital Camera - Black
```

```
 </h2>
 <BR>
<img src="http://images.bestbuy.com/BestBuy_US/images/products/5430/
➥   5430135_sa.jpg" alt="http://http://images.bestbuy.com/BestBuy_US/images/
➥   products/5430/5430135_sa.jpg">
<BR>
Model: DSCWX100/B      SKU: 5430135 <BR>
Customer Reviews:  4.9 of 5 Stars(14 reviews)
<BR>
Best Buy
http://www.bestbuy.com
<BR>
Sale Price: $199.99<BR>
Regular Price: $219.99<BR>
In Stock <BR>

<h3>
   Product Description
   <ul>
   <li>10x optical/20x clear image zoom </li>
   <li>2.7" Clear Photo LCD display</li>
   <li>1080/60i HD video</li>
   <li>Optical image stabilization</li>
   </ul>
</h3>
<BR>
Sample Customer Reviews<BR>
<BR>
Impressive - by: ABCD, November 29, 2012 <BR>

At 4 ounces this is a wonder. With a bright view screen and tons of features,
    this camera can't be beat.
<BR>
5.0/5.0 Stars<BR>
<BR>
Nice Camera, easy to use, panoramic feature by: AbcdE, November 26, 2012 <BR>
Great for when you don't feel like dragging the SLR around. Panoramic feature
    and video quality are very good.<BR>
4.75/5.0 Stars<BR>
<BR>
</body>
</html>
```

Although RDFa supports the entire GoodRelations vocabulary,[5] we're electing to limit our markup to the Google-supported properties listed in table 6.1. We encourage you to generate rich snippets for your web page by using the tools provided by GoodRelations.[6] You should heed the additional recommendations from the developers of GoodRelations (http://wiki.goodrelations-vocabulary.org/Quickstart).

---

[5] "GoodRelations Language Reference, V1.0, Release Oct. 1, 2011, http://www.heppnetz.de/ontologies/goodrelations/v1.html.

[6] Google Webmaster Tools, "Product properties: GoodRelations and hProduct," May 27, 2013, http://support.google.com/webmasters/bin/answer.py?hl=en&answer=186036.

The following listing is an annotated version of the basic HTML shown in listing 6.5. This web page is for the Sony camera from our wish list in chapter 4. We selected the camera because it's a product often marketed online, and GoodRelations will enable us to annotate the sale price, the vendor, the manufacturer, and product reviews.

Listing 6.6 Sample listing 6.5 using GoodRelations

```
<!DOCTYPE html>
<html version="HTML+RDFa 1.1" lang="en">
<head>
<title>Illustrating RDFa and GoodRelations</title>
<meta content="text/html; charset=UTF-8" http-equiv="Content-Type" />
<base href =
"http://rosemary.umw.edu/~marsha/other/sonyCameraRDFaGRversion3.html" />
</head>

<body id="camera"
prefix = "
review: http://purl.org/stuff/rev#
rdf: http://www.w3.org/1999/02/22-rdf-syntax-ns#
rdfs: http://www.w3.org/2000/01/rdf-schema#
xsd: http://www.w3.org/2001/XMLSchema#
foaf: http://xmlns.com/foaf/0.1/
rel: http://purl.org/vocab/relationship
v: http://rdf.data-vocabulary.org/# "
>
```

Generated using the URL in the footnote but modified to centralize all prefix declarations under body tag[7]

```
<!—Company related data—Put this on your main page -->
  <div typeof="gr:BusinessEntity" about="#company">
    <div property="gr:legalName" content="Linked Data Practitioner's
  Guide"></div>
    <div property="vcard:tel" content="540-555-1212"></div>
    <div rel="vcard:adr">
      <div typeof="vcard:Address">
        <div property="vcard:country-name" content="United States"></div>
        <div property="vcard:locality" content="Fredericksburg"></div>
        <div property="vcard:postal-code" content="22401"></div>
        <div property="vcard:street-address" content="1234 Main
  Street"></div>
      </div>
    </div>
    <div rel="foaf:page" resource=""></div>
  </div>

  <div typeof="gr:Offering" about="#offering">
    <div rev="gr:offers" resource="http://www.example.com/#company"></div>
    <div property="gr:name" content="Cyber-shot DSC-WX100"
  ml:lang="en"></div>
    <div property="gr:description" content="18.2-Megapixel
  Digital Camera - Black &lt;li&gt;10x optical/20x
  clear image zoom &lt;/li&gt; &lt;li&gt;2.7&quot; Clear Photo LCD
```

---

[7] Generated using http://www.ebusiness-unibw.org/tools/grsnippetgen/.

```
display&lt;/li&gt; &lt;li&gt;1080/60i HD video&lt;
/li&gt; &lt;li&gt;Optical image stabilization&lt;/li&gt;"
xml:lang="en"></div>
<div property="gr:hasEAN_UCC-13" content="0027242854031"
datatype="xsd:string"></div>
<div rel="foaf:depiction"
resource="http://images.bestbuy.com/BestBuy_US/images/products
/5430/5430135_sa.jpg"></div>
<div rel="gr:hasPriceSpecification">
  <div typeof="gr:UnitPriceSpecification">
    <div property="gr:hasCurrency" content="USD"
datatype="xsd:string"></div>
    <div property="gr:hasCurrencyValue" content="199.99"
datatype="xsd:float"></div>
    <div property="gr:hasUnitOfMeasurement" content="C62"
datatype="xsd:string"></div>
  </div>
</div>

<div rel="gr:hasBusinessFunction"
resource="http://purl.org/goodrelations/v1#Sell"></div>
<div rel="foaf:page" resource="http://www.example.com/dscwx100/"></div>
<div rel="gr:includes">
  <div typeof="gr:SomeItems" about="#product">
    <div property="gr:category" content="ProductOrServiceModel"
xml:lang="en"></div>
    <div property="gr:name" content="Cyber-shot DSC-WX100"
xml:lang="en"></div>
    <div property="gr:description" content="18.2-Megapixel Digital
Camera - Black &lt;li&gt;10x optical/20x clear image zoom &lt;/li&gt;
&lt;li&gt;2.7&quot; Clear Photo LCD display&lt;/li&gt;
&lt;li&gt;1080/60i HD video&lt;/li&gt; &lt;li&gt;Optical image
stabilization&lt;/li&gt;" xml:lang="en"></div>
    <div property="gr:hasEAN_UCC-13" content="0027242854031"
datatype="xsd:string"></div>
    <div rel="foaf:depiction"
resource="http://images.bestbuy.com/BestBuy_US/images/products/
5430/5430135_sa.jpg"></div>
    <div rel="foaf:page"
resource="http://www.example.com/dscwx100/"></div>
  </div>
</div>
</div>

<h2> Sony - Cyber-shot DSC-WX100 <BR>
18.2-Megapixel Digital Camera - Black </h2>
<BR>
<img src="http://images.bestbuy.com/BestBuy_US/images/products/5430/
5430135_sa.jpg" alt="http://http://images.bestbuy.com/BestBuy_US/images/
products/
5430/5430135_sa.jpg">
<BR>

<span rel="v:hasReview">
  <span typeof="v:Review-aggregate" about="#review_data">
```

```
Customer Reviews:
<span property="v:average" datatype="xsd:string"> 4.9 </span>
of <span property="v:best">5.0</span> Stars (<span property="v:count"
    datatype="xsd:string">14 </span>reviews)
<BR>
  </span>
</span>
Best Buy <BR>
<div rel="foaf:page" resource="http://www.bestbuy.com"></div>
<BR>

<span rel="gr:hasPriceSpecification">
<span typeof="gr:UnitPriceSpecification">
Sale Price: $<span property="gr:hasCurrencyValue v:lowprice"
    datatype="xsd:float">199.99</span><BR>
Regular Price: $<span property="gr:hasCurrencyValue v:highprice"
    datatype="xsd:float">219.99</span><BR>
</span>
</span>
Availability: <div rel="gr:hasInventoryLevel">
        <div typeof="gr:QuantitativeValue">
          <div property="gr:hasMinValue" content="1" datatype="xsd:float">In-
    stock</div>
        </div>
  </div>
  <BR>


<h3>
Product Description
<ul>
<li>10x optical/20x clear image zoom </li>
<li>2.7" Clear Photo LCD display</li>
<li>1080/60i HD video</li>
<li>Optical image stabilization</li>
</ul>
</h3>
<BR>


Sample Customer Reviews<BR>
<BR>

<br />Product Reviews:
<div rel="review:hasReview v:hasReview">
<span typeof="v:Review-aggregate review:Review">
<br />Average:
<span property="review:rating v:average" datatype="xsd:float">4.5</span>, avg.:
<span property="review:minRating" datatype="xsd:integer">0</span>, max:
<span property="review:maxRating" datatype="xsd:integer">5</span> (count:
<span property="review:totalRatings v:votes"
datatype="xsd:integer">45</span>)<br />
</span>
</DIV>

<div rel="review:hasReview v:hasReview" typeof="v:Review">
Impressive - by: <span property="v:reviewer">ABCD</span>, <span
```

Additional properties that improve the accessibility of your data

In RDFa, in the absence of a resource attribute, the typeof attribute on the enclosing div implicitly sets the subject of the properties marked up within that div.

Sample of a review aggregate

```
➥    property="v:dtreviewed" content="2012-11-29">November 29, 2012
➥    </span><BR>
<span property="v:summary">At 4 ounces this is a wonder. with a bright view
➥    screen and tons of features this camera can't be beat </span>
<span property="v:value">5.0</span>of
<span property="v:best">5.0</span> Stars<BR>
</div>
<BR>
<BR>

<div rel="review:hasReview v:hasReview" typeof="v:Review">
Nice Camera, easy to use, panoramic feature by: <span property="v:reviewer">
➥    AbcdE</span>, <span property="v:dtreviewed" content="2012-11-26">November

➥    26, 2012 </span><BR>
<span property="v:summary">Great for when you don't feel like dragging the
➥    SLR around. Panoramic feature and video quality are very good.</span><BR>
<span property="v:value">4.75</span> of
<span property="v:best">5.0</span> Stars<BR>
</div>
<BR>
<div rel="gr:hasBusinessFunction"
resource="htt;://purl.org/goodrelations/v1#Sell"></div>           From
<div property="gr:hasEAN_UCC-13" content="0027242854031"          GoodRelations
➥    datatype="xsd:string"></div>                                  website
<div rel="foaf:page" resource=""></div>
<div rev="gr:offers" resource="http://www.bestbuy.com"></div>
</div>
</body>
</html>
```

As you can glean from examining listing 6.6, the GoodRelations vocabulary fulfilled its expectations. Every business-related item on the page is associated with its meaning. Martin Hepp recommends that developers follow the original Google patterns[8] for marking up their pages with the following additions. These additions will make your data understood by all RDFa-aware search engines, shopping comparison sites, and mobile services. The Google recommendations are for Google only. The additional items are as follows:

- Add "about" attributes for turning your key data elements into identifiable resources so you can refer to your offer data.
- Add "datatype" attributes for all literal values to fulfill valid RDF requirements.
- Add alt="Product image" to all images for XHTML compatibility.
- Add foaf:page link. Empty quotation marks are sufficient for this link if it doesn't exist.
- Add gr:hasEAN_UCC-13 for the EAN/ISBN13 code. The UPC code can be easily translated to this format by appending a leading zero. This is useful for linking your offer to datasheets provided by their manufacturers.

---

[8] Google Webmaster Tools, "Product properties: GoodRelations and hProduct," May 27, 2013, http://support.google.com/webmasters/bin/answer.py?hl=en&answer=186036.

- Add the `gr:hasBusinessFunction` to make clear you're selling the item.
- Add `gr:offers` link to the company via the `rev` attribute. This can also be inserted on your main page.

Hence, in compliance with Martin Hepp's recommendations, listing 6.6 includes the following code:

```
<div rel="gr:hasBusinessFunction"
resource="http://purl.org/goodrelations/v1#Sell"></div>
<div property="gr:hasEAN_UCC-13" content="0027242854031"
datatype="xsd:string"></div>
<div rel="foaf:page" resource=""></div>
<div rev="gr:offers" resource="http://www.bestbuy.com"></div>
```

Notice the data type associated with each of the literal currency values.

```
Sale Price: $<span property="gr:hasCurrencyValue v:lowprice"
datatype="xsd:float">199.99</span><BR>
Regular Price: $<span property="gr:hasCurrencyValue v:highprice"
datatype="xsd:float">219.99</span><BR>
```

6.2.3   *A closer look at selections of RDFa GoodRelations*

Breaking down the document section by section, the start of the document contains these statements:

```
<!DOCTYPE html>
<html version="HTML+RDFa 1.1" lang="en">
<head>
<title>Illustrating RDFa and GoodRelations</title>
<meta content="text/html; charset=UTF-8" http-equiv="Content-Type" />
<base href = "http://www.example.com/sampleProduct/">
</head>
```

These statements identify the document type as HTML5 and set the `html version` attribute to HTML+RDFa1.1. These settings will ensure that most clients extract the RDF and recognize its existence. The purpose of the `<base href…>` statement is to provide an absolute URI for reference, and it should contain the URI of the company web reference.

> **NOTE**   Use the actual URI associated with the publication of the product's document as the expression within the quotes.

Including the `prefix` statement in the `<body…>` statement, shown in the next listing, establishes access to the schema at each of these locations for the entire `body` section of the document and establishes each vocabulary within this namespace.

> **Listing 6.7   Excerpt showing centralization of prefix information**

```
<body id="camera"
prefix = "
review: http://purl.org/stuff/rev#
rdf: http://www.w3.org/1999/02/22-rdf-syntax-ns#
rdfs: http://www.w3.org/2000/01/rdf-schema#
```

```
xsd: http://www.w3.org/2001/XMLSchema#
foaf: http://xmlns.com/foaf/0.1/
rel: http://purl.org/vocab/relationship
v: http://rdf.data-vocabulary.org/# "
>
```

Sections of code in listing 6.8 were generated using the GoodRelations snippet generator at http://www.ebusiness-unibw.org/tools/grsnippetgen/. We modified the output from the snippet generator. The namespace declarations were removed to simplify the example and replace the xmlns statements with their HTML5 equivalents. We also consolidated and centralized all the prefix declarations.

The excerpt highlighted in this listing describes the company web page, the legal name of the company, and its country, city, ZIP code, and physical address.

Listing 6.8   Excerpt of company information

```
<div typeof="gr:BusinessEntity" about="#company">
  <div property="gr:legalName"
  content="Linked Data Practitioner's Guide"></div>
  <div property="vcard:tel" content="540-555-1212"></div>
  <div rel="vcard:adr">
    <div typeof="vcard:Address">
      <div property="vcard:country-name" content="United States"></div>
      <div property="vcard:locality" content="Fredericksburg"></div>
      <div property="vcard:postal-code" content="22401"></div>
      <div property="vcard:street-address"
  content="1234 Main Street"></div>
    </div>
  </div>
  <div rel="foaf:page" resource=""></div>
</div>
```

The next listing, also generated using the online form at http://www.ebusiness-unibw.org/tools/grsnippetgen/, was modified to reflect the existing presence of the prefix declarations. It annotates the individual product information. It includes the product name, description, digital image of the product, UPC, seller, and cost.

Listing 6.9   Excerpt of product information

```
<div typeof="gr:Offering" about="#offering">
  <div rev="gr:offers" resource="http://www.example.com/#company"></div>
<div property="gr:name" content="Cyber-shot DSC-WX100"
  xml:lang="en"></div>
  <div property="gr:description" content="18.2-Megapixel Digital Camera
  - Black &lt;li&gt;10x optical/20x clear image zoom &lt;/li&gt;
  &lt;li&gt;2.7&quot; Clear Photo LCD display&lt;/li&gt;
  &lt;li&gt;1080/60i HD video&lt;/li&gt; &lt;li&gt;Optical image
  stabilization&lt;/li&gt;" xml:lang="en"></div>
  <div property="gr:hasEAN_UCC-13" content="0027242854031"
  datatype="xsd:string"></div>
  <div rel="foaf:depiction"
resource="http://images.bestbuy.com/BestBuy_US/images/products/5430/
```

```
5430135_sa.jpg"></div>
  <div rel="gr:hasPriceSpecification">
    <div typeof="gr:UnitPriceSpecification">
      <div property="gr:hasCurrency"
content="USD" datatype="xsd:string"></div>
        <div property="gr:hasCurrencyValue"
content="199.99" datatype="xsd:float"></div>
        <div property="gr:hasUnitOfMeasurement"
content="C62" datatype="xsd:string"></div>
    </div>
  </div>
</div>
```

Listing 6.10 highlights the annotation of an individual product review. You'll notice that the entire review is wrapped in a `<div rel=…>` to establish a relationship between our Sony camera and this review. Listing 6.6 contains two individual reviews and one aggregate review. All three are similarly annotated. Because the aggregate review represents a composite review, you'll notice that some of the represented properties are different from those in the next listing.

Listing 6.10   Excerpt showing annotation of an individual product review

```
<div rel="review:hasReview v:hasReview" typeof="v:Review">
Nice Camera, easy to use, panoramic feature by: <span
   property="v:reviewer"> AbcdE</span>, <span property="v:dtreviewed"
     content="2012-11-26">November 26, 2012 </span><BR>
<span property="v:summary">Great for when you don't feel like dragging
   the SLR around. Panoramic feature and video quality are very
     good.</span><BR>
<span property="v:value">4.75</span> of
<span property="v:best">5.0</span> Stars<BR>
</div>
```

6.2.4   *Extracting Linked Data from GoodRelations-enhanced HTML document*

As we illustrated in section 6.1, entering the HTML document shown in listing 6.6 into the validator and RDF 1.1 distiller (http://www.w3.org/2012/pyRdfa/) generates the Turtle content shown in the next listing. As we mentioned earlier in this chapter, this output can be retained and published. It can be used as input to other applications. In section 6.4, we'll illustrate mining this Linked Data using SPARQL.

Listing 6.11   Turtle statements derived from listing 6.6

```
@prefix foaf: <http://xmlns.com/foaf/0.1/> .
@prefix gr: <http://purl.org/goodrelations/v1#> .
@prefix rev: <http://purl.org/stuff/rev#> .
@prefix v: <http://rdf.data-vocabulary.org/#> .
@prefix vcard: <http://www.w3.org/2006/vcard/ns#> .
@prefix xsd: <http://www.w3.org/2001/XMLSchema#> .

<http://rosemary.umw.edu/~marsha/other/sonyCameraRDFaGRversion3.html
   #company> a gr:BusinessEntity;
     gr:legalName "Linked Data Practitioner's Guide"@en;
```

```
        vcard:adr [ a vcard:Address;
              vcard:country-name "United States"@en;
              vcard:locality "Fredericksburg"@en;
              vcard:postal-code "22401"@en;
              vcard:street-address "1234 Main Street"@en ];
        vcard:tel "540-555-1212"@en;
        foaf:page
➥       <http://rosemary.umw.edu/~marsha/other/sonyCameraRDFaGRversion3.html> .


<http://www.example.com/#company> gr:offers
➥   <http://rosemary.umw.edu/~marsha/other/sonyCameraRDFaGRversion3.html
➥   #offering> .


<http://rosemary.umw.edu/~marsha/other/sonyCameraRDFaGRversion3.html
➥   #offering> a gr:Offering;
        gr:description "18.2-Megapixel Digital Camera - Black
➥   <li>10x optical/20x clear image zoom </li>
➥   <li>2.7\" Clear Photo LCD display</li>
➥   <li>1080/60i HD video</li>
➥   <li>Optical image stabilization</li>"@en;
        gr:hasBusinessFunction gr:Sell;
        gr:hasEAN_UCC-13 "0027242854031"^^xsd:string;
        gr:hasPriceSpecification [ a gr:UnitPriceSpecification;
              gr:hasCurrency "USD"^^xsd:string;
              gr:hasCurrencyValue "199.99"^^xsd:float;
              gr:hasUnitOfMeasurement "C62"^^xsd:string ];
        gr:includes
➥   <http://rosemary.umw.edu/~marsha/other/sonyCameraRDFaGRversion3.html
➥   #product>;
        gr:name "Cyber-shot DSC-WX100"@en;
        foaf:depiction
➥   <http://images.bestbuy.com/BestBuy_US/images/products/5430/
        5430135_sa.jpg>;
        foaf:page <http://www.example.com/dscwx100/> .


<http://rosemary.umw.edu/~marsha/other/sonyCameraRDFaGRversion3.html
➥   #product> a gr:SomeItems;
        gr:category "ProductOrServiceModel"@en;
      gr:description "18.2-Megapixel Digital Camera - Black
➥   <li>10x optical/20x clear image zoom </li>
➥   <li>2.7\" Clear Photo LCD display</li>
➥   <li>1080/60i HD video</li> <li>Optical image stabilization</li>"@en;
        gr:hasEAN_UCC-13 "0027242854031"^^xsd:string;
        gr:name "Cyber-shot DSC-WX100"@en;
        foaf:depiction
➥   <http://images.bestbuy.com/BestBuy_US/images/products/5430/
        5430135_sa.jpg>;
        foaf:page <http://www.example.com/dscwx100/> .


<http://rosemary.umw.edu/~marsha/other/sonyCameraRDFaGRversion3.html#
➥   review_data> a v:Review-aggregate;
        v:average " 4.9"^^xsd:string;
        v:best "5.0"@en;
        v:count "14"^^xsd:string .
```

```
<http://www.bestbuy.com> gr:offers
    <http://rosemary.umw.edu/~marsha/other/sonyCameraRDFaGRversion3.html> .

<http://rosemary.umw.edu/~marsha/other/
    sonyCameraRDFaGRversion3.html> gr:hasBusinessFunction
    <http://rosemary.umw.edu/~marsha/other/#Sell>;
    gr:hasEAN_UCC-13 "0027242854031"^^xsd:string;
    gr:hasInventoryLevel [ a gr:QuantitativeValue;
            gr:hasMinValue "1"^^xsd:float ];
    gr:hasPriceSpecification [ a gr:UnitPriceSpecification;
            gr:hasCurrencyValue "199.99"^^xsd:float,
                "219.99"^^xsd:float;
            v:highprice "219.99"^^xsd:float;
            v:lowprice "199.99"^^xsd:float ];
    rev:hasReview _:_7a58d778-3981-4844-96e6-71b32fe1b439,
        _:_8d4ade4e-7085-4104-9a4e-d6131abe5853,
        _:_c6154cb1-03bf-4ba9-b237-67e0984a7a86;
    v:hasReview _:_7a58d778-3981-4844-96e6-71b32fe1b439,
        _:_8d4ade4e-7085-4104-9a4e-d6131abe5853,
        _:_c6154cb1-03bf-4ba9-b237-67e0984a7a86,
        <http://rosemary.umw.edu/~marsha/other/sonyCameraRDFaGRversion3.html
    #review_data>;
    foaf:page <http://rosemary.umw.edu/~marsha/other/
        sonyCameraRDFaGRversion3.html>,
            <http://www.bestbuy.com> .

_:_7a58d778-3981-4844-96e6-71b32fe1b439 a v:Review;
    v:best "5.0"@en;
    v:dtreviewed "2012-11-26"@en;
    v:reviewer " AbcdE"@en;
    v:summary "Great for when you don't feel like dragging the SLR
    around. Panoramic feature and video quality are very good."@en;
    v:value "4.75"@en .

_:_8d4ade4e-7085-4104-9a4e-d6131abe5853 a rev:Review,
        v:Review-aggregate;
    rev:maxRating 5;
    rev:minRating 0;
    rev:rating "4.5"^^xsd:float;
    rev:totalRatings 45;
    v:average "4.5"^^xsd:float;
    v:votes 45 .

_:_c6154cb1-03bf-4ba9-b237-67e0984a7a86 a v:Review;
    v:best "5.0"@en;
    v:dtreviewed "2012-11-29"@en;
    v:reviewer "ABCD"@en;
    v:summary "At 4 ounces this is a wonder. with a bright view screen and
tons of features this camera can't be beat "@en;
    v:value "5.0"@en .
```

_:_7a58d778-3981-4844-96e6-71b32fe1b439 represents a blank node. Refer to chapter 2 for a more complete explanation.

_:_8d4ade4e-7085-4104-9a4e-d6131abe5853 represents a blank node. Refer to chapter 2 for a more complete explanation.

_:_c6154cb1-03bf-4ba9-b237-67e0984a7a86 represents a blank node. Refer to chapter 2 for a more complete explanation.

In this section we've embedded RDFa using the GoodRelations vocabulary. This specialized vocabulary will enable you to embed product, service, and company information in your web pages. This additional information improves SEO and click-through rates. Stay tuned; we understand that GoodRelations is in the process of being integrated into schema.org.

6.3   *Embedding RDFa using the schema.org vocabulary*

Schema.org is a collaborative initiative by three major search engines: Yahoo!, Bing, and Google. Its purpose is to create and support a common set of schema for structured data markup on web pages and to provide a common means for webmasters to mark up their pages so that the search results are improved and human users have a more satisfying experience. We'll follow a progression similar to what we did in section 6.2. We'll take a brief look at the schema.org vocabulary and apply it by embedding RDFa into the same basic HTML page that describes our Sony camera.

6.3.1   *An overview of schema.org*

The designers of schema.org provided a single common vocabulary and markup syntax (Microdata[9]) that's supported by the major search engines. This approach enables webmasters to use a single syntax and avoid tradeoffs based on which markup type is supported by which search engine. As you can see in table 6.4, schema.org supports a broad collection of object types and isn't limited to e-commerce terminology.

Table 6.4 Commonly used schema.org object types by category

Parent type	Subtypes
Creative works	CreativeWork, Article, Blog, Book, Comment, Diet, ExercisePlan, ItemList, Map, Movie, MusicPlaylist, MusicRecording, Painting, Photograph, Recipe, Review, Sculpture, SoftwareApplication, TVEpisode, TVSeason, TVSeries, WebPage, WebPageElement
MediaObject (Embedded non-text objects)	AudioObject, ImageObject, MusicVideoObject, VideoObject
Event	BusinessEvent, ChildrensEvent, ComedyEvent, DanceEvent, EducationEvent, Festival, FoodEvent, LiteraryEvent, MusicEvent, SaleEvent, SocialEvent, SportsEvent, TheaterEvent, UserInteraction, VisualArtsEvent
Organization	Corporation, EducationalOrganization, GovernmentOrganization, LocalBusiness, NGO, PerformingGroup, SportsTeam
Intangible	Audience, Enumeration, JobPosting, Language, Offer, Quantity, Rating, StructuredValue
Person	

---

[9] Defining the HTML microdata mechanism, HTML Microdata W3C Working Draft May 24, 2011, http://dev.w3.org/html5/md-LC/.

Table 6.4 Commonly used schema.org object types by category *(continued)*

Parent type	Subtypes
Place	LocalBusiness, Restaurant, AdministrativeArea, CivicStructure, Landform, LandmarksOrHistoricalBuildings, LocalBusiness, Residence, TouristAttraction
Product	
Primitive Types	Boolean, Date, DateTime, Number, Text, Time

NOTE The schema.org specification is accessible from http://schema.org/docs/schemas.html.

Unlike RDF, schema.org was not designed to

- Provide resource description for purposes other than discovery
- Publish data not displayed on web pages
- Facilitate machine-to-machine communication
- Support other ontologies outside of those agreed on by the partners of schema.org

Subsequent feedback from the web community encouraged the developers of schema.org to accept and adopt RDFa Lite as an alternative syntax to encode schema.org terms. Schema.org members are search engines, which really care about scalability, thus making the use of RDFa Lite strongly preferred. The difference is that RDFa 1.1 is a complete syntax for RDF (and can thus express anything that RDF can). RDFa Lite consists of only five simple attributes: vocab, typeof, property, resource, and prefix. One of the convenient features about RDFa 1.1 Lite and RDFa 1.1 is that a number of commonly used prefixes (http://www.w3.org/2011/rdfa-context/rdfa-1.1.html) are predefined. Therefore, you can omit declaring them and just use them, but the W3C recommended style is to include the prefix declarations.

The full specification for RDFa 1.1 Lite is at http://www.w3.org/TR/rdfa-lite/. RDFa 1.1 Lite is a subset of RDFa and consists of just five attributes that are used together with HTML tags to enable web developers to mark up their sites with Linked Data. We'll briefly discuss these attributes and then develop an example illustrating how RDFa 1.1 Lite works with HTML to enable meaningful markup of web pages.

Table 6.5 Properties of the schema.org Product class

Property	Type	Description
aggregateRating	AggregateRating	Based on a collection of reviews or ratings, this is the overall rating of the item.
brand	Organization	The brand of the product, for example, Sony, Minolta.
description	Text	A brief narrative about the item.

Table 6.5 Properties of the schema.org `Product` class *(continued)*

Property	Type	Description
image	URI	The URI of an image of the item.
manufacturer	Organization	The manufacturer of this product.
model	Text	The model identifier for this product.
name	Text	The name of the product.
offers	Offer	An offer to sell this product.
productID	Text	The product identifier, such as a UPC code.
review	Review	A review of this product.
URI	URI	The URI of this product.

As we mentioned in section 6.1, HTML without RDFa annotations to the browser looks like this:

```
Headline
Some image
More text
Bulleted list
More text
```

Adding RDFa markup will add meaning to all this text and enable the search engines to interpret this content as a human reader would. The search engines will "see" this:

```
Product name
Product image
Product description
Product rating
More product description
Consumer reviews
```

Obviously, this is a more meaningful web page.

6.3.2 *Enhancing HTML with RDFa Lite using schema.org*

Using schema.org with RDFa 1.1 Lite is similar to annotating a web page with RDFa except you limit your terms to those defined in the Lite subset. This example was intentionally restricted to just those terms defined in schema.org. Although doing so was certainly not required, we thought it the best approach given the purpose of our illustration.

   As we illustrated in section 6.1, we'll start with a plain HTML file designed around an item from our chapter 4 wish list, shown in listing 6.12, without semantic annotations and then enhance that web document with schema.org using RDFa 1.1 Lite notation. The enhanced document is in listing 6.13. As we illustrated in section 6.2, the web page contains product information for the Sony Cyber-shot DSC-WX100 that we added to our wish list in chapter 4.

   In prior examples, we used multiple vocabularies and specified which ones using prefix statements. In this case, we need only designate a single vocabulary, schema.org, which will be our default vocabulary, for example:

```
<div vocab = "http://schema.org/" typeof= "Product">
Some other text
</div>
```

We've actually defined two attributes: the default vocabulary that we're going to use and the type of the object we'll be describing. We also need to identify the properties of the object that we'll be describing. Looking more closely at the schema.org `Product` class summarized in table 6.5, we find that it has a number of properties/attributes that we'll use to enhance our Sony camera web page.

Listing 6.12 Basic HTML

```
<html>
<head>
<title>SONY Camera</title>
<meta content="text/html; charset=UTF-8" http-equiv="Content-Type" />
</head>

<body>

<h2> Sony - Cyber-shot DSC-WX100 <BR>
  18.2-Megapixel Digital Camera - Black
</h2>
 <BR>
<img
➥    src="http://images.bestbuy.com/BestBuy_US/images/products/5430/
➥    5430135_sa.jpg"
➥    alt="http://http://images.bestbuy.com/BestBuy_US/images/
➥    products/5430/5430135_sa.jpg">
<BR>
Model: DSCWX100/B      SKU: 5430135 <BR>
Customer Reviews:  4.9 of 5 Stars(14 reviews)
<BR>
Best Buy
http://www.bestbuy.com
<BR>
Sale Price: $199.99<BR>
Regular Price: $219.99<BR>
In Stock <BR>

<h3>
  Product Description
```

```
<ul>
<li>10x optical/20x clear image zoom </li>
<li>2.7" Clear Photo LCD display</li>
<li>1080/60i HD video</li>
<li>Optical image stabilization</li>
</ul>
</h3>
<BR>
Sample Customer Reviews<BR>
<BR>
Impressive - by: ABCD, November 29, 2012 <BR>

At 4 ounces this is a wonder. With a bright view screen and tons of features,
    this camera can't be beat
<BR>
5.0/5.0 Stars<BR>
<BR>
Nice Camera, easy to use, panoramic feature by: AbcdE, November 26, 2012 <BR>
Great for when you don't feel like dragging the SLR around. Panoramic feature
    and video quality are very good.<BR>
4.75/5.0 Stars<BR>
<BR>
</body>
</html>
```

6.3.3 *A closer look at selections of RDFa Lite using schema.org*

As you examine listing 6.13, you'll notice extensive use of the <span></span> and
<div></div> HTML tags with their property attributes. The values associated with
those properties are from table 6.5, the properties of the schema.org Product class.
One difference is the use of the typeof attribute when the property is of a non-basic
type. For example,

```
<div property="offers" typeof="AggregateOffer">
```

designates the encapsulated property as type offers and that an item classified as
offers is of typeof AggregateOffer.

Listing 6.13   HTML sample with RDFa markup from the schema.org vocabulary

```
<!DOCTYPE html>
<html version="HTML+RDFa 1.1" lang="en">
<head>
<title>Illustrating RDFa 1.1 Lite and schema.org</title>

<meta content="text/html; charset=UTF-8" http-equiv="Content-Type" />
<base href = "http://www.example.com/sampleProduct"/>
</head>

<body vocab="http://schema.org/">
<div typeof="Product">
 <h2 > <span property="brand" typeof="Organization">Sony </span>          Product
 <span property="name"> Cyber-shot DSC-WX100 </span>                      description
 <span property="description">18.2-Megapixel Digital Camera - Black
➥   </span></h2>
```

```
<BR>
<img property="image" src="http://images.bestbuy.com/BestBuy_US/images/
    products/5430/5430135_sa.jpg" alt="http://images.bestbuy.com/BestBuy_US/
    images/products/5430/5430135_sa.jpg">
<BR>
Model: <span property="model">DSCWX100/B </span>   SKU: <span
⇒   property="productID">5430135 </span>
<div property="aggregateRating" typeof="AggregateRating">
Customer Reviews:   <span property="ratingValue">4.9</span> of
<span property="bestRating">5.0</span> Stars (<span property="ratingCount">14
⇒   </span>reviews)
<BR>
</div>
Best Buy <BR>
<span property="URI">http://www.bestbuy.com </span>
<BR>
<div property="offers" typeof="AggregateOffer">
Sale Price: $<span property="lowPrice">199.99</span><BR>
Regular Price: $<span property="highPrice">219.99</span><BR>
In Stock <BR>
</div>
<h3>
Product Description
<div property="description">
<ul>
<li>10x optical/20x clear image zoom </li>
<li>2.7" Clear Photo LCD display</li>
<li>1080/60i HD video</li>
<li>Optical image stabilization</li>
</ul>
</div>
</h3>
<BR>
Sample Customer Reviews<BR>
<BR>
<div property="review" typeOf="Review">
Impressive - by: <span property="author">ABCD</span>,
<span   property="datePublished" content="2012-11-29">November 29, 2012
⇒   </span><BR>
At 4 ounces this is a wonder. with a bright view screen and tons of
⇒   features this camera can't be beat
<span property="ratingValue">5.0</span> of
<span property="bestRating">5.0</span> Stars<BR>
</div>
<BR>
<BR>
<div property="review" typeOf="Review">
Nice Camera, easy to use, panoramic feature by: <span
⇒   property="author">AbcdE</span>, <span property="datePublished"
⇒   content="2012-11-26">November 26, 2012 </span><BR>
Great for when you don't feel like dragging the SLR around. Panoramic feature
⇒   and video quality are very good.<BR>
<span property="ratingValue">4.75</span> of
<span property="bestRating">5.0</span> Stars<BR>
```

Review aggregate

Single person review

```
</div>
<BR>
</div>
</body>
</html>
```

6.3.4   *Extracting Linked Data from a schema.org enhanced HTML document*

The resulting Turtle obtained from entering the HTML document shown in listing 6.13 into the validator and RDF 1.1 distiller (http://www.w3.org/2012/pyRdfa/) is illustrated in the following listing. As we mentioned previously, this output can be retained and published. It can be used as input to other applications. In section 6.4, we'll illustrate mining similar Linked Data using SPARQL.

Listing 6.14   Resulting Turtle from HTML annotated with schema.org vocabulary

```
@prefix rdfa: <http://www.w3.org/ns/rdfa#> .
@prefix schema: <http://schema.org/> .

<http://www.example.com/sampleProduct> rdfa:usesVocabulary schema: .

[] a schema:Product;
    schema:aggregateRating [ a schema:AggregateRating;
            schema:bestRating "5.0"@en;
            schema:ratingCount "14"@en;
            schema:ratingValue "4.9"@en ];
    schema:brand [ a schema:Organization ];
    schema:description """

10x optical/20x clear image zoom
2.7" Clear Photo LCD display
1080/60i HD video
Optical image stabilization

"""@en,
        "18.2-Megapixel Digital Camera - Black "@en;
    schema:highPrice "219.99"@en;
    schema:image <http://images.bestbuy.com/BestBuy_US/images/products/5430/
      5430135_sa.jpg>;
    schema:lowPrice "199.99"@en;
    schema:model "DSCWX100/B "@en;
    schema:name " Cyber-shot DSC-WX100 "@en;
    schema:offers """
Sale Price: $199.99
Regular Price: $219.99
In Stock
"""@en;
    schema:productID "5430135 "@en;
    schema:review [ a schema:Review;
            schema:author "AbcdE"@en;
            schema:bestRating "5.0"@en;
            schema:datePublished "2012-11-26"@en;
            schema:ratingValue "4.75"@en ],
        [ a schema:Review;
            schema:author "ABCD"@en;
```

```
        schema:bestRating "5.0"@en;
        schema:datePublished "2012-11-29"@en;
        schema:ratingValue "5.0"@en ];
  schema:URI "http://www.bestbuy.com "@en .
```

NOTE   [ ] represents a blank node. Refer to chapter 2 for additional explanation.

Annotating your data with the schema.org vocabulary and RDFa 1.1 Lite will provide a more satisfying result from SEO, expose your information to more consumers, and contribute to the community of publically accessible published Linked Data.

6.4   *How do you choose between using schema.org or GoodRelations?*

As a web developer, how do you choose between GoodRelations and schema.org? This question isn't easy to answer and may not have a one-size-fits-all response. When schema.org was introduced, web authors who wanted to improve their SEO and target the major search engines—Google, Microsoft, Yahoo!, and Yandex—would select schema.org and annotate their web pages using the microdata syntax. But now that schema.org supports RDFa 1.1 Lite, web authors have more options.

The W3C, the developers of RDFa, took the feedback they received from Google, Microsoft, and Yahoo! very seriously and proposed RDFa Lite in response to their concerns. The schema.org community was concerned about the complexity of RDFa. Manu Sporny, the chair of the W3C RDF Web Applications Working Group, addressed this: "With RDFa 1.1, our focus has been on simplifying the language for Web authors. In some cases, we've simplified the RDFa markup to only require two HTML attributes to markup some of the schema.org examples. In most cases you only need three HTML attributes to express a concept that will enhance your search ranking… it's as simple as that."[10] With the support of RDFa 1.1 Lite, a developer can annotate a page using the schema.org vocabulary and if needed supplement those annotations with vocabulary from other sources, including GoodRelations.

The advantage of using RDFa 1.1 Lite with either schema.org or GoodRelations is that a web author can apply other features of the full RDFa standard because RDFa Lite is a subset of RDFa. For the time being, features outside of RDFa Lite would be ignored by the schema.org community. Consequently, at the moment, the choice between GoodRelations or schema.org seems to be one of best fit for the task at hand. Examine the vocabularies and determine which one addresses your needs. Because they can be used in conjunction with each other, we think that the choice is one of personal preference.

6.5   *Extracting RDFa from HTML and applying SPARQL*

RDF extracted from the RDFa-enhanced HTML files can be queried using SPARQL. The following listing illustrates a SPARQL query selecting the individual reviews and yields

---

[10] Eric Franzon, "Schema.org announces intent to support RDFa Lite!" November 11, 2011, http://semanticweb.com/breaking-schema-org-announces-intent-to-support-rdfa-lite_b24623#more-24623.

the results. The source being queried is a file copy of the Turtle extracted by the validator and RDF 1.1 distiller (http://www.w3.org/2012/pyRdfa/). This output is shown after the listing.

Listing 6.15   Sample SPARQL query to select reviews

```
prefix v: <http://rdf.data-vocabulary.org/#>
prefix rev: <http://purl.org/stuff/rev#>

SELECT ?date ?summary ?value
FROM <http://rosemary.umw.edu/~marsha/other/sonyCameraGRversion3.ttl>

WHERE {
  ?review a v:Review
    ; v:dtreviewed ?date
    ; v:summary ?summary
    ; v:value ?value .
} LIMIT 10
```

This query selects a review that identifies a date, narrative summary, and a rating value and extracts the date of the review, its narrative summary, and the numeric value of the rating. As we'd expect based on chapter 5, we have three columns of output representing the date, narrative summary, and numeric value. Following are the results of this query showing the two reviews selected.

```
-----------------------------------------------------------------------------
-----------------------------------------------------------------------------
| date          | summary
                                    | value     |
=============================================================================
=============================================================================
| "2012-11-29"@en | "At 4 ounces this is a wonder. With a bright view screen
    and
 tons of features, this camera can't be beat "@en      | "5.0 "@en  |
| "2012-11-26"@en | "Great for when you don't feel like dragging the SLR
    around.
 Panoramic feature and video quality are very good."@en | "4.75 "@en |
-----------------------------------------------------------------------------
-----------------------------------------------------------------------------
```

In this example, we applied a SPARQL query to RDFa extracted from our HTML page describing our Sony camera. The query selected the individual person reviews and extracted the date, summary, and star value contained in each review. Our HTML page contained two reviews.

6.6   *Summary*

We've illustrated three techniques for enhancing your web pages with RDFa 1.1. Section 6.1 illustrated how to use RDFa and the FOAF vocabulary to add structured data and semantic meaning to your HTML content. Section 6.2 illustrated how to annotate your HTML content with RDFa and the GoodRelations business-oriented vocabulary to add structured data and hence semantic meaning to a product description and sales information. Section 6.3 accomplished the same goal but is limited to RDFa 1.1 Lite because it's supported by schema.org.

In the next chapter, we'll be examining data reuse and RDF databases, and we'll be building an application illustrating spidering Linked Data.

RDF database fundamentals

7

This chapter covers

- An overview of RDF databases
- A comparison of RDF and relational databases
- Collecting Linked Data in an RDF database

This chapter will enable you to recognize the benefits of Linked Data modeling over other forms of modeling. The chapter is not intended as a thorough analysis of different database models but will present sufficient content to enable you to understand the features associated with RDF databases. We'll highlight the differences between the traditional relational database approach and RDF databases. We'll explain why the Linked Data community finds RDF databases useful and the types of problems such systems solve. We'll demonstrate how to transform data from Excel, CSV, and XML formats to Turtle for ease of integration into other applications. The final section of this chapter will develop a real-world example involving the collection and reuse of Linked Data as well as storing this content into an RDF database.

7.1 Classifying RDF databases

In general, databases can be classified in two broad categories, relational and NoSQL (Not Only SQL). RDF databases are just one of the many types of NoSQL

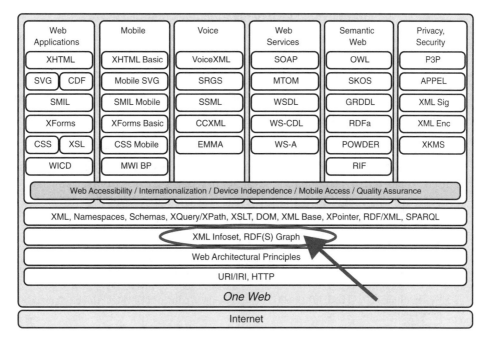

Figure 7.1 W3C technology stack

databases and the only type based on an international family of standards. RDF databases are also the only ones whose semantic meaning is formally defined. As you can see from figure 7.1, RDF is an integral component of the technology that powers the underlying layer supporting the Semantic Web.

RDF is one of three defined data models that underlie all other W3C standards. Linked Data uses RDF as its data model because RDF is the standard for representing data on the web. It's built upon the well-established lower-level standards like HTTP and URIs. Given the growth exhibited in the Linked Open Data cloud and increased use of RDFa to enhance web pages, we expect that RDF data will still be usable even decades from now.

In previous chapters, we described RDF as a generic, graph-based data model that represents data in the form of triples. These triples are records containing three values (subject, predicate, object) containing (URI, URI, URI) or (URI, URI, value). There are basic forms that can be used to store this data. In chapter 4, we developed individual files of Turtle statements. Interestingly, we're unlikely to view such files as a self-contained database, but in the RDF world they are. Each individual file can be queried using SPARQL and the extracted results harvested and used in data aggregations or as input to other applications. For instance, our aggregation of data from the Internet Movie Database and Best Buy RDFa could have been output to a Turtle file for future processing. But searching large files of triples can be a slow process.

An RDF database system needs to satisfy several challenges, as summarized here:

- Triples must be capable of being uniquely identified.
- Given a subject and predicate, searches should be efficient and execute quickly.
- Given a predicate and object, searches should be efficient and execute quickly.
- The RDF graph represented in the data must be preserved.

Note that many RDF databases use relational databases as their storage layer (although many others are purpose-built). Such relational RDF stores can be classified in three categories as summarized in table 7.1. These categories refer to the model used to store the data. Interestingly, relational database management systems have demonstrated that they can efficiently host large amounts of data. Hence, they may also be used to store RDF. The challenge of such systems is to properly translate a SPARQL query into SQL. SQL isn't designed for storage and retrieval of RDF data, whereas SPARQL is able to query an RDF graph represented in RDF triples.

Table 7.1   Classifications of relational RDF stores

Category	Description
Vertical (triple) table stores	Each RDF triple is stored directly in a three-column table (subject, predicate, object).
Property (*n*-ary) table stores	Multiple RDF properties are modeled as *n*-ary table columns for a single subject.
Horizontal (binary) table stores	RDF triples are modeled as one horizontal table or into a set of vertically partitioned binary tables where each individual table represents an RDF property.

In general, RDF databases are triplestores. A triplestore is a system that has some form of persistent storage of RDF data and lets you run SPARQL queries against that data. Many of these systems are based on reusing and adapting well-established techniques from relational databases. One basic approach would be to create a single table of three columns where the first column holds the subject, the second the predicate, and the third column the object. The basic three-column table can be optimized, but as of yet there are no best practices. Optimization techniques include indexing, applications of various hash functions, and restructuring of the basic table approach.

7.1.1   Selecting an RDF database systems

A large variety of databases are available, and the challenge is to find the one best suited for your project. Table 7.2 lists a few commonly used triplestores.

Table 7.2   Commonly used triplestores

Name	URL
4Store	http://www.4store.org/
Allegro-Graph	http://www.franz.com/agraph/allegrograph

Table 7.2 Commonly used triplestores *(continued)*

Name	URL
BigData	http://www.bigdata.com/
Fuseki	http://jena.apache.org/documentation/serving_data/index.html
Mulgara	http://mulgara.org/
Oracle	http://www.oracle.com/technetwork/database/options/semantic-tech/index.html
OWLIM	http://www.ontotext.com/owlim
Redland RDF Library	http://librdf.org/
Sesame	http://www.openrdf.org/
StarDog	http://stardog.com/
Virtuoso	http://virtuoso.openlinksw.com/

At the end of the day, the choice of database system for a Linked Data deployment should be guided by criteria such as the persistence strategy, the size of data to be served, and the relative frequencies of access and update. A reliable persistence strategy ensures data preservation, consistency, and integrity. Additional criteria for evaluation will likely include consideration of hardware and software requirements, cost, SPARQL support, ability to be embedded in an existing system, live backup capability, and security level. You'll need to critically examine each option in detail to determine whether it will meet your needs.

7.1.2 *RDF databases versus RDBMS*

There are several important differences between RDF databases and relational databases. We'll examine the differences in transactional models and schema descriptions, the breaching of traditional knowledge containers, and the elimination of data warehouses.

DIFFERENCE IN TRANSACTIONAL MODELS

Relational databases exhibit reliability, efficiency, and consistency. Most support the ACID model:

- *Atomicity* of transactions ensures that if any transaction in a multistep operation fails, then all associated transactions are rolled back. The database is unchanged.
- *Consistency* of each transaction means that no element of an atomic transaction may violate the database's business rules. Any transaction violating a rule results in failure and the database remains unchanged. This supports atomicity.

- *Isolation* between multiple transactions means that transactions must occur and complete sequentially. No transaction may see the intermediate product of another.
- *Durability* ensures that a successful transaction is permanently preserved through the use of backups and transaction logs.

The independence, flexibility, and distributed nature of the Web make enforcing rigid ACID expectations impossible. NoSQL databases, which include RDF databases, view ACID expectations as overly rigorous and hindering the operation of a database. Instead, NoSQL databases favor a softer model known as the BASE model. A BASE model embraces three tenets:

- *Basic availability* of the data even in the event of multiple failures. NoSQL databases spread data across many storage systems with a high degree of replication. If one segment of data is disrupted, then it expects other segments to be available and so prevent a complete database outage.
- *Soft* state abandons the consistency requirement of the ACID model. This model places the responsibility for data consistency with the developer and is not maintained by the database.
- *Eventual* consistency means that NoSQL systems expect that at some point data will converge to a consistent state, with no guarantees as to when this will occur.

DIFFERENCE IN SCHEMA DESCRIPTION

Data is transformed into useful information by adding context. For example, 888771234 alone is not particularly meaningful. But in a different format, 888-77-1234, many of us would guess that it could be a U.S. Social Security Number. Even better, if this number were in Jane Doe's file, in a field labeled SSN, then you'd likely assume that Jane Doe's Social Security Number is 888-77-1234. Data published using Linked Data standards provides such context.

In a relational database this data could be stored in a table like table 7.3, Database Table A, where field names represent the schema that might be defined in a data dictionary but more likely is not.

Table 7.3   Database Table A

id	last	first	ssn	date
1001	Doe	Jane	888771234	11-12-1959

Figure 7.2 shows a schema associated with the ssn field of a representative relational database. The schema is generic and doesn't offer any description of the meaning of the field. You are left to make your own association between the field name and its meaning. You need to rely on the database designer to have chosen meaningful names.

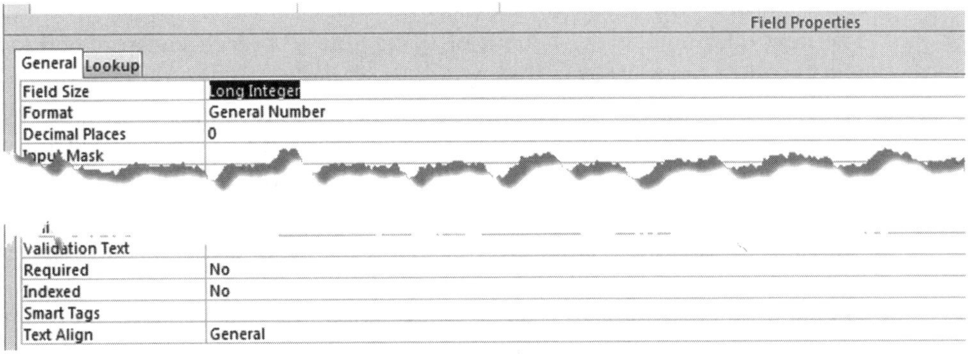

Figure 7.2   Documented schema for ssn field of a representative SQL database

In contrast, using an RDF database, this data would be represented in an unambiguous manner, as shown in figure 7.3, with documented schema. The following listing shows Jane Doe's information represented in RDF using an unambiguous schema.

Listing 7.1   Jane Doe record formatted in RDF

```
@base <http://www.example.com/~jdoe/foaf.ttl#>.
@prefix foaf: <http://xmlns.com/foaf/0.1/> .
@prefix vcard: <http://www.w3.org/2001/vcard-rdf/3.0#> .
@prefix datacite: <http://purl.org/spar/datacite/> .

    <me> a foaf:Person;
        foaf:family_name "Doe";
        foaf:givenname "Jane";
        foaf:name "Jane Doe";
        vcard:BDAY "1959-12-11";
        datacite:social-security-number "888771234".
```

You could access the URI associated with any predicate and see the schema associated with that term, for example, a Social Security Number, as shown in figure 7.3. We think the choice of which schema description is more meaningful is obvious.

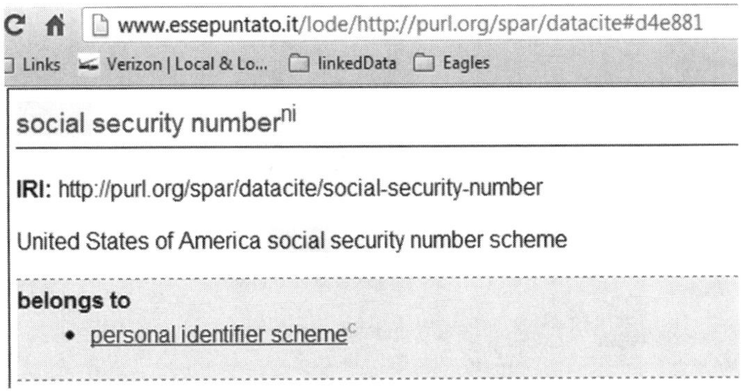

Figure 7.3   Datacite schema for Social Security Number

BREACHING OF TRADITIONAL KNOWLEDGE CONTAINERS

The next difference is the benefit of being able to breach encapsulated containers. This benefit can be illustrated by a simple example. Let's consider two independent websites. One site fronts an MS SQL database of all Grammy awards (http://www.example.com/grammyWinners); the other site fronts a large MySQL database of biographies of music artists (http://www.example.com/artistBios). These sites were started independently of each other and do not collaborate. The Grammy awards DB contains all Grammy-winning productions and a list of artists who wrote, performed, or produced these works. It doesn't contain any artist information except for the artist's name and date of birth. The second site of music artist biographies contains a full listing of many current and former artists/performers, complete biographies of each artist/performer, and a list of associated music works.

What information might you, as a user of each of these systems, be interested in extracting? Users of http://www.example.com/grammyWinners would benefit from selecting a Grammy winner's name and having personal biographical information displayed. Unfortunately, the biographical information is stored in a separate database at http://www.example.com/artistBios. Figure 7.4 illustrates the independence and separation of these two databases.

Users of http://www.example.com/artistBios would benefit from being able to select an artist's musical work and having its Grammy award statistics displayed. Unfortunately, the Grammy award statistics are stored in http://www.example.com/grammyWinners.

Any sharing of data between these two sites can't be accomplished by joining the tables contained in their separate databases. They're unlikely to share primary keys, metadata, or identifiers, and their individual database server systems are likely incompatible. Collaboration would entail working together to design a common data format and common artist IDs (vocabulary alignment). This sort of information sharing across incompatible, independently designed data systems requires time, additional cost, and human intervention to provide contextual interpretation of the different datasets.

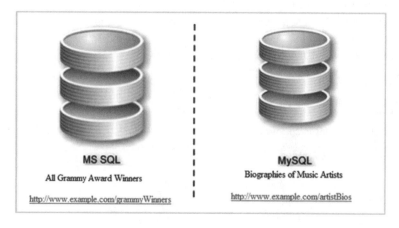

MS SQL

All Grammy Award Winners

http://www.example.com/grammyWinners

MySQL

Biographies of Music Artists

http://www.example.com/artistBios

Figure 7.4   Independent and separate relational databases

Contrast this scenario with one where each dataset is stored using structured data in RDF format (Linked Data). We'd expect both sites to follow the Linked Data principles in structuring their data. They'd use a common, standard vocabulary (base ontology) in describing their data, refer to URIs appropriately, and publish that data on a query-able endpoint so that both sites could communicate across the Web. This common, standard vocabulary would enable the following:

- Each site would be able to query the other using common terms.
- The Grammy winners site could now query the artist names on the artist biographies site at will and gain more detail about a specific artist.
- The artist biographies site could query the Grammy winners site and gain more detail about a production's Grammy status.

Most important, this collaboration is possible because of the inherent characteristics of Linked Data. Thus, independently designed and maintained datasets can share their knowledge domains by being interlinked and queried together.

ELIMINATION OF DATA WAREHOUSES

The final difference is the elimination of the need for building data warehouses. The process necessary to build such a warehouse is illustrated in figure 7.5. Traditionally, combining resources from multiple databases required the construction of a data warehouse. Data warehouses are centralized data repositories that integrate data from various transactional, legacy, or external systems, applications, and sources. The collection and housing of this data are focused on the isolation and optimization of queries without any impact on the systems that support a business' primary transactions.

This integration of multiple large databases into a single repository, as depicted in figure 7.5, is achieved at great expense and time. A major portion of this expense is the extraction, transformation, and loading processes. The alignment of database schemas is called vocabulary alignment.

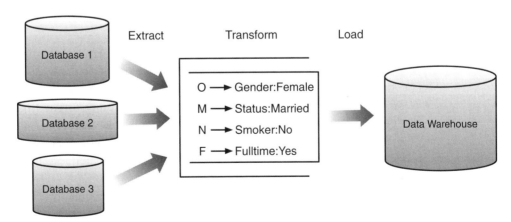

Figure 7.5 Diagram of the process of constructing a data warehouse from independent relational databases

Data warehouses, as such, aren't needed when using RDF stores. The integration of multiple data sources is made easier in Linked Data by three mechanisms:

- Use of the same URIs to name resources whenever possible
- Reuse of common vocabularies wherever possible
- Use of `owl:sameAs` to indicate that a particular resource is identical (or nearly identical) to another resource

These mechanisms allow for rapid alignment of resources after their creation.

7.1.3   Benefits of RDF database systems

We've already illustrated a number of advantages of using RDF database systems in comparison to RDBMS. We've illustrated the ease with which knowledge containers can be breached. We've illustrated that data warehouses aren't needed with RDF databases. Also, all RDF databases offer additional benefits as listed and described in table 7.4.

Table 7.4   Summary of benefits of RDF databases

Benefit	Description
SPARQL	You enjoy the use of a powerful standard query language.
Ease of collaboration	Standard serialization formats provide import/export capability based on well-defined, standardized, implementation-independent formats such as N-Triples/N-Quads.
Data portability	You can switch RDF storage solutions in-house, use multiple different solutions concurrently, and share data with others.
No vendor lock-in	If RDF database solution A isn't working out, you can switch to RDF database solution B or C; there's no need to transform the data.
Tool chain portability	Your RDF-based code doesn't need to change just because you switch RDF database programs.

In general, the Linked Data community prefers RDF triplestores over other systems for the following reasons:

- *Access*—Linked Data may be queried with SPARQL much more naturally (and more capably) than with SQL. SPARQL can perform distributed queries (using the FROM and FROM NAMED clauses), something that the SQL standard doesn't support.
- *Distributed queries of Linked Data*—These allow many interesting use cases, such as leaving data sources in place (without copying) while querying.
- *Fit for purpose*—RDF databases store and allow access to RDF data using the RDF data model. This allows RDF to be accessed and manipulated in ways natural to that data model.
- *Efficiency*—Some RDF databases allow access to and manipulation of RDF more quickly than other mechanisms.

In this overview of RDF databases we've covered criteria that you need to consider in selecting an RDF database, the differences of RDF databases over RDBMS, and other benefits of using RDF databases. We've stressed how using RDF facilitates the integration and aggregation of distributed and diverse data stores. In the next sections, we'll demonstrate how non-RDF sources can be transformed and aggregated. We'll demonstrate applying such aggregations in solving more complex problems.

7.2 Transforming spreadsheet data to RDF

In building applications, you're likely to find that data you need is already available in non-RDF storage like Excel spreadsheets, comma-separated value (.csv) files, and SQL RDBMS. To facilitate integrating these diverse data formats, you need to transform the data into RDF. There are tools available to help you transform your data. The W3C maintains a list of tools that convert data from many non-RDF formats to RDF. You can find this list at http://www.w3.org/wiki/ConverterToRdf. You can always create your own tools.

In this section we'll demonstrate how you can use Python to transform data from MS Excel format to Turtle. The free Lingfo Python library has built-in capabilities that handle reading binary Excel files. This library is available from http://pypi.python.org/pypi/xlrd. Reference http://wiki.python.org/moin/CheeseShopTutorial for installation instructions. Another excellent resource is "Integrate disparate data sources with Semantic Web technology" (http://www.ibm.com/developerworks/xml/library/x-disprdf) by Bob DuCharme. In this article DuCharme illustrates integrating data from Excel spreadsheets (XLS files), CSV files obtained from http://finance.yahoo.com, and RDF data from DBpedia. The source files DuCharme uses in his application are available from the link at the end of his article.

7.2.1 A basic RDF conversion of MS Excel

Manually converting large amounts of data to an RDF format is often too time-consuming or too complex to be worth doing. The Python script shown in listing 7.2 is modeled after DuCharme's sources and presents an automated process of converting an Excel spreadsheet to RDF. It accesses the Excel spreadsheet as entered by the user and outputs valid Turtle. This is a useful and generic script that outputs the column labels as predicates formatted as URIs using the URI associated with the prefix `field`. Listing 7.2 illustrates the process of transforming a spreadsheet into RDF, but it doesn't support the Linked Data principles as put forth by Tim Berners-Lee "to include links to other URIs" that are resolvable. This RDF output is still usable but has limited utility to localized queries. You'd need to be aware of the column labels and use them in your SPARQL queries. In the real world, you'd want to map the column labels to resolvable URIs such as those in FOAF or vCard.

> **Listing 7.2 Python script to convert an Excel spreadsheet to Turtle**

```
# Convert inputFile.xls spreadsheet to Turtle.
#
import xlrd[1]
```

See the URL in the footnote for Lingfo information.[1]

---

[1] "Lingfo—Python 'xlrd' package for extracting data from Excel files," 0.6.1 final, http://www.lexicon.net/sjmachin/xlrd.htm.

```
import sys                                    Command-line arguments
                                              supplied using Python
if(len(sys.argv) < 2):                        xls2rdf.py input.xls.
    inputFile = input( 'Enter
➥  "source:\\\\subdirectory\\\\inputFile.xls " \n==>' )
else:                                                 Use the Lingfo
    inputFile = sys.argv[1]                    ◁──┐   library to obtain
                                                  │   the Excel
book = xlrd.open_workbook(inputFile)       ◁──────┘   spreadsheet.
sheet = book.sheet_by_index(0) # Get the first sheet
rowCount = sheet.nrows
colCount = sheet.ncols                                 Output the prefix
print "@prefix field: <http://www.example.com/fieldNames#>."  ◁──┐ statements.
print "@prefix rdf: <http://www.w3.org/1999/02/22-rdf-syntax-ns#>."   Process
                                                       spreadsheet and
for rowNum in range(rowCount):              ◁───────── output Turtle.
  rowValues = sheet.row_values(rowNum,start_colx=0, end_colx=None)
  if (rowNum == 0):                            ◁──────┐ First row has
    propertyNames = rowValues                         │ property names.
    for i in range(colCount):
      propertyNames[i] = propertyNames[i].replace(" ","")   ◁──┐ Remove
  else:                                      ◁────────┐          │ any spaces
    print "<field:%s>" % str(rowNum)          Property values, so │ in names.
    for i in range(colCount-1):               output them as RDF.
      print ' field:%s "%s";'%(propertyNames[i],rowValues[i])
    print ' field:%s "%s".'%(propertyNames[colCount-1],rowValues[colCount-
➥  1])
```

When the script from listing 7.2 is applied to the spreadsheet shown in figure 7.6, Turtle output is obtained.

	A	B	C	D
1	FirstName	LastName	State	EmailAddress
2	Lucas	Aladdin	VA	luke@example.com
3	Pat	Albert	MD	albert@example.com
4	Susan	Alfred	PA	sue@example.com
5	Bob	Anker	FL	bob@example.com
6	Dolores	Ayres	CA	XYXYXY@example.com
7	Rita	Basit	VA	rita@example.com
8	Peter	Becker	MD	pete@example.com
9	Frank	Becker	PA	frank@example.com
10	Joshua	Bernstein	FL	slowone@example.com
11	Alex	Bernstein	CA	alex@example.com
12	Bruce	Bernstein	VA	bruce@example.com
13	Herb	Bloom	MD	herb@example.com
14	Bruce	Bloomfield	PA	bruce@example.com
15	Beth	Braun	FL	beth@example.com
16	Judith	Braun	CA	judith@example.com

Figure 7.6 Sample Excel spreadsheet

The following Turtle output was produced by the Python script shown in listing 7.2.

```
@prefix field: <http://www.example.com/fieldNames#>.
@prefix rdf: <http://www.w3.org/1999/02/22-rdf-syntax-ns#>.
<field:1>
 field:FirstName "Lucas";
 field:LastName "Aladdin";
 field:State "VA";
 field:EmailAddress "luke@example.com".
<field:2>
 field:FirstName "Pat";
 field:LastName "Albert";
 field:State "MD";
 field:EmailAddress "albert@example.com".
```

This output is valid RDF but not useful Linked Data because it isn't linked anywhere and it doesn't provide mapping information. It doesn't follow the Linked Data principles introduced in chapter 1. Generating meaningful URIs is tedious and typically requires human involvement. The Python script in listing 7.3 illustrates the process and produces meaningful Turtle Linked Data that follows the principles of Linked Data.

7.2.2 Transforming MS Excel to Linked Data

In reviewing the following listing, you'll notice that you need to supply the links to the vocabularies associated with the Linked Data terms that match the column headings and the actual Linked Data terms associated with each column heading. The output from this script is useful Linked Data and is shown following the listing.

Listing 7.3 Python script that converts a spreadsheet to useful Linked Data

```
import xlrd                          See the URL in the          Command-line arguments
import sys                           footnote for Lingfo         supplied using Python
                                     information.²               xls2rdf.py input.xls
if(len(sys.argv) < 2):
    inputFile = input( 'Enter filename of spreadsheet as \n'  +
                      '"source:\\\\subdirectory\\\\inputFile.xls " \n==>' )
else:
    inputFile = sys.argv[1]
#inputFile = "c:\\users\\zaidman\\desktop\\sample1.xls"
book = xlrd.open_workbook(inputFile)                          Use the Lingfo library
sheet = book.sheet_by_index(0) # Get the first sheet          to obtain the Excel
rowCount = sheet.nrows                                        spreadsheet.
colCount = sheet.ncols
prefix=""

print "Gathering mapping information to transform spreadsheet data to "
print "Linked Data vocabulary\n\n"
prompt =  'Enter "<url>" of where the rdf form of this spreadsheet will'
prompt = prompt + ' be published \n'
baseurl = input(prompt)
```

---

[2] "Lingfo—Python 'xlrd' package for extracting data from Excel files," 0.6.1 final, http://www.lexicon.net/sjmachin/xlrd.htm.

```
print 'Now gathering prefix information \n'
print 'Enter "prefix,<URL of vocabulary>"\n'
line = input('Enter ""[return] when all prefix information has been
➥     entered \n')
count = 0;
while (line <> ""):
    count +=1                                                  First row
    prefix= prefix + line +'|'                            has property
    print 'Enter next "prefix,<URL of vocabulary>"\n'         names.
    line = input('or enter ""[return] when all prefixes have
➥  been entered\n')
print '\nPreparing to gather predicate information for column headings\n'
propertyNames = sheet.row_values(0,start_colx=0, end_colx=None)
for i in range(colCount):
    propertyNames[i]=input('prefix:term for ' + propertyNames[i] + ' ==> ')

print '\n\n'
print '@prefix base: ' + baseurl                        Output the prefix
stmts=prefix.split("|");                                statements.
for i in range(count):
    items=stmts[i].split(",")
    print '@prefix ' + items[0]+': ' + items[1]         Process
#Process spreadsheet                                    spreadsheet.
rowNum=1
while (rowNum <rowCount):
    rowValues = sheet.row_values(rowNum,start_colx=0, end_colx=None)
    print "<base:%s>" % str(rowNum)
    for i in range(colCount-1):
      print '%s "%s";'%(propertyNames[i],rowValues[i])
    print '%s "%s".'%(propertyNames[colCount-1],rowValues[colCount-1])
    rowNum +=1
```

The output illustrates that common RDF Linked Data vocabularies are being used in transforming the spreadsheet into useful Turtle Linked Data. The output file from such a script could be queried using SPARQL.

```
@prefix base: http://www.example.com/sample.ttl#
@prefix foaf: http://xmlns.com/foaf/0.1/
@prefix v: http://www.w3.org/2006/vcard/ns#
<base:1>
foaf:firstName "Lucas";
foaf:lastName "Aladdin";
v:region "VA";
v:email "luke@example.com".
<base:2>
foaf:firstName "Pat";
foaf:lastName "Albert";
v:region "MD";
v:email "albert@example.com".
```

The script shown in listing 7.3 is less than eloquent. But it does illustrate the need for human involvement in preparing a useful transformation from non-RDF data to useful Turtle. It also illustrates that the process is straightforward and can be automated. Further modification of the process could include retaining the mapping information in a mapping file, enabling the user to modify an existing mapping file for use with a related spreadsheet, and automatic detection of available mapping files. Although these enhancements would make the tools more useful, that's not their purpose in this illustration, and thus we chose to present the simple version. Other applications will illustrate more sophisticated techniques.

7.2.3 Finding RDF converter tools

If you're not so eager to prepare your own scripts, an alternate option is to use tools already available. The W3C maintains an index of Converter to RDF tools, also known as RDFizers (http://www.w3.org/wiki/ConverterToRdf), which convert application data from an application-specific format into RDF. Such tools include converters for Excel spreadsheets, Quicken Interchange Format, and plug-ins for SQL databases like MySQL. The list of available converters is extensive and too long to include here.

In this section, we've demonstrated two applications that can be used to convert data in CSV format to Turtle format. To further illustrate the utility of integrating diverse and distributed RDF data, we present an application in section 7.3 that demonstrates the collection of diverse data formats, their conversion to RDF, and the storage of this aggregated RDF data in a Fuseki Triplestore.

7.3 Application: collecting Linked Data in an RDF database

This application is a demonstration of combining data in Linked Data format from multiple sources on the Web. The feeds that we will use come from two U.S. government agencies:

- The U.S. Environmental Protection Agency's (EPA) SunWise Program (http://www.epa.gov/sunwise/)
- The National Oceanic and Atmospheric Administration's (NOAA) National Digital Forecast Database (NDFD)[3]

The SunWise program is a large effort by the EPA aimed at educating the public on how to protect themselves from the sun. NOAA's NDFD is a collection of digital forecasts of the most relevant weather information from field offices around the United States. This information includes everything from maximum and minimum temperatures to wave heights along coastal areas.

7.3.1 Outlining the process

The application we demonstrate here uses three data sources. It retrieves XML data from NOAA web services, CSV data from the EPA's SunWise Program, and a local file of postal ZIP codes. The ZIP codes contained in our file are all of the postal codes associated with the U.S. state of Virginia, but your input file could contain those postal codes of interest to you. The ZIP code file used for this example is available at http://linkeddatadeveloper.com/Projects/Linked-Data/resources/va-zip-codes.txt.

---

[3] "What is the NDFD?", updated October 4, 2012, http://www.nws.noaa.gov/ndfd/.

Each line of va-zipcodes.txt contains a single ZIP code. Please remember to adjust the name of this file to match your application. A portion of the ZIP code file is shown here:

```
20101
20102
20103
20104
20105
. . .
24649
24651
24656
24657
24658
```

We'll store our transformed and aggregated data using a Fuseki RDF database from the Apache Jena project. Fuseki includes a lightweight, in-memory database perfect for working with small amounts of RDF data. In order to execute our application, you'll need to install Fuseki and set permissions by following the instructions at http://jena.apache.org/documentation/serving_data/index.html. You should already have Python installed from chapter 4.

Our application creates an output file of the Turtle data mined from the NOAA and EPA sources. This file is later loaded into the Fuseki database for query. A sample of the contents of this file is shown in the following listing.

Listing 7.4   Turtle from weather data

```
@prefix rdfs: <http://www.w3.org/2000/01/rdf-schema#> .
@prefix wh: <http://www.example.com/WeatherHealth/Schema#> .

<http://www.example.com/WeatherHealth/ZipCodes/20101> wh:weather_for
<http://www.example.com/WeatherHealth/ZipCodes/20101/01-09-13> .
<http://www.example.com/WeatherHealth/ZipCodes/20101/01-09-13>
    wh:max_temp 57
  ; wh:min_temp 34
  ; wh:uv_value 2
  ; wh:uv_alert "False"
.

<http://www.example.com/WeatherHealth/ZipCodes/24658>
    wh:weather_for
    <http://www.example.com/WeatherHealth/ZipCodes/24658/01-09-13> .
<http://www.example.com/WeatherHealth/ZipCodes/24658/01-09-13>
    wh:max_temp 58
  ; wh:min_temp 39
  ; wh:uv_value 1
  ; wh:uv_alert "False"
.
```

7.3.2   *Using Python to aggregate our data sources*

The application itself is provided in listing 7.5. The program follows this process:

1 Aggregate the data as mined from the EPA and NOAA sources based on selected ZIP codes.

2 Transform the aggregated data into Turtle.

3 Store this Turtle content in the file weatherData.ttl.

4 Load the contents of weatherData.ttl into the Fuseki in-memory database.

5 Query the database for the maximum temperature and UV value expected for a given ZIP code.

Listing 7.5 Finding maximum temperature and UV index for all ZIP codes in Virginia

```
#! /usr/bin/python
import os
import urllib
import urllib2
from urllib2 import Request, urlopen, URLError
import csv
from cStringIO import StringIO
import xml.etree.ElementTree as ET
from datetime import date
import subprocess
from time import sleep

# Variables, input, and output files
input = open('va-zip-codes.txt', 'r')
output = open('weatherData.ttl', 'w')
today = date.today().strftime("%m-%d-%y")

print "\nStarting Fuseki..."
os.chdir("/Users/LukeRuth/Desktop/jena-fuseki-0.2.5/")
args1 = ['./fuseki-server', '--update', '--mem', '/ds']
subprocess.Popen(args1)

sleep(10)
print "\n"

print >>output, "@prefix rdfs: <http://www.w3.org/2000/01/rdf-schema#> ."
print >>output, "@prefix wh:
    <http://www.example.com/WeatherHealth/Schema#> .\n"

# Cycle through every zip code in the input file
for line in input:
    zip = line

    zip = zip.rstrip()

    noaaQuery =
 "http://graphical.weather.gov/xml/sample_products/browser_interface/
    ndfdXMLclient.php?ZIP CodeList=" + zip +
    "&product=time-series&maxt=maxt&mint=mint"
    epaQuery =
    "http://iaspub.epa.gov/enviro/efservice/getEnvirofactsUVDAILY/ZIP/"
    + zip + "/CSV"
```

Include necessary libraries.

Modify the reference to this file to match your input.

Modify the reference to this file to be the location of the desired Turtle output file.

Start Fuseki server.

The directory in this command must match the location of the Fuseki Server on your system.

Wait for the server to respond.

Print prefixes.

Assign ZIP code to variable zip and remove trailing newline character.

Build up query URLs to issue.

```
noaaReq = urllib2.Request(url=noaaQuery)
try:
    noaaContents = urllib2.urlopen(noaaReq).read()
except URLError, e:
    if hasattr(e, 'reason'):
        print'We failed to reach a server.'
        print 'Reason: ', e.reason
    elif hasattr(e, 'code'):
        print 'The server couldn\'t fulfill the request.'
        print 'Error code: ', e.code
else:
    # Parse and obtain desired NOAA xml contents
    root = ET.fromstring(noaaContents)
    for temperature in root.findall(".//value/..[@type='maximum']"):
        maxTemp = temperature.find('value').text

    for temperature in root.findall(".//value/..[@type='minimum']"):
        minTemp = temperature.find('value').text

try:
    epaContents = urllib2.urlopen(epaQuery).read()
except URLError, e:
    if hasattr(e, 'reason'):
        print'We failed to reach a server.'
        print 'Reason: ', e.reason
    elif hasattr(e, 'code'):
        print 'The server couldn\'t fulfill the request.'
        print 'Error code: ', e.code
else:
    epaContents = epaContents.rstrip()
    # Loop through EPA CSV file and assign values to variables
    reader = csv.DictReader(StringIO(epaContents), delimiter=',')
    for row in reader:
        uvValue = row['UV_VALUE']
        uvAlert = row['UV_ALERT']
```

Retrieve NOAA contents and assign to variable noaaContents—catch and print any errors.

Retrieve EPA contents and assign to variable epaContents—catch and print any errors.

```
print >>output, "<http://www.example.com/WeatherHealth/ZipCodes/" +
zip + "> wh:weather_for
<http://www.example.com/WeatherHealth/ZipCodes/" +
zip + "/" + today + "> ."
print >>output, "<http://www.example.com/WeatherHealth/ZipCodes/"
+ zip + "/" + today + ">"
```

Start making Turtle.

```
# Only print values that are present
if (maxTemp):
    print >>output, " wh:max_temp " + maxTemp
if (minTemp):
    print >>output, " ; wh:min_temp " + minTemp
if (uvValue):
    print >>output, " ; wh:uv_value " + uvValue

if (uvAlert == "0"):
    print >>output, " ; wh:uv_alert \"False\""
```

```
        elif (uvAlert == "1"):
            print >>output, " ; wh:uv_alert \"True\""


        print >>output, ". \n";

# Close zip code input and Turtle output files
input.close()
output.close()
```
→ **Load data file into Fuseki database.**

```
print "Loading Data..."
args2 = ["./s-put", "http://localhost:3030/ds/data", "default", "/Users/
    LukeRuth/Desktop/LinkedData_WeatherHealthApp/Chapter7/weatherData.ttl"]
subprocess.Popen(args2)
```

```
sleep(10)
print "\n"
```
← **Wait for the server to respond.**

→ **Query Fuseki.**

```
print "Executing Query..."
args3 = ["./s-query", "--service",
    "http://localhost:3030/ds/query",
    "SELECT ?day ?maxTemp ?uvValue WHERE { ?day
    <http://www.example.com/WeatherHealth/Schema#max_temp> ?maxTemp ;
     <http://www.example.com/WeatherHealth/Schema#uv_value>
    ?uvValue . } LIMIT 1"]
subprocess.Popen(args3)
```

```
sleep(10)
print "\nScript Complete.\n"
```
← **Wait for the server to respond.**

7.3.3 Understanding the output

This query asks, "Today, in this ZIP code, what is the maximum temperature expected and the UV value?" The query *would* run for all the ZIP codes (which is a big, cumbersome query) had we not put LIMIT 1 on it. The output as produced by listing 7.5 can be found in the following listing. You can reduce the execution time by reducing the number of ZIP codes in the input file. You can obtain results for all of the ZIP codes in the input file by removing the limit from the SPARQL query.

Listing 7.6 Output from Listing 7.5

```
Starting Fuseki...                          ←── Starting Fuseki.
09:48:34 INFO  Server    :: Dataset: in-memory
09:48:35 INFO  Server    :: Dataset path = /ds
09:48:35 INFO  Server    :: Fuseki 0.2.5 2012-10-20T17:03:29+0100
09:48:35 INFO  Server    :: Started 2013/01/09 09:48:35 EST on port 3030


Loading Data...
09:55:17 INFO  Fuseki    :: [1] PUT http://localhost:3030/ds/data?default
09:55:17 INFO  Fuseki    :: [1] 204 No Content


Executing Query...
09:55:27 INFO  Fuseki    :: [2] GET http://localhost:3030/ds/
    query?query=SELECT+%3Fday+%3FmaxTemp+%3FuvValue+WHERE+%7B+%3Fday+%3Chttp
    %3A%2F%2Fwww.example.com%2FWeatherHealth%2FSchema%23max_temp%3E+%3FmaxTe
```

Loading Turtle data into the database.

Executing our SPARQL query.

```
      mp+%3B+%3Chttp%3A%2F%2Fwww.example.com%2FWeatherHealth%2FSchema%23uv_val
      ue%3E+%3FuvValue+.+%7D+LIMIT+10
09:55:27 INFO  Fuseki    :: [2] Query = SELECT ?day ?maxTemp ?uvValue WHERE {
      ?day <http://www.example.com/WeatherHealth/Schema#max_temp> ?maxTemp ;
      <http://www.example.com/WeatherHealth/Schema#uv_value> ?uvValue . }
      LIMIT 10
09:55:27 INFO  Fuseki    :: [2] OK/select
09:55:27 INFO  Fuseki    :: [2] 200 OK
{                                                    ⟵── Output of query.
  "head": {
    "vars": [ "day" , "maxTemp" , "uvValue" ]
  } ,
  "results": {
    "bindings": [
      {
        "day": { "type": "uri" , "value": "http://www.example.com/
    WeatherHealth/ZIP Codes/20191/01-09-13" } ,
        "maxTemp": { "datatype": "http://www.w3.org/2001/XMLSchema#integer" ,
      "type": "typed-literal" , "value": "57" } ,
        "uvValue": { "datatype": "http://www.w3.org/2001/XMLSchema#integer" ,
      "type": "typed-literal" , "value": "2" }
    ]
  }
}
```

> **Results show a high of 57 with a UV index of 2.**

```
Script Complete.
```

This application illustrates how easy it is to use RDF as a common data model for data integration. In just a dozen statements, you can collect and transform the NOAA weather data from XML format into Turtle, as shown here:

```
noaaQuery =
⟹  "http://graphical.weather.gov/xml/sample_products/browser_interface/
⟹  ndfdXMLclient.php?
⟹  ZIP CodeList=" + zip + "&product=time-series&maxt=maxt&mint=mint"

noaaReq = urllib2.Request(url=noaaQuery)

# Parse and obtain desired NOAA xml contents
root = ET.fromstring(noaaContents)
for temperature in root.findall(".//value/..[@type='maximum']"):
    maxTemp = temperature.find('value').text

for temperature in root.findall(".//value/..[@type='minimum']"):
    minTemp = temperature.find('value').text
print >>output, "<http://www.example.com/WeatherHealth/ZIP Codes/" +
⟹  zip + "> wh:weather_for
⟹  <http://www.example.com/WeatherHealth/ZIP Codes/" + zip + "/" +
⟹  today + "> ."
    print >>output, "<http://www.example.com/WeatherHealth/ZIP Codes/"
⟹  + zip + "/" + today + ">"

    # Only print values that are present
    if (maxTemp):
        print >>output, " wh:max_temp " + maxTemp
```

```
if (minTemp):
    print >>output, " ; wh:min_temp " + minTemp

print >>output, ". \n";
```

Similar statements collect and transform the EPA data from CSV to Turtle.

This application illustrates how diverse data formats may be aggregated, converted to RDF, combined, stored in an RDF database, and queried to produce results that solve specific problems. In this case, we're able to determine the anticipated maximum temperature and UV value for each ZIP code in Virginia. Combining these independent data sources was critical to enabling us to query the NOAA and EPA datasets together and determine the maximum temperature expected and the UV value for today, in the specified ZIP code. Ultimately, the final output could be considered when issuing alerts so that residents in at-risk communities can exercise caution when participating in outdoor activities.

7.4 Summary

This chapter helped you understand the differences between the traditional relational database approach and RDF databases. After reading this chapter you understand the advantages of RDF databases over RDBMS. You understand why the Linked Data community finds RDF databases useful and the types of problems such systems are best fit to solve. In general, integrating information already in RDF format is painless. But data that you need and would like to use is often stored in non-RDF sources. The good news is that much of this data can be transformed into RDF for ease of integration into other applications.

We've identified available resources to help you accumulate data from diverse non-RDF resources, and we've demonstrated this process by building an application that collects such sources and stores the aggregation in an RDF database. Now you're about ready to build some of your own Linked Data applications. Chapter 8 will familiarize you with ways to describe your RDF data so it may be discovered on the Web, and chapter 9 will familiarize you with more sophisticated tools like Callimachus and the advanced problems that Callimachus can help you solve.

Datasets

8

This chapter covers

- The Description of a Project vocabulary for describing projects
- The Vocabulary of Interlinked Datasets for describing datasets
- The purpose and preparation of a sitemap for describing sites
- Techniques for linking to other datasets
- How to join the Linked Open Data cloud

In previous chapters we've stressed the importance of applying the principles of Linked Data. You'll recall that one of these principles is to use HTTP URIs so that the references are resolvable and define the item without equivocation. By using vocabularies like Description of a Project (DOAP) to describe software projects, Vocabulary of Interlinked Datasets (VoID) to describe datasets, and sitemaps for describing websites, you support the principles of Linked Data and facilitate connecting to other datasets and enable yourself to publish your data on the Linked Open Data (LOD) cloud. This chapter will familiarize you with these vocabularies and best practices for publication.

This chapter will provide an introduction to the ways that new Linked Data should be described and linked into the larger Linked Data world. Just as FOAF describes people, DOAP describes projects, VoID describes datasets, and semantic sitemaps describe the Linked Data offerings on a site. Once those descriptions are in place, the next step is to ensure that you meet the guidelines of the LOD cloud by linking out to other datasets and (optionally) asking DBpedia to link to your data. Then, you can follow the published guidelines for joining the LOD cloud.

Here are some definitions that you should keep in mind as you read this chapter:

- A *dataset* is a collection of related data that's published, maintained, or aggregated by a single provider. It's often available as RDF and accessible, for example, through dereferenceable HTTP URIs or a SPARQL endpoint.
- An *RDF link* is an RDF triple whose subject and object are contained in different datasets. In addition, these datasets may be on different servers.
- A *linkset* is a collection of RDF links between two datasets.
- *Metadata* is data about data.

8.1 Description of a Project

Completing an open-source project is certainly an accomplishment, but attracting users and contributors can be a task in itself. What information would potential users and/or contributors need to know about your project, and how can you provide it? Users and contributors would need the name, description, its homepage, a download page and mirror site, a license type, limitations like specific OS and programming language requirements, the category of the project, and how to report bugs and determine known bugs. You can represent all this and more using DOAP. In addition, you can connect a DOAP file to your project's registration in various online catalogs.

Edd Dumbill (http://eddology.com/about) created DOAP in 2004. DOAP is an XML/RDF vocabulary to describe software projects and in particular open source projects. A DOAP file is a machine-readable document that's used to share information about a project. Listing 8.1 is a sample DOAP file.

A DOAP file can be used to easily import projects into directories, automate the updating of these directories, exchange data between directories, configure resources like mailing lists, and provide support for package maintainers who bundle resources for distribution. In short, you can save a lot of time by creating and maintaining a DOAP file.

There are many online catalogs in which you can register your product and announce the existence and purpose of your project. Some of these catalogs are:

- Freecode (http://freecode.com/)
- The Free Software Directory (http://directory.fsf.org/wiki/Main_Page)
- The GNOME Project (http://www.GNOME.org/)
- The Open Source Directory (http://osdir.com/)
- SourceForge (http://sourceforge.net)

The process of manually registering is time-consuming. In addition, each new release requires someone to visit each catalog's site and update the project information. Fortunately, the Semantic Web provides a mechanism for the automation of catalog registration and maintenance. You can take advantage of this by publishing and maintaining a DOAP file for your project.

8.1.1   *Creating a DOAP profile*

Now we're going to show you how to create a DOAP profile for Callimachus, an open source project developed by 3 Round Stones. We did this using DOAP A Matic, which provides a simple mechanism for preparing this profile. The resulting minimal DOAP descriptor is illustrated in listing 8.1 This file was prepared using DOAP A Matic: http://crschmidt.net/semweb/doapamatic/. The DOAP profile for Callimachus is published at http://3roundstones.com/callimachus/callimachus.doap. You could prepare a DOAP profile using an editor but we recommend that you use DOAP A Matic. The resulting profile is in XML, and unless you're familiar with XML, creating this file from scratch is difficult.

Listing 8.1   Example DOAP file for Callimachus

```
<Project xmlns:rdf=http://www.w3.org/1999/02/22-rdf-syntax-ns#
    xmlns:rdfs="http://www.w3.org/2000/01/rdf-schema#"
    xmlns=http://usefulinc.com/ns/doap#
    xmlns:foaf=http://xmlns.com/foaf/0.1/
    xmlns:admin="http://webns.net/mvcb/">
<name>The Callimachus Project</name>
<shortname>Callimachus</shortname>
<shortdesc>
Callimachus is the leading Open Source platform for navigating,
    managing, and visualizing applications using the Web of Data.
</shortdesc>
<description>
Callimachus is the leading Open Source platform for navigating, managing,
    and visualizing applications using the Web of Data. Use Callimachus to
    create and deploy mobile and Web apps using open data and enterprise
    content using open Web standards.
</description>
<homepage rdf:resource="http://callimachusproject.org/"/>
<wiki rdf:resource="http://callimachusproject.org/docs/?view"/>
<download-page
    rdf:resource="http://code.google.com/p/callimachus/downloads/list"/>
<bug-database
    rdf:resource="http://code.google.com/p/callimachus/issues/list"/>
<category rdf:resource="http://dbpedia.org/resource/Category:Semantic_Web"/>
<programming-language>Java</programming-language>
<programming-language>JavaScript</programming-language>
<license rdf:resource="http://usefulinc.com/doap/licenses/asl20"/>
<maintainer>
<foaf:Person>
<foaf:name>James Leigh</foaf:name>
<foaf:homepage rdf:resource="http://3roundstones.com"/>
```

This is the Apache License Selection from the list of available licenses.

```
<foaf:mbox_sha1sum>ded445287ad3645499f20d61f1f1fbd3f17b7917</
    foaf:mbox_sha1sum>
</foaf:Person>
</maintainer>
<developer>
<foaf:Person>
<foaf:name>David Wood</foaf:name>
<foaf:homepage rdf:resource="http://3roundstones.com"/>
<foaf:mbox_sha1sum>abe8c5daaf522b41c7550a48360be9379e59db2c</
    foaf:mbox_sha1sum>
</foaf:Person>
</developer>
<helper>
<foaf:Person>
<foaf:name>Luke Ruth</foaf:name>
<foaf:homepage rdf:resource="http://3roundstones.com"/>
<foaf:mbox_sha1sum>8e9e08a4cc834f24b69e8fbee7d786493a3f3f9c</
    foaf:mbox_sha1sum>
</foaf:Person>
</helper>
<repository>
<SVNRepository>
<browse rdf:resource="http://code.google.com/p/callimachus/source/browse/"/>
<location rdf:resource="http://callimachus.googlecode.com/svn/trunk/"/>
</SVNRepository>
</repository>
</Project>
```

Figure 8.1 represents the form available from DOAP A Matic. A closer examination of the contents of listing 8.1 shows that each item corresponds to the contents of the form. Figure 8.1 is the first screen of this form. You'll notice that some of the text of the descriptions isn't visible. You should note that the length of the text isn't limited by the width of the text box for the short and full descriptions. The tool automatically supplies the URL of the license as selected. In our case, the corresponding license is Apache License 2.0. You'll also note that we skipped categories that weren't relevant, like "Download Mirror."

Clicking the Generate button, at the bottom of the form but not visible in figure 8.1, converts the information entered in the form to RDF/XML, as shown in listing 8.1. You can then copy the output and retain it for future editing and/or publishing. The DOAP RDF/XML file can be enhanced by adding additional statements using a text editor and manually inserting relevant content. In examining listing 8.1, you'll notice that the FOAF vocabulary is used to describe the people associated with the project, such as the maintainer and the developer. If reading listing 8.1 is difficult because of the RDF/XML format, remember that you can copy and paste the DOAP A Matic output into a converter like the one found at http://www.rdfabout.com/demo/validator/ that converts and displays the equivalent Turtle file.

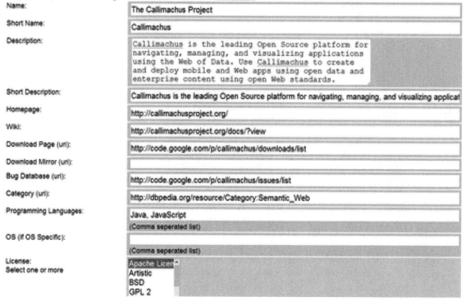

Figure 8.1   Sample of DOAP A Matic's form

8.1.2   *Using the DOAP vocabulary*

You should be aware of the full DOAP vocabulary so that you can add additional relevant content. The DOAP vocabulary currently contains three kinds of classes:

- *Project*—The main project resource
- *Version*—An instance of released software
- *Repository*—A source code repository

For convenience, a summary of the DOAP classes and properties is contained in table 8.1.

Table 8.1   DOAP classes and selected properties

Project class		
name	category—URI of assigned type	license—URI of associated license
shortname	wiki—URI of assigned wiki	download-page—URI of where the project can be obtained
homepage	bug-database—URI for bug reporting	download-mirror—URI of mirror site
old-homepage	screenshots—URI of a web page of screenshots	repository—a doap:Repository for the source code

Table 8.1 DOAP classes and selected properties *(continued)*

Project **class**		
`created`—YYYY-MM-DD format	`mailing-list`—URI of such list	`release`—a `doap:Version` for current release
`description`	`programming-language`	`maintainer`—`foaf:Person` for project maintainer or leader
`shortdesc`	`os`—specific OS limitations, omit if not OS specific	`developer`—`foaf:Person` of project developer
`documenter`—`foaf:Person` of documentation contributor	`translator`—`foaf:Person` of a translation contributor	
Repository **class**		
`anon-root`—path of the root of the anonymously accessible repository	`module`—module name of source code within the repository	`browse`—URL of web browser interface to the repository
`location`—base URL of archive		
Version **class**		
`branch`—a string indicating the branch of this version, such as stable, unstable, GNOME26	`name`—a release name, such as Lion	`created`—date of release in YYYY-MM-DD form
`revision`—revision number of the release; e.g., 2.5		

For a complete description, access the DOAP schema at the DOAP namespace, http://usefulinc.com/ns/doap. A more readable version of the full schema can be displayed by using Morten Frederiksen's Schema Reader (http://xml.mfd-consult.dk/ws/2003/01/rdfs/), an online service for transforming an RDF schema to human-readable form. A sample of the output from this service is shown in figure 8.2.

After you've completed a DOAP file, you should use a validator like the RDF Validator and Converter found at http://www.rdfabout.com/demo/validator/ to ensure that the content of the document is valid RDF. Then you need to publish it in a publicly accessible space where it can be obtained via an HTTP or HTTPS request. After publication, your project description will be available to aggregator sites that pull in project information from different sources and combine them into a single database. You can either notify an aggregator directly of the location of your DOAP file or you can register it at one of the sites from which an aggregator harvests such files. Harvesting of updates would be automatic. In general, the DOAP file is stored with the project. Project maintainers do not need to visit the aggregator site to maintain their records. As needed, simply update your local DOAP file and wait for the aggregator site to harvest the new information. That's the beauty of the automated maintenance of this data.

Namespace: http://usefulinc.com/ns/doap#

Classes

Project	A project.
[Project]	*isDefinedBy:* ⚡ http://usefulinc.com/ns/doap#
	subClassOf: ⚡ http://xmlns.com/wordnet/1.6/Project
	subClassOf: ⚡ http://xmlns.com/foaf/0.1/Project
Version	Version information of a project release.
[Version]	*isDefinedBy:* ⚡ http://usefulinc.com/ns/doap#
Specification	A specification of a system's aspects, technical or otherwise.
[Specification]	*isDefinedBy:* ⚡ http://usefulinc.com/ns/doap#
	subClassOf: ⚡ http://www.w3.org/2000/01/rdf-schema#Resource
Repository	Source code repository.
[Repository]	*isDefinedBy:* ⚡ http://usefulinc.com/ns/doap#
Subversion Repository	Subversion source code repository.
	isDefinedBy: ⚡ http://usefulinc.com/ns/doap#
[SVNRepository]	*subClassOf:* ⚡ http://usefulinc.com/ns/doap#Repository
BitKeeper Repository	BitKeeper source code repository.
	isDefinedBy: ⚡ http://usefulinc.com/ns/doap#
[BKRepository]	*subClassOf:* ⚡ http://usefulinc.com/ns/doap#Repository
CVS Repository	CVS source code repository.

Figure 8.2 Sample of DOAP schema transformed with Frederiksen's schema viewer

Unfortunately, expectations about the content of a DOAP file may differ among online catalog services. One such service, the Apache Software Foundation (ASF), at http:// projects.apache.org/guidelines.html, provides a form to assist you in creating an ASF-compatible DOAP file at http://projects.apache.org/create.html. You can find a sample of an ASF DOAP file in the following listing. Once you determine where the file will be stored, send an email to <site-dev@apache.org> so it may be included in the project listings. The URL of this DOAP file must use HTTP and *not* HTTPS.

Listing 8.2 An ASF DOAP file for the Callimachus Project

```xml
<?xml version="1.0"?>
<?xml-stylesheet type="text/xsl"?>
<rdf:RDF xml:lang="en"
        xmlns="http://usefulinc.com/ns/doap#"
        xmlns:rdf="http://www.w3.org/1999/02/22-rdf-syntax-ns#"
        xmlns:asfext="http://projects.apache.org/ns/asfext#"
        xmlns:foaf="http://xmlns.com/foaf/0.1/">
<!--
    Licensed to the Apache Software Foundation (ASF) under one or more
    contributor license agreements.  See the NOTICE file distributed with
    this work for additional information regarding copyright ownership.
```

```
    The ASF licenses this file to You under the Apache License, Version 2.0
    (the "License"); you may not use this file except in compliance with
    the License.  You may obtain a copy of the License at

        http://www.apache.org/licenses/LICENSE-2.0

    Unless required by applicable law or agreed to in writing, software
    distributed under the License is distributed on an "AS IS" BASIS,
    WITHOUT WARRANTIES OR CONDITIONS OF ANY KIND, either express or implied.
    See the License for the specific language governing permissions and
    limitations under the License.
-->
  <Project rdf:about="http://callimachusproject.org/">
    <created>2013-01-31</created>
    <license rdf:resource="http://usefulinc.com/doap/licenses/asl20" />
    <name>Apache The Callimachus Project</name>
    <homepage rdf:resource="http://callimachusproject.org/" />
    <asfext:pmc rdf:resource="http://abdera.apache.org" />
    <shortdesc>Callimachus is the leading Open Source platform
    for navigating, managing, and visualizing applications using
    the Web of Data.</shortdesc>
    <description>Callimachus is the leading Open Source platform
    for navigating, managing, and visualizing applications using
    the Web of Data. Use Callimachus to create and deploy mobile
    and Web apps using open data and enterprise content using open
    Web standards.</description>
    <bug-database
    rdf:resource="http://code.google.com/p/callimachus/issues/list" />
    <download-page
    rdf:resource="http://code.google.com/p/callimachus/downloads/list" />
    <programming-language>Java</programming-language>
    <category rdf:resource="http://projects.apache.org/category/content" />
    <release>
      <Version>
        <name>Callimachus</name>
        <created>2010-12-21</created>
        <revision>1.0</revision>
      </Version>
    </release>
    <repository>
      <SVNRepository>
        <location
    rdf:resource="http://callimachus.googlecode.com/svn/trunk/"/>
        <browse
    rdf:resource="http://code.google.com/p/callimachus/source/browse/"/>
      </SVNRepository>
    </repository>
    <maintainer>
      <foaf:Person>
        <foaf:name>James Leigh</foaf:name>
          <foaf:mbox rdf:resource="mailto:james@example.com"/>
      </foaf:Person>
    </maintainer>
  </Project>
</rdf:RDF>
```

Additional content expected by ASF.

Notice that the mailbox reference isn't encrypted using shalsum.

The expectations for a GNOME DOAP file are similar to those produced by DOAP A Matic. GNOME provides specific guidance at https://live.GNOME.org/Maintainers-Corner. One difference is that the email entries aren't encrypted. An additional requirement is that the DOAP file needs to be named according to the name of your module (for example, callimachus.doap) and located in the top directory in the master repository. The differences among these DOAP files are minor. Once you prepare a basic DOAP file, you can use a text editor to customize the contents for various catalogs.

As we've just discussed, you should document and publicize your open source project using a DOAP profile. The preparation of this document will enable aggregators to compile your project's information in their databases. You maintain the original document in your space, and the aggregator will automatically update their records.

8.2   *Documenting your datasets using VoID*

Publishers are increasingly interested in making their content searchable, linkable, and easier to aggregate and reuse. Social media sites and search engines want to expose their content to the right users, in a rich and attractive form. A dataset publisher needs to be able to publish metadata about their dataset so that the dataset can be discovered and aggregated by search engines and Web spiders. Consumers need to know the contents of your dataset, its location, which vocabularies are used, and other datasets to which this dataset refers. This metadata needs to provide clear licensing information so that consumers can determine how they might use the data and how to attribute credits. Consumers need to have information about the access interfaces. The Vocabulary of Interlinked Datasets can support these needs, and the publication of a VoID file about your dataset will facilitate its use by others.

8.2.1   *The Vocabulary of Interlinked Datasets*

VoID was introduced in 2009. It's an RDF schema vocabulary for expressing metadata about RDF datasets. It's intended as a bridge between the publishers and users of RDF data, with applications ranging from data discovery to cataloging and archiving of datasets. This section presents an overview of the VoID vocabulary. It contains terms that enable you to express general metadata, access metadata, structural metadata, and links between datasets. It also provides deployment advice and discusses the discovery of VoID descriptions. Table 8.2 shows an overview of this vocabulary.

A complete listing and associated descriptions can be found at http://www.w3.org/TR/void.

General metadata includes information such as a title and description, the license of the dataset, and information about its subject. It utilizes the Dublin Core model (http://www.w3.org/TR/void/#metadata). Some of these properties are the name of the dataset, the creator and publisher, date of creation, and date of most recent modification. *Access metadata* describes how RDF data can be accessed using protocols such as RDF Data Dumps, SPARQL endpoints, and resolvable HTTP URIs.

Table 8.2 VoID at a glance

Classes			
Dataset	DatasetDescription	Linkset	TechnicalFeature
Properties			
class	classPartition	classes	dataDump
distinctObjects	distinctSubjects	documents	entities
exampleResource	feature	inDataset	linkPredicate
objectsTarget	openSearchDescription	properties	property
property-Partition	rootResource	sparqlEndpoint	subjectsTarget
subset	target	triples	uriLookupEndpoint
uriRegexPattern	uriSpace	vocabulary	

Structural metadata provides high-level information about the schema and internal structure of a dataset and can be helpful when exploring or querying datasets. This includes information such as the vocabularies used in the dataset, statistics about the size of the dataset, and examples of typical resources in the dataset. This information is useful for tasks such as querying and data integration.

Descriptions of links between datasets provide information about the relationship between multiple datasets. The void:target property is used to name the two datasets. Every linkset must have exactly two distinct void:targets. void:target has subproperties, void:subjectsTarget and void:objectsTarget. These can be used to state the subject-object direction of the links explicitly: the subjects of all link triples are in the dataset named void:subjectsTarget and the objects in void:objectsTarget.

A linkset may not have more than one void:subjectsTarget or more than one void:objectsTarget. There are two different notions of "directionality" for RDF links: the dataset providing the subjects of the triples uses void:subjectsTarget and the dataset containing the objects uses void:objectsTarget. The dataset containing the links expresses this by making the linkset a void:subset of the respective target datasets.

This is especially important when referring to owl:sameAs links. This property is symmetric, so its subjects and objects are exchangeable. The question is usually which publisher made the links available as part of its dataset. The publisher should make its linkset a void:subset of the target dataset.

8.2.2 *Preparing a VoID file*

This section will explain how to use the ve^2 editor to prepare a VoID file. We'll illustrate two such files; the first one is for a fictitious dataset and demonstrates how to express the interlinking of two separate datasets, as shown in the following listing. The second, shown in listing 8.4, is for our Bonobo dataset, which isn't interlinked but should be meaningful to you because we discussed this dataset in chapter 2.

Listing 8.3   Sample VoID file for a fictitious dataset

```
@prefix rdf: <http://www.w3.org/1999/02/22-rdf-syntax-ns#> .
@prefix rdfs: <http://www.w3.org/2000/01/rdf-schema#> .
@prefix foaf: <http://xmlns.com/foaf/0.1/> .
@prefix dcterms: <http://purl.org/dc/terms/> .
@prefix void: <http://rdfs.org/ns/void#> .
@prefix : <#> .                                             We assume that the empty
                                                            prefix is bound to the base
                                                            URL of the current file.
## your dataset
:myDS rdf:type void:Dataset ;
 foaf:homepage <http://example.org/> ;
 dcterms:title "Example Dataset" ;
 dcterms:description "A simple dataset in RDF." ;
 dcterms:publisher <http://example.org/me> ;
 dcterms:source <http://example.org/source.xml> ;
 dcterms:license <http://opendatacommons.org/licenses/pddl/1.0/> ;
 void:sparqlEndpoint <http://dbpedia.org/sparql> ;
 void:uriLookupEndpoint <http://lookup.dbpedia.org> ;
 void:vocabulary <http://purl.org/dc/terms/> ;
 void:exampleResource <http://example.org/resource/ex> ;
 void:subset :myDS-DS1 .
## datasets you link to
                                                            Interlinking
                                                            to :DSI
:DS1 rdf:type void:Dataset ;
 foaf:homepage <http://dbpedia.org/> ;
 dcterms:title "DBpedia" ;
 dcterms:description "Linked Data version of Wikipedia." ;
 void:exampleResource <http://dbpedia.org/resource/Ludwig_van_Beethoven> .

:myDS-DS1 rdf:type void:Linkset ;
 void:linkPredicate <http://www.w3.org/2002/07/owl#sameAs> ;
 void:target :myDS ;
 void:target :DS1 .
```

To prepare a dataset for publication, you'll need a void file that you publish alongside the dataset. We recommend that you use ve^2—the VoID editor (http://lab.linked-data.deri.ie/ve2/). This tool walks you through the preparation of this file and provides a form that enables you to enter relevant information about your dataset.

ve^2, maintained by Michael Hausenblas (http://mhausenblas.info/), has multiple capabilities. It enables you to prepare a VoID file, inspect it, and announce it. All you need to do is point your browser at http://lab.linkeddata.deri.ie/ve2/. The editor enables you to specify most of the metadata that you'll need. But you can always copy and paste the output into a text editor and insert additional information if needed.

Figure 8.3 is a screen shot of using ve^2 to generate the VoID file for listing 8.4. This figure illustrates the ease with which you can create a VoID file.

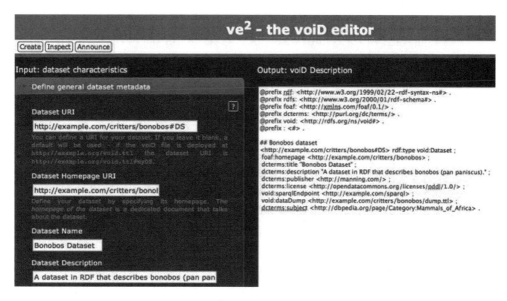

Figure 8.3   Sample of creation screen of ve²

You can find the VoID file by using ve² to insert content related to our Bonobo dataset, in the following listing. We chose this illustration because you're familiar with this dataset from chapter 2.

Listing 8.4   A sample void.ttl file for a fictitious Bonobo dataset

```
@prefix rdf: <http://www.w3.org/1999/02/22-rdf-syntax-ns#> .
@prefix rdfs: <http://www.w3.org/2000/01/rdf-schema#> .
@prefix foaf: <http://xmlns.com/foaf/0.1/> .
@prefix dcterms: <http://purl.org/dc/terms/> .
@prefix void: <http://rdfs.org/ns/void#> .
@prefix : <#> .

## Bonobos dataset
<http://example.com/critters/bonobos#DS> rdf:type void:Dataset ;
 foaf:homepage <http://example.com/critters/bonobos> ;
 dcterms:title "Bonobos Dataset" ;
 dcterms:description "A dataset in RDF that describes bonobos (pan
   paniscus)." ;
 void:exampleResource <http://example.org/critters/bonobos/Mary> ;
 dcterms:publisher <http://manning.com/> ;
 dcterms:license <http://opendatacommons.org/licenses/pddl/1.0/> ;
 void:sparqlEndpoint <http://example.com/sparql> ;
 void:dataDump <http://example.com/critters/bonobos/dump.ttl> ;
 dcterms:subject <http://dbpedia.org/page/Category:Mammals_of_Africa> .
```

> **We assume that the empty prefix is bound to the base URL, site of publication, of the current file.**

> **Sample URL showcasing data**

As we've just discussed, you need to be able to publish metadata about your dataset so that the dataset can be discovered and aggregated by search engines and web spiders. The preparation and publication of a VoID file about your dataset is the way to accomplish this.

8.3   *Sitemaps*

Webmasters need to inform search engines about pages on their sites that are available for crawling. Sitemaps support this effort. In general, a sitemap is an XML file that lists URLs for a site along with additional metadata about each URL. Using a sitemap, webmasters can provide information about each URL:

- Last update
- Frequency of updates
- The relative level of importance of this URL
- Metadata about specific types of content on your site
- Running time, category, and family-friendly status of a video
- Subject matter, type, and license of an image

The content of a sitemap helps search engines more effectively crawl your site. A sitemap is especially useful in identifying dynamic web content that's provided on the fly.

Web crawlers usually discover pages from links both within your site and from other sites. Sitemaps supplement this data and enable crawlers that support sitemaps to pick up all URLs specified in the map. Sitemaps are especially useful if your site is new and has few links to it and if your site has a large archive of content pages that are poorly linked to each other. Using sitemaps is no guarantee that search engines will include your web pages in their results, but it will improve your chances for discovery.

Fortunately, the W3C has a standard protocol defining these documents. This format, Sitemap 0.90, is described at http://www.sitemaps.org/protocol.html. More good news is that Google, Yahoo!, and Microsoft have jointly adopted this protocol, thus simplifying how webmasters and online publishers submit their sites' contents for indexing. A semantic sitemap facilitates the consumption of published RDF data by Semantic Web browsers and search engines. Semantic sitemaps are an extension of the Sitemap 0.90 protocol. Semantic sitemaps enable the smart selection of data access methods by clients and crawlers alike. This additional information will announce the presence of RDF data and deal with specific RDF publishing needs. Section 8.3.1 will briefly address the format and preparation of a sitemap that follows the 0.90 protocol. We'll then address the extensions that you'd use to generate a semantic sitemap.

8.3.1   *Non-semantic sitemaps*

Follow the guidelines on http://www.sitemaps.org/protocol.html in preparing a sitemap and verify that the file is syntactically correct. You can find an XML validation tool at http://www.w3schools.com/xml/xml_validator.asp. Here are some guidelines that you should be especially careful to follow:

- All data values must be entity-escaped (http://www.sitemaps.org/protocol.html#escaping).
- The file itself must be UTF-8 encoded (save the file using this format) and encoded for readability by the web server on which it's located.

- All URLs in a sitemap must be from a single host.
- A sitemap file can contain no more than 50,000 URLs and must be no larger than 50 MB when uncompressed; break larger sitemaps into multiple smaller sitemaps.
- List multiple sitemaps in a sitemap index file (http://www.sitemaps.org/protocol.html) and then submit the index file.

The following listing shows a basic sitemap that contains just one URL and uses all required and optional tags.

Listing 8.5 Sample XML sitemap

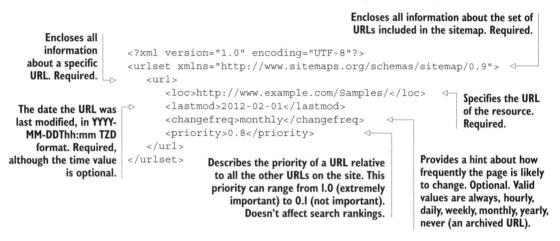

You can create your sitemap manually using a text editor. Alternatively, there are a number of tools (http://code.google.com/p/sitemap-generators/wiki/SitemapGenerators) available that can help you generate your sitemap. After you've prepared your sitemap file, place it on your web server. The location of a sitemap file determines the set of URLs that can be included in that sitemap. A sitemap file located at http://example.com/Sample/sitemap.xml can include any URLs starting with http://example.com/Sample/ but may not include URLs starting with http://example.com/catalog/.

Now you need to inform the search engines that support this protocol of its existence. You can do this by the following methods:

- Submitting it to them via the search engine's submission interface.
- Specifying the location in your site's robots.txt file. Robots.txt is a regular text file that through its name has special meaning to the majority of robots on the Web. For example, the robots.txt file at http://www.example.com/robots.txt would contain the line `Sitemap: http://www.sitemaphost.com/sitemap1.xml`.
- Sending an HTTP request.

Search engines can then retrieve your sitemap and make the URLs available to their crawlers.

8.3.2 Semantic sitemaps

In this section, we'll discuss the extensions that are needed to prepare a semantic sitemap. This additional information is intended to improve crawling performance, enable a complete crawl of disconnected datasets, efficiently discover scattered and poorly linked RDF documents, identify and catalog SPARQL endpoints, enable site operators to make delegated authorities visible, identify RDF dumps, and perform closed-world queries about self-contained data. Semantic sitemaps enable the efficient indexing of large datasets because they require no crawling on your site. You can download the schema for semantic sitemaps at http://www.sitemaps.org/schemas/sitemap/0.9/sitemap.xsd. You can find the schema for semantic sitemap index files at http://www.sitemaps.org/schemas/sitemap/0.9/siteindex.xsd. The following listing illustrates a semantic sitemap. A second example is in listing 8.7 and again uses our Bonobo example.

Listing 8.6 Sitemap XML file that uses semantic crawling extensions[1]

Dataset is labeled as the Example Corp. Product Catalog.

Namespace for the sitemapextension vocabulary

```
<?xml version="1.0" encoding="UTF-8"?>
<urlset xmlns="http://www.sitemaps.org/schemas/sitemap/0.9"
    xmlns:sc="http://sw.deri.org/2007/07/sitemapextension/scschema.xsd">
  <sc:dataset>
    <sc:datasetLabel>Example Corp. Product Catalog</sc:datasetLabel>
    <sc:datasetURI>http://example.com/catalog.rdf#catalog</sc:datasetURI>
    <sc:linkedDataPrefix slicing="subject-object">
http://example.com/products/</sc:linkedDataPrefix>
    <sc:sampleURI>http://example.com/products/widgets/X42</sc:sampleURI>
    <sc:sampleURI>http://example.com/products/categories/all</sc:sampleURI>
    <sc:sparqlEndpointLocation slicing="subject-object">
    http://example.com/sparql
    </sc:sparqlEndpointLocation>
    <sc:dataDumpLocation>
http://example.com/data/catalogdump.rdf.gz
    </sc:dataDumpLocation>
    <sc:dataDumpLocation>
    http://example.org/data/catalog_archive.rdf.gz </sc:dataDumpLocation>
    <sc:dataDumpLocation>
http://example.org/data/product_categories.rdf.gz</sc:dataDumpLocation>
      #E, #F
    <changefreq>weekly</changefreq>
  </sc:dataset>
</urlset>
```

Its Semantic Web identifier is http://example.com/catalog.rdf#catalog; it would be reasonable to expect further RDF annotations about the dataset at http://example.com/catalog.rdf.

Dataset contents have identifiers starting with http://example.com/products/, and descriptions of them are served as linked data.

Updates to the dataset should be expected weekly.

The dump of the entire dataset is split into three parts.

---

[1] http://sw.deri.org/2007/07/sitemapextension/#examples

Table 8.3 lists the tags that can be used in a semantic sitemap. After preparation, the semantic sitemap needs to be published by saving it on your server and noting its existence in the corresponding robots.txt file.

Table 8.3 Semantic sitemap extensions

Semantic sitemap tags	Description
sc:dataset	Declares a dataset
sc:linkedDataPrefix	A prefix for Linked Data hosted on a server
sc:sparqlEndpointLocation	The location of a SPARQL protocol endpoint
sc:sparqlGraphName	Specifies the URI of a named graph within the SPARQL endpoint
sc:dataDumpLocation	Location of an RDF data dump file
sc:datasetURI	Optional URI that identifies the current dataset
sc:datasetLabel	Optional name of the dataset
sc:sampleURI	Points to a representative sample within the dataset; useful for human exploration of the dataset

The following listing illustrates a possible semantic sitemap for our Bonobo site. We'll reference this sitemap in the next section when we address linking to external data.

Listing 8.7 Sample semantic sitemap for our Bonobo example

```
<?xml version="1.0" encoding="UTF-8"?>
<urlset xmlns="http://www.sitemaps.org/schemas/sitemap/0.9"
    xmlns:sc="http://sw.deri.org/2007/07/sitemapextension">
  <sc:dataset>
    <sc:datasetLabel>
    Bonobos Dataset
    </sc:datasetLabel>
    <sc:datasetURI>http://example.com/critters/bonobos#DS
    </sc:datasetURI>
    <sc:sampleURI>http://example.com/critters/bonobos/Mary
    </sc:sampleURI>
    <sc:linkedDataPrefix sc:slicing="subject-object">
      http://example.com/critters/bonobos/</sc:linkedDataPrefix>
  <sc:sparqlEndpoint sc:slicing="subject-object">
    http://example.com/sparql
  </sc:sparqlEndpoint>
  <sc:dataDump>http://example.com/critters/bonobos/dump.ttl
  </sc:dataDump>
    <changefreq>weekly</changefreq>
  </sc:dataset>
</urlset>
```

URL pointing to sample data

A base URL is included in <sc:linkedData Prefix>.

8.3.3 *Enabling discovery of your site*

Just as Google can index your web pages, Sindice can index your semantic content using semantic sitemaps (http://www.sindice.com/developers/publishing), as illustrated in figure 8.4. Content providers need to do the following:

- Publish data as machine-readable pages using RDF or RDFa standards.
- Enable effective discovery and synchronization using your sitemap.xml and robots.txt files. Be sure to include `lastmod`, `changefreq`, and `priorityfields` so Sindice and others can limit their downloads to only new and changed pages.
- Tell Sindice about your site. Individual pages from your site can quickly be updated into Sindice by sending an automatic notification using the Sindice Ping API. For example:

```
curl -H "Accept: text/plain" --data-binary
    'http://www.example.com/mypage.html'
    http://sindice.com/api/v2/ping
```

NOTE `'http://www.example.com/mypage.html'` needs to be replaced with the actual URL at which your data is published. This URL needs to be publicly accessible.

An alternative method is to use the submit form, which can be found at http://sindice.com/main/submit.

- Check that your site has been discovered and synchronized. A day or even some hours after submitting your site, you can search Sindice to determine how many of your pages have been indexed. Substitute your domain into the following searches to find which pages have been indexed today or over the past week: http://sindice.com/search?q=date:today+domain:www.example.com and http:// sindice.com/search?q=date:last_week+domain:www.example.com.

Both VoID and semantic sitemaps can include sample URLs within a dataset. But the bonobo example developed in chapter 2 doesn't contain instances of bonobos; it merely provides a description of bonobos in general. Therefore, we can't really provide an example URL. If you needed to, you could add a description of a specific bonobo to the dataset, like this:

```
http://example.com/critters/bonobos/Mary a dbpedia:Bonobo;
rdfs:label "Mary the bonobo".
```

Once you have a specific bonobo, you could add it as a sample URL to the VoID and semantic sitemap.

The sitemap triple would be

```
<sc:sampleURI>http://example.com/critters/bonobos/Mary
</sc:sampleURI>
```

The VoID sample URL triple would be

```
void:exampleResource <http://example.org/critters/bonobos/Mary> .
```

Figure 8.4 Sindice sitemap availability submission form

In our discussion of sitemaps, we've demonstrated how to prepare a sitemap so that you can inform search engines about pages on your site that are available for crawling.

8.4   *Linking to other people's data*

You'll recall our small bonobo dataset from chapter 2, repeated in listing 8.8. Assume we're interested in publishing this dataset on the LOD cloud. This dataset would be more useful if we publish it with links to other related datasets already published. To that end, we're going to find related content on the LOD cloud so we can add links to our data.

One method for finding and selecting target datasets for interlinking is the "follow-your-nose" principle. In this method, you manually inspect the content by following URIs step by step. This is obviously labor intensive and time-consuming—by all measures expensive. A better approach would be to use semantic indexers, like Sindice (http://sindice.com) or a Web of Data browser like OpenLink Data Explorer (http://linkeddata.uriburner.com/ode/). In addition, if a site's semantic sitemap indicates the availability of a SPARQL endpoint, then the dataset could be queried. Let's see what we can find regarding bonobos using Sindice and OpenLink Data Explorer.

Listing 8.8   Bonobo example data in Turtle format from chapter 2

```
@prefix dbpedia:     <http://dbpedia.org/resource/> .
@prefix dbpedia-owl: <http://dbpedia.org/ontology/> .
@prefix foaf:     <http://xmlns.com/foaf/0.1/> .
@prefix ex: <http://example.com/> .
@prefix rdf:     <http://www.w3.org/1999/02/22-rdf-syntax-ns#> .
@prefix rdfs: <http://www.w3.org/2000/01/rdf-schema#> .
```

```
@prefix vcard: <http://www.w3.org/2006/vcard/ns#> .
@prefix xsd: <http://www.w3.org/2001/XMLSchema#> .

dbpedia:Bonobo
    rdf:type    dbpedia-owl:Eukaryote , dbpedia-owl:Mammal ,
dbpedia-owl:Animal ;
    rdfs:comment "The bonobo, Pan paniscus, previously called the pygmy
chimpanzee and less often, the dwarf or gracile chimpanzee, is a great ape
and one of the two species making up the genus Pan; the other is Pan
troglodytes, or the common chimpanzee. Although the name \"chimpanzee\" is
sometimes used to refer to both species together, it is usually understood
as referring to the common chimpanzee, while Pan paniscus is usually
referred to as the bonobo."@en ;
    foaf:depiction    <http://upload.wikimedia.org/wikipedia/commons/a/a6/
    Bonobo-04.jpg> ;
    foaf:name    "Bonobo"@en ;
    rdfs:seeAlso http://eol.org/pages/326448/overview   .

<http://dbpedia.org/resource/San_Diego_Zoo> rdfs:label "San Diego Zoo"@en ;
    <http://semanticweb.org/wiki/Property:Contains> dbpedia:Bonobo ;
    vcard:adr  _:1 ;
    dbpedia:Exhibit  _:2 ;
    a ex:Zoo

  .

<http://dbpedia.org/resource/Columbus_Zoo_and_Aquarium> rdfs:label
    "Columbus Zoo and Aquarium"@en ;
    <http://semanticweb.org/wiki/Property:Contains> dbpedia:Bonobo ;
    a ex:Zoo

  .

_:1 vcard:locality "San Diego" ;
    vcard:region "California" ;
    vcard:country-name "USA"

  .

_:2 rdfs:label "Pygmy Chimps at Bonobo Road"@en ;
    <http://dbpedia.org/property/dateStart> "1993-04-03-08:00"^^xsd:date ;
    <http://semanticweb.org/wiki/Property:Contains> dbpedia:Bonobo

  .

ex:Zoo a rdfs:Class .
```

Location of the "Bonobos are mammals" triple

This triple includes an external link to the Encyclopedia of Life.

Starting with Sindice.com, we searched for "bonobo." We got more than 8,000 hits, but not all of them refer to RDF data, as shown in figure 8.5. We decided to narrow the choices using the advanced search option.

As you can see in figure 8.6, we were able to narrow our search to about 3,000 documents. Looking at the selected members of the LOD cloud shown in figure 8.7, you can see that dbpedia.org and wordnet.rkbexplorer are both present, so these RDF links would help us reach our goal of 50 RDF links. You should manually examine these datasets to determine their relevance to your dataset. In fact, the results contain references to musicbrainz, which refers to a musician whose stage name is Bonobo.

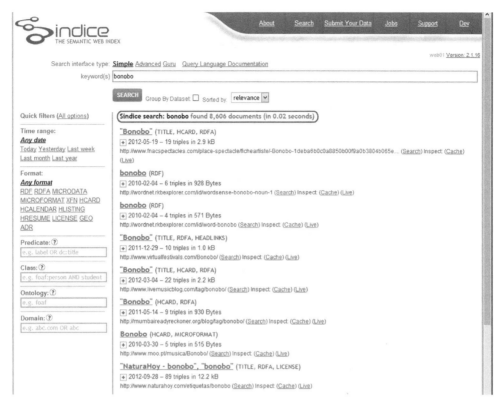

Figure 8.5   Basic Sindice search for "bonobo"

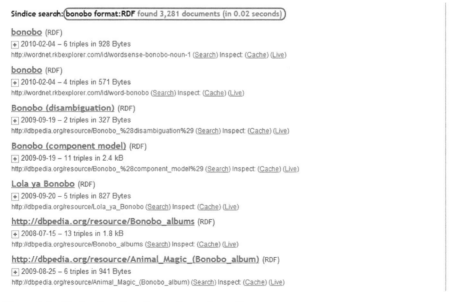

Figure 8.6   Sindice bonobo advanced search results

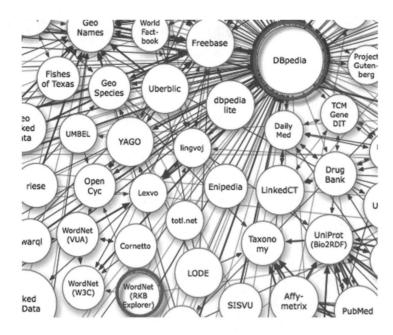

Figure 8.7 Selection from the LOD cloud diagram

All in all, we found more than 100 datasets relevant to bonobos, including:

- rdf.opiumfield.com (2080)
- www.bbc.co.uk (198)
- foaf.qdos.com (27)
- www.spin.de (16)
- users.livejournal.com (8)

- dbpedia.org (296)
- api.hi5.com (85)
- identi.ca (18)
- oai.rkbexplorer.com (13)
- products.semweb.bestbuy.com (7)

We'll augment our RDF dataset and update our VoID file to show these links. These triples will be inserted; see listing 8.9.

```
rdfs:seeAlso http://www.bbc.co.uk/nature/species/Bonobo.rdf ;
rdfs:seeAlso http://www.bbc.co.uk/nature/adaptations/Visual_perception#p00bk61z ;
rdfs:seeAlso http://wordnet.rkbexplorer.com/id/word-bonobo ;
```

Listing 8.9 Extended bonobo example data in Turtle format

```
@prefix dbpedia:     <http://dbpedia.org/resource/> .
@prefix dbpedia-owl: <http://dbpedia.org/ontology/> .
@prefix foaf:        <http://xmlns.com/foaf/0.1/> .
@prefix ex: <http://example.com/> .
@prefix rdf:    <http://www.w3.org/1999/02/22-rdf-syntax-ns#> .
@prefix rdfs: <http://www.w3.org/2000/01/rdf-schema#> .
@prefix vcard: <http://www.w3.org/2006/vcard/ns#> .
@prefix xsd: <http://www.w3.org/2001/XMLSchema#> .

dbpedia:Bonobo
    rdf:type    dbpedia-owl:Eukaryote , dbpedia-owl:Mammal ,
```

```
dbpedia-owl:Animal ;
    rdfs:comment "The bonobo, Pan paniscus, previously called the pygmy
chimpanzee and less often, the dwarf or gracile chimpanzee, is a great ape
and one of the two species making up the genus Pan; the other is Pan
troglodytes, or the common chimpanzee. Although the name \"chimpanzee\" is
sometimes used to refer to both species together, it is usually understood
as referring to the common chimpanzee, while Pan paniscus is usually
referred to as the bonobo."@en ;
    foaf:depiction      <http://upload.wikimedia.org/wikipedia/commons/a/a6/
      Bonobo-04.jpg> ;
    foaf:name      "Bonobo"@en ;
    rdfs:seeAlso http://eol.org/pages/326448/overview  ;
        rdfs:seeAlso http://www.bbc.co.uk/nature/species/Bonobo.rdf ;
        rdfs:seeAlso
            http://www.bbc.co.uk/nature/adaptations/
    Visual_perception#p00bk61z ;
        rdfs:seeAlso http://wordnet.rkbexplorer.com/id/word-bonobo .
```

Additional RDF links

```
<http://dbpedia.org/resource/San_Diego_Zoo> rdfs:label "San Diego Zoo"@en ;
    <http://semanticweb.org/wiki/Property:Contains> dbpedia:Bonobo ;
    vcard:adr _:1 ;
    dbpedia:Exhibit _:2 ;
    a ex:Zoo

.


<http://dbpedia.org/resource/Columbus_Zoo_and_Aquarium> rdfs:label
    "Columbus Zoo and Aquarium"@en ;
    <http://semanticweb.org/wiki/Property:Contains> dbpedia:Bonobo ;
    a ex:Zoo

.


_:1 vcard:locality "San Diego" ;
    vcard:region "California" ;
    vcard:country-name "USA"

.


_:2 rdfs:label "Pygmy Chimps at Bonobo Road"@en ;
    <http://dbpedia.org/property/dateStart> "1993-04-03-08:00"^^xsd:date ;
    <http://semanticweb.org/wiki/Property:Contains> dbpedia:Bonobo

.


ex:Zoo a rdfs:Class .
```

We also need to modify the VoID file to reflect the links to these external datasets. The modified file is shown in the following listing. These external dataset links are single-directional. Our dataset references them, but they don't reference our bonobo dataset.

Listing 8.10 Modified VoID file showing links to external datasets

```
@prefix rdf: <http://www.w3.org/1999/02/22-rdf-syntax-ns#> .
@prefix rdfs: <http://www.w3.org/2000/01/rdf-schema#> .
@prefix foaf: <http://xmlns.com/foaf/0.1/> .
@prefix dcterms: <http://purl.org/dc/terms/> .
@prefix void: <http://rdfs.org/ns/void#> .
```

```
@prefix : <#> .

## your dataset
<http://example.com/critters/bonobos#DS> rdf:type void:Dataset ;
 foaf:homepage <http://example.com/critters/bonobos> ;
 dcterms:title "Bonobos Dataset" ;
 dcterms:description "A dataset in RDF that describes bonobos
➥    (pan paniscus)l" ;
 dcterms:publisher <http://manning.com/> ;
 dcterms:license <http://opendatacommons.org/licenses/pddl/1.0> ;
 void:sparqlEndpoint <http://example.com/sparql> ;
 void:dataDump <http://example.com/critters/bonobos/dump.ttl> ;
 void:exampleResource <http://example.org/critters/bonobos/Mary> ;
 void:subset :myDS-DS1 ;
 void:subset :myDS-DS2 .

## datasets you link to
```

Defining the
relationship to
www.bbc.co.uk, DSI

```
# interlinking to :DS1
:DS1 rdf:type void:Dataset ;
 foaf:homepage <http://www.bbc.co.uk> ;
 dcterms:title "bbc" ;
 dcterms:description "rdf of bonobo data" ;
 void:exampleResource <http://www.bbc.co.uk/nature/species/Bonobo.rdf> .

:myDS-DS1 rdf:type void:Linkset ;
 void:linkPredicate <http://www.w3.org/2000/01/rdf-schema#seeAlso> ;
 void:target <http://example.com/critters/bonobos#DS> ;
 void:target :DS1 .

# interlinking to :DS2
:DS2 rdf:type void:Dataset ;
 foaf:homepage <http://wordnet.rkbexplorer.com> ;
 dcterms:title "wordnet" ;
 dcterms:description "rdf dictionary" .
```

Defining the relationship to
wordnet.rkbexplorer.com, DS2

```
:myDS-DS2 rdf:type void:Linkset ;
 void:linkPredicate <http://www.w3.org/2000/01/rdf-schema#seeAlso> ;
 void:target <http://example.com/critters/bonobos#DS> ;
 void:target :DS2 .
```

8.5   *Examples of using owl:sameAs to interlink datasets*

A critical component in the ability to interlink RDF datasets is the use of owl:sameAs. This property enables machines to merge resource descriptions if the resources described are linked with owl:sameAs. Owl:sameAs is part of OWL and is frequently used to support Linked Data integration across identified resources and across distributed datasets. It provides an alternative means to rdfs:seeAlso to refer to an external equivalent resource. It plays a critical role in supporting the Linked Data principles as put forth by Tim Berners-Lee "to include links to other URIs" so that discovery of related data is promoted. The following listing shows examples of using owl:sameAs. The first example is an extraction of a fragment from a FOAF document. The use of `owl:sameAs` here enables the integration of information from this FOAF document and that stored on my Facebook and Twitter accounts.

Listing 8.11 Extract from FOAF document illustrating `owl:sameAs`

```
@base <http://rosemary.umw.edu/~marsha/foaf.ttl#> .
@base <http://rosemary.umw.edu/~marsha/foaf.ttl#> .
@prefix admin: <http://webns.net/mvcb/> .
@prefix foaf: <http://xmlns.com/foaf/0.1/> .
@prefix rdf: <http://www.w3.org/1999/02/22-rdf-syntax-ns#> .
@prefix rdfs: <http://www.w3.org/2000/01/rdf-schema#> .
@prefix owl: <http://www.w3.org/2002/07/owl#> .

<me> a foaf:Person;
    foaf:family_name "Zaidman";
    foaf:givenname "Marsha";
    foaf:homepage <http://rosemary.umw.edu/~marsha>;
        owl:sameAs <http://www.facebook.com/marsha.zaidman>;
        owl:sameAs <https://twitter.com/MarshaZman>.
```

Additional prefix statement to make the OWL ontology accessible

Identifies the references to my Facebook account and my Twitter account as matching resources in the remote documents

More recent uses of `owl:sameAs` connect resources from Linked Data sources. The example shown in the following listing illustrates that *the New York Times* is adding links to a Geonames URI, a DBpedia URI, and a Freebase URI. All links are now equivalent to *The New York Times* resource (http://data.nytimes.com/69949648080753147811), and all contents at these links may be integrated.

Listing 8.12 Illustration of using `owl:sameAs` to connect linked resources

```
<http://data.nytimes.com/69949648080753147811>
owl:sameAs <http://data.nytimes.com/rhode_island_geo>  ;
owl:sameAs <http://dbpedia.org/resource/Rhode_Island>  ;
owl:sameAs <http://rdf.freebase.com/ns/en.rhode_island>  ;
owl:sameAs <http://sws.geonames.org/5224323/>   .
```

To reiterate, the use of `owl:sameAs` in this context will enable machine aggregation of the data in the specified equivalent links. But such simple aggregation may introduce errors. For example, the use of `owl:sameAs` may combine context-dependent descriptions provided in different data sources. To appreciate the problem, you have to understand entailment. *Entailments* are the sets of facts that can be deduced from the meaning of Semantic Web data. The crucial difference between plain-old data and Linked Data is that Linked Data includes these entailments. Consider the English-language statement "bananas are yellow." Because it's expressed in a language, it has meaning in addition to the single fact that bananas are yellow. If we also assert that a specific object is a banana, then there is an entailment that the object is also yellow.

You should be aware that the common usage of `owl:sameAs` may raise questions. As an example involving the population of the state of Rhode Island (figure 8.8), *the*

The New York Times **Linked Open Data** BETA

Rhode Island

http://data.nytimes.com/69949648080753147811

geo:lat	41.7503782
geo:long	-71.4997825
nyt:topicPage	http://topics.nytimes.com/top/classifieds/realestate/locations/newengland/index.html
owl:sameAs	http://data.nytimes.com/rhode_island_geo
owl:sameAs	http://dbpedia.org/resource/Rhode_Island
owl:sameAs	http://rdf.freebase.com/ns/en.rhode_island
owl:sameAs	http://sws.geonames.org/5224323/

Figure 8.8 ***The New York Times*** **LOD on Rhode Island**

The New York Times is using `owl:sameAs` to show the equivalence of http://data.nytimes.com/69949648080753147811 to http://rdf.freebase.com/ns/en.rhode_island and to http://sws.geonames.org/5224323/. Unfortunately, the populations reported for Rhode Island using these two sources are 1,051,302 and 1,050,292, respectively. Each value could be true in a certain context. But in answering a simple question, "What is the population of Rhode Island?" web users expect a single response and not a set of alternatives. This occurs because an OWL reasoner conflated the context-dependent descriptions. A *reasoner* is a program that performs logical operations, such as the operations defined in OWL. Naturally, a human reader would understand that these populations are associated with different years.

Properly applying `owl:sameAs` is important to the integration of data in related resources. But the use of `owl:sameAs` has known issues. Some of them stem from possible misuse of the term. In general, the fundamental problem with the use of URIs as identifiers and the use of `owl:sameAs` is one of context and the implicit import of properties. These equivalences are drawn because `owl:sameAs` is both symmetric and transitive. Unfortunately, `owl:sameAs` is often used when describing the "same thing but in different contexts" or "two things that are very similar to each other" but is better described using `owl:equivalentTo`. Realistically, the proper application of `owl:sameAs` is a value judgment that can be made only by the creator of the data.

As our final activity in linking to other people's data, DBpedia now allows you to inform them of new datasets and ask that they link to you. We'll discuss this in section 8.6. The GitHub repository, https://github.com/dbpedia/dbpedia-links, has complete information.

8.6 Joining Data Hub

By now you're probably eager to join the LOD cloud and share your data with others. The process that you need to follow to share your data on Data Hub (formerly CKAN) is available at http://datahub.io/en/about. For convenience, we'll briefly discuss the process here:

1 Navigate to http://datahub.io/. Figure 8.9 shows the Data Hub welcome screen. Click the link to the dataset submission page, shown in figure 8.10.

2 To add your dataset to Data Hub, you need to follow the process outlined at http://www.w3.org/wiki/TaskForces/CommunityProjects/LinkingOpenData/ DataSets/CKANmetainformation. This includes documentation and naming expectations and is outlined here for your convenience. See figure 8.11 for the actual form. Describe your dataset with the following information:

   a. Data Hub name (unique ID for your dataset on Data Hub, in the form of [a-z0-9-]{2+}+"THE NAME OF YOUR DATASET")
   b. Title (full name of your dataset)
   c. URL (link to dataset homepage)
   d. Number of triples (approximate number of RDF triples in the dataset)
   e. Links (separate links for each dataset to which your dataset links)

3 Data Hub tags

   a. Tag your newly added dataset with "lod."
   b. Tag it with "nolinks" if your dataset doesn't have any incoming links (inlinks) or outgoing links (outlinks).

4 Provide as much additional information as possible (for example, SPARQL endpoint, VoID description, license, and the topic of the dataset). This information helps the community to know more about the development state of the Web of Linked Data. Recommended documentation is described at http://www.w3.org/wiki/TaskForces/CommunityProjects/LinkingOpenData/ DataSets/CKANmetainformation.

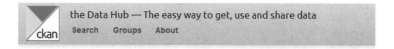

Figure 8.9   Data Hub welcome page

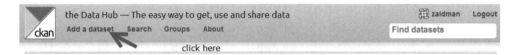

Figure 8.10   Data Hub Add a Dataset selection

In completing the submission form, be sure to include license information so that others will understand how they may use your data. The more complete your information, the more useful your dataset will be to future users.

NOTE   Before creating a new Data Hub package, double-check that a package doesn't already exist for your dataset by navigating to http://datahub.io/dataset or selecting the Search option, visible in figure 8.10.

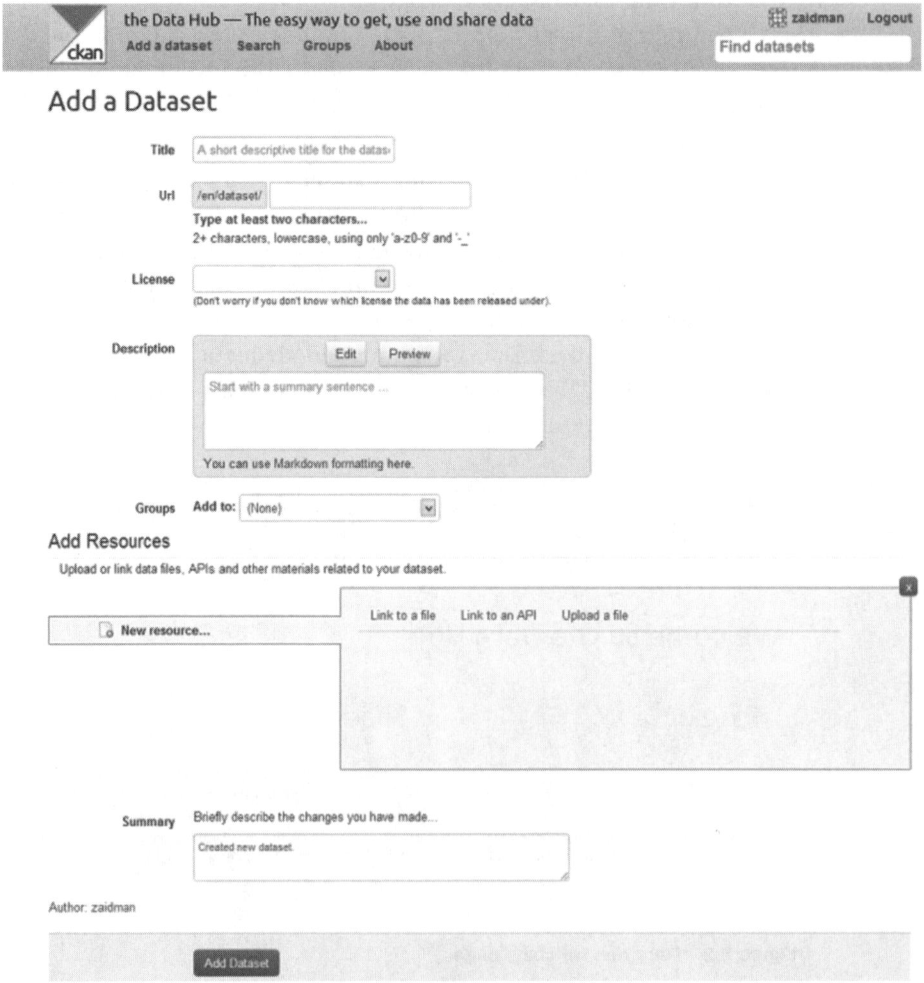

Figure 8.11   Data Hub Add a Dataset submission page

This section addressed joining Data Hub, which enables you to join the LOD cloud and publicize your dataset to others.

8.7 Requesting outgoing links from DBpedia to your dataset

As we mentioned in chapter 1, you should do your best to publish 5-Star data that has both inlinks and outlinks. One way to generate inlinks to your dataset is by requesting DBpedia to provide links to your data. dbpedia-links is a version-controlled repository that contains outgoing links in N-Triples format for DBpedia. You accomplish this by pointing your browser to https://github.com/dbpedia/dbpedia-links and then using the GitHub interface to upload links to your dataset using their GUI.

Follow these steps as outlined to create these outgoing links from DBpedia to your dataset.

1 Navigate to https://github.com/dbpedia/dbpedia-links.
2 Log in to your own GitHub account. (You can create an account if you need one.)
3 Fork the repository, https://github.com/dbpedia/dbpedia-links, into your GitHub space. The fork operation enables you to use the dbpedia-links repository as a starting point for your own. Simply click the Fork button; see figure 8.12.

Figure 8.12 GitHub screenshot of Fork option

4 To add links to a previous unlinked dataset, do the following:

Create a folder with the dataset domain, for example, http://datasets/bonobo.info.

Put your triples into a .nt file, for example, http://datasets/bonobo.info/bonobo_links.nt.

bonobo_links would contain N-Triples like `<http://dbpedia.org/resource/Bonobo> owl:sameAs <http://example.com/species/Bonobo>`.

In addition to `owl:sameAs`, these N-Triples may also contain a few other predicates like `umbel:isLike` and `skos:{exact|close|...}Match`.

Then copy in the metadata.ttl stub from one of the other examples in the repository.

NOTE The metadata.ttl file isn't used yet and so is just a stub. You should verify that this is still the case when you submit your request.

N-Triples

N-Triples is a subset of Turtle, and all tools that support Turtle input will support N-Triples. Each line of an N-Triple file represents a single statement of information or a comment. Each statement has three components: the subject, the predicate, and the object.

Each component is separated by white space and each statement ends in a period.

Subjects may take the form of a full URI or a blank node. Predicates must be a full URI, and objects may be a full URI, a blank node, or a literal. This format will be adopted as a standard in the latter part of 2013.

---

5 To modify an existing dataset, follow the steps outlined in step 4, but modify an existing .nt file or create a separate one.

6 Finalize your edits by sending a pull request via GitHub; see figure 8.13. This operation requests that DBpedia add your triples to their repository.

Figure 8.13   GitHub screenshot of Pull Request option

NOTE   All information uploaded to the dbpedia-links repository will be considered as public domain, and you'll lose all rights to it. It will be relicensed under the same license as DBpedia uses.

When establishing DBpedia outgoing links, please honor the conventions posted at the GitHub repository: https://github.com/dbpedia/dbpedia-links.

8.8   Summary

In this chapter, we've illustrated how you can best share your datasets and projects on the Web. We've illustrated how you can optimize the inclusion of your projects and datasets in Semantic Web search results. This optimization is best achieved by publishing DOAP files of your projects and VoID files for your datasets along with a semantic sitemap. Ultimately, you can publish your qualified datasets on the LOD cloud. Chapter 9 will acquaint you with the Callimachus Project and illustrate how it can support your Linked Data applications.

Part 4

Pulling it all together

What is Callimachus? How can you use it to generate web pages from RDF data? How can you use Callimachus to build web applications? What's the current state of Linked Data on the Semantic Web? What does the future hold for Linked Data on the Semantic Web?

By this point, you've traveled a long way in your understanding, appreciation, and application of Linked Data on the Web. These final three chapters help you regroup. Part 4 introduces you to an advanced tool and walks you through an extension of the weather application originally presented in chapter 7. This new weather application looks nice and has some functionality you'll want to use in your own applications. It's based on RDF data you created from data feeds at a couple of open data sites provided by the U.S. government. We summarize the process of publishing Linked Data from preparation to publication and clarify easily overlooked steps like minting URIs and customizing vocabularies. We expect you to find this a helpful reference as you prepare your own datasets for publication.

Callimachus: a Linked Data management system

This chapter covers

- An introduction to the Callimachus Project
- Getting started with Callimachus
- Using HTML templates to create web pages
- Creating and editing RDF data using the Callimachus template system
- Creating a web application with Callimachus

This chapter will bring together much of what you learned from the previous chapters. At this point in the book, you're ready to build a web app using Linked Data. Having a platform for Linked Data development will make your work easier and faster. This chapter will introduce you to the Callimachus Project. We'll show you how to get started with Callimachus and how to use it to build web applications using Linked Data.

The project team calls Callimachus a Linked Data management system, but it might be better thought of as an application server for Linked Data. Callimachus is open source software released under the Apache 2.0 license. Callimachus provides browser-based development tools to easily create web applications using RDF data.

Callimachus has several major features:

- A template system to automatically generate web pages for each member of an OWL class. OWL classes are technically either equivalent to or subclasses of RDF Schema classes (depending on the OWL profile used), but for our purposes you can think of them as being equivalent.
- An ability to retrieve data at runtime and convert it to RDF.
- An ability to associate SPARQL queries with URLs, to parameterize those queries, and to use their results with charting libraries.
- An implementation of persistent URLs (PURLs).
- A structured writing system based on DocBook and including a visual editing environment.

In short, Callimachus allows you to navigate, visualize, and build applications on Linked Data. The data may be stored locally or gathered from the Web. It may even be converted into RDF as it's brought into Callimachus. These features make Callimachus an excellent tool for Linked Data developers.

We won't cover all of those features here because they're already described in the Callimachus documentation. Instead, we'll show you how to build web pages from RDF classes using a Callimachus template; create a simple note-taking application that creates, edits, and views notes; and extend the weather application from chapter 7. You can then explore the rest of its capabilities on your own.

The Callimachus Project is named for an ancient Greek researcher at the Library of Alexandria, Callimachus of Cyrene. He was the first person in recorded history to have a demonstrated need for graph data structures. In Callimachus's day, books consisted of rolls of papyrus. The title, author, and subject of each book were written on a leather tag sewn onto the edge of the paper. Those tags are the precursors to the tags we find in HTML, XML, and other markup languages. The Callimachus Project's logo comes from these tags, as shown in figure 9.1

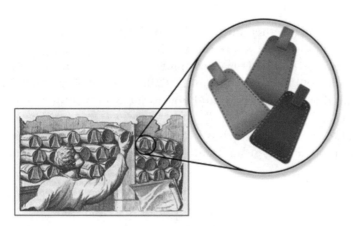

Figure 9.1   The Callimachus logo's origin in literal tags

Callimachus is a new type of application server that allows applications to build on Linked Data. You could compare it to application servers that build on structured data in a relational database or document management systems that operate on documents. Callimachus is one of a new category of Linked Data products that include Virtuoso Open-Source Edition[1] and commercial products such as TopBraid Composer.[2]

9.1 Getting started with Callimachus

First, obviously, you need to get a Callimachus instance up and running. Start by downloading the most recent release from the project's website, http://callimachus-project.org. Follow the installation directions provided in its documentation to set up your own Callimachus server. Start the server and resolve the service's URL in your web browser. You should see a welcome screen similar to the one in figure 9.2 if everything goes well.

Please note that as of this writing Callimachus 1.2 requires Java Development Kit (JDK) 1.7, not just a Java Runtime Environment (JRE). Earlier Java versions aren't supported.

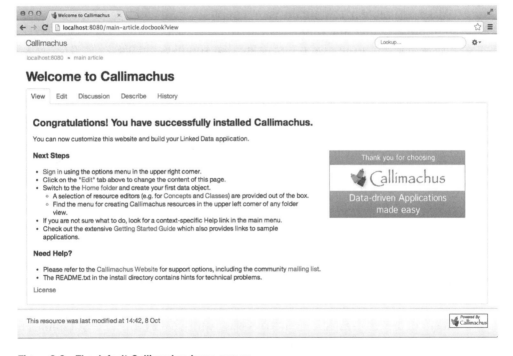

Figure 9.2   The default Callimachus home screen

---

[1] OpenLink Software, Virtuose Open-Source Edition, "What's New," http://virtuoso.openlinksw.com/dataspace/doc/dav/wiki/Main/.

[2] Explanation of editions and licensing, http://www.topquadrant.com/products/TB_Composer.html.

One of the easiest and most useful things you can do with Callimachus is generate web pages based on RDF data. The next section will show you how to load RDF data into Callimachus and use its template system to generate web pages for each instance of a class of RDF resources.

9.2   Creating web pages using RDF classes

The first thing to do with Callimachus is to add RDF data to it, accomplished via the Callimachus file manager. Log into Callimachus using the initial user you established and select the Home Folder option from the main menu. As of this writing, the main menu is accessed by selecting the gear icon in the upper right in the default theme. You can use the file manager to make subfolders and add or remove RDF and other resources, just like a file manager on your computer. The difference with the Callimachus file manager is that resources aren't really in a filesystem; the file manager views are generated at runtime from RDF. This allows RDF resources to reside in an RDF database, while binary resources, like images or HTML pages, reside in a Binary Large Object (BLOB) store.

9.2.1   Adding data to Callimachus

Make a subfolder to contain your sample data so you don't pollute the home folder. We called ours *bonobos*, but you can give it any name that you like. You create a subfolder by selecting the gear icon in the upper-left corner of the Callimachus folder view and selecting the Folder option. Figure 9.3 shows the pull-down menu from the gear icon and the Folder option being selected.

You'll need to be logged into Callimachus to make folders or add content. If you don't see the gear icon, but you do see a link that says "Sign in," please log in first.

Next, you'll create some sample data. You'll make a Turtle file containing a couple of bonobos named Mary and Bonny. You'll need to say that these two bonobos are each instances of the `dbpedia:Bonobo` class and also that `dbpedia:Bonobo` is an OWL class. Earlier examples showed the assignment of `dbpedia:Bonobo` as an RDFS class, which isn't sufficient for Callimachus. Callimachus can only associate resources with OWL classes. Listing 9.1 shows our sample data. Note that we've described each bonobo using a label and a comment so we have some information to show about them. Labels and comments provide a reasonable minimum level of human-readable information about any RDF resource and help to make your data self-commenting.

Figure 9.3   Creating a folder in Callimachus

Listing 9.1   Some bonobos in Turtle format

```
@prefix dbpedia:    <http://dbpedia.org/resource/> .
@prefix ex: <http://localhost:8080/bonobos/> .
@prefix rdf:    <http://www.w3.org/1999/02/22-rdf-syntax-ns#> .
@prefix rdfs: <http://www.w3.org/2000/01/rdf-schema#> .

dbpedia:Bonobo a owl:Class
        ;rdfs:label "Bonobo" .

ex:Mary a dbpedia:Bonobo
  ; rdfs:label "Mary"
  ; rdfs:comment "Mary is a pleasant bonobo."
  .

ex:Bonny a dbpedia:Bonobo
  ; rdfs:label "Bonny"
  ; rdfs:comment "Bonny is not very nice. She throws things at visitors."
  .
```

Your prefix here should match your personal Callimachus instance's host name and path.[3]

Making bonobos into an OWL class

Statements about the bonobo called Mary

Statements about the bonobo called Bonny

Save the contents of listing 9.1 to a file. Navigate into your new folder (you should already be there) and select the Upload button (upward-pointing arrow in a circle) to upload your sample data file. You should see something similar to figure 9.4 when the file has been uploaded to your folder.

9.2.2   *Telling Callimachus about your OWL class*

The sample data contains an OWL class, but Callimachus doesn't automatically associate imported classes with resources. This is actually a good idea, because you might not want Callimachus to automatically generate web pages for instances of all classes. Some people have created datasets that use tens of thousands of classes, which might get very confusing. So, you need to tell Callimachus about your Bonobo class. You do that by making an equivalent Callimachus class and associating the two.

You can explore all the OWL classes in a file by clicking that file, clicking the gear dropdown in the top right of the screen, and selecting "Explore OWL classes in this graph." This is the Callimachus Class Explorer and is shown in figure 9.5. You can see the dbpedia:Bonobo class (shown as just the suffix Bonobo). It has a description of "null" because

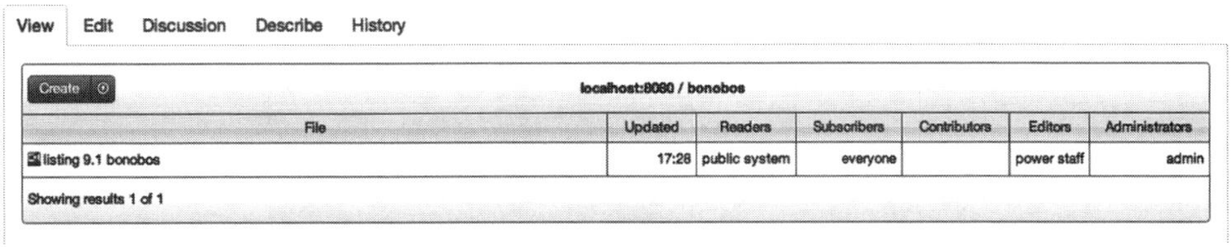

Figure 9.4   Creating a view of the bonobo data

---

[3]   For example, by default configuration, data URIs should start with http://localhost:8080/.

we didn't add an `rdfs:comment` describing it in our sample data.[4] The Assign Templates link next to the class name may be used to generate an equivalent Callimachus class and assign Callimachus templates to the class. Click that link now.

You'll be taken to a New Class page where the Callimachus equivalent class will be created. Call your class `Bonobo` to match the `dbpedia:Bonobo` class, give it a comment if you like, and then select the small icon to the upper right of the View Template label in the Page Templates section. Figure 9.6 shows how this looks.

Figure 9.5   The list of `owl:Classes` found in the bonobo folder

9.2.3   *Associating a Callimachus view template to your class*

A Callimachus view template is used to generate web pages (views) of a class instance. Every class instance will be viewed using the same template. You'll find that adding a new view template will present the opportunity to create a new one or to point to one already in the file manager. In this case, you'll create a new one and use

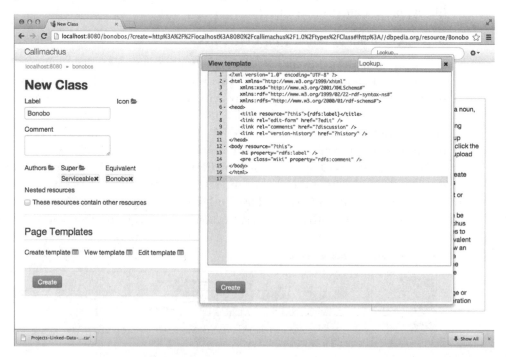

Figure 9.6   Creating a Callimachus class for bonobos and assigning a view template to it

---

[4] It's always better to describe your data. As an exercise, you could add an `rdfs:comment` describing the `dbpedia:Bonobo` class to your sample data and upload it again. You'd then see your description in the Class Explorer.

the default template provided. The following listing shows the default view template and its components.

Listing 9.2   The bonobo view template

```
<?xml version="1.0" encoding="UTF-8" ?>
<html xmlns="http://www.w3.org/1999/xhtml"
      xmlns:xsd="http://www.w3.org/2001/XMLSchema#"
      xmlns:rdf="http://www.w3.org/1999/02/22-rdf-syntax-ns#"
      xmlns:rdfs="http://www.w3.org/2000/01/rdf-schema#">
<head>
    <title resource="?this">{rdfs:label}</title>
    <link rel="edit-form" href="?edit" />
    <link rel="comments" href="?discussion" />
    <link rel="describedby" href="?describe" />
    <link rel="version-history" href="?history" />
</head>
<body resource="?this">
    <h1 property="rdfs:label" />
    <pre class="wiki" property="rdfs:comment" />
</body>
</html>
```

XML namespaces in this XHTML document serve the same purpose as PREFIXes in Turtle or SPARQL.

"?this" is replaced at execution time with the URI of the requested resource (a particular bonobo).

A header based on the object of the rdfs:label triple

A preformatted text area based on the object of the rdfs:comment triple

You'll notice that Callimachus templates are just XHTML with some (very) minor syntax added to them. Those of you who are familiar with other template languages such as PHP or JSP might be surprised by how little extra syntax there is. In fact, the added syntax is just RDFa. RDFa attributes are used to provide hints to Callimachus on how to locate the RDF data you'd like to present.

The RDFa in Callimachus templates is parsed to generate SPARQL queries to locate the right data in Callimachus's underlying RDF database, so Callimachus introduces minor extensions to standard XHTML+RDFa but keeps them to a minimum. The full template language is described in the Callimachus documentation.

Save your new template by clicking the Create button in the template pop-up window and providing a filename. We generally use the class name followed by the type of template as a name, so we called this one bonobo view.xhtml.

Next, save your class using the Create button on the New Class page. You'll be redirected to a view of the saved class construct.

The class resource page has a link in the gear drop-down in the upper right called Bonobos Resources. Selecting it will show you the two resources that are members of this class. They both came from your sample data: Mary and Bonny. Figure 9.7 shows you the list. Adding more named bonobos to your sample data will add more entries onto this list. Selecting a resource from this list will use the view template to generate a web page about each bonobo.

Bonobo Resources

A B C D E F G H I J K L M N O P Q R S T U V W X Y Z #

B   **M**

Bonny   Mary

Figure 9.7   The list of bonobo resources

Figure 9.8 shows you what you'll see by selecting the link to Mary. A web page is drawn for the bonobo Mary that uses the two RDF triples defined in the view template, one using an `rdfs:label` and the other using an `rdfs:comment`. The page for Bonny looks identical, with the obvious exception that the label will be Bonny and the comment will be Bonny's comment.

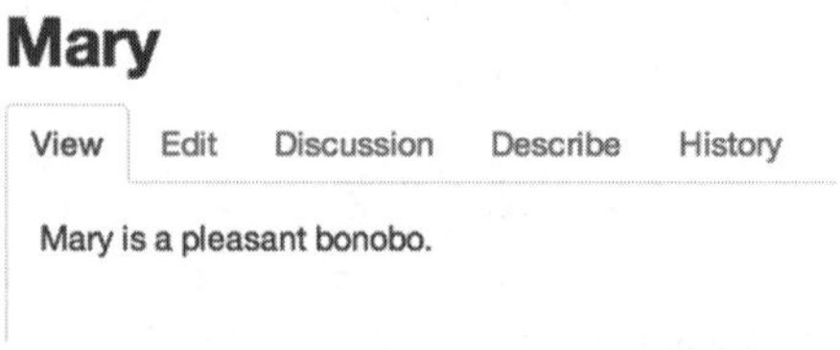

Mary

View	Edit	Discussion	Describe	History

Mary is a pleasant bonobo.

Figure 9.8   The bonobo instance called Mary, rendered via the bonobo view template

If you want to extend this example, take the following steps:

1 Add more data to the sample data file. You might, for example, describe the hair color of each bonobo or say what they like to eat. You do that by adding RDF about each resource.
2 Replace the data file on the server with the one you edited. Alternatively, you could edit the Turtle in place on the server by selecting the Edit option from the data file's description page.
3 Extend the view template to display the new information. You can do this by finding the view template in the folder, selecting it, and then selecting Edit.

Your generated pages should now show the new data!

This section provided an introduction to generating web pages from RDF data. Of course, some web pages contain forms that allow user input. Callimachus uses that capability to allow you to create and edit RDF data from dynamically created web pages so casual users never need to see RDF serializations directly (unless they want to).

The next section describes the create and edit templates and shows how they can be used to quickly make a simple web application for taking notes.

9.3   *Creating and editing class instances*

This section describes a simple note-taking application. It uses the Callimachus create and edit templates to produce and modify RDF class instances without the need to first upload RDF. The application will allow users to fill out a form to create a new note, view notes that have been created, and edit them as desired. Each note will be named with a label and contain information in a comment. The user who last modified a note and the date and time of creation will be shown when a note is viewed.

You'll need to be logged into Callimachus in order to create the components of the notes application.

Figure 9.9 shows the structure of the notes application. Start by creating a Callimachus folder to hold the application and then a subfolder to store the notes that will be created. The top-level folder will contain four files: a note class and the three templates associated with that class. The templates are used to create, view, and edit a note. You'll need to create a class from the gear menu. Call the class `Note`, and make sure to create the three templates while you're in the class-creation interface, just as you did for the

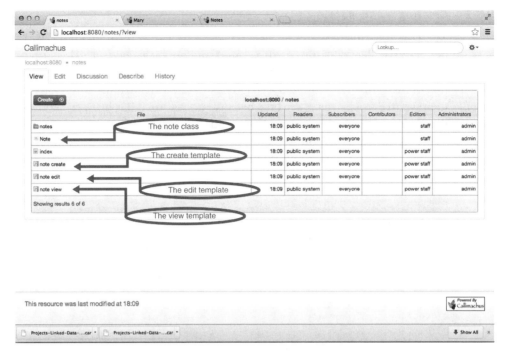

Figure 9.9   The Note class's page

bonobo view in the previous section. You can accept the default contents for each of the templates for now and edit them after you read the details about the desired functionality in the following listings.

Figure 9.10 shows how the Note class should look when you've finished creating it.

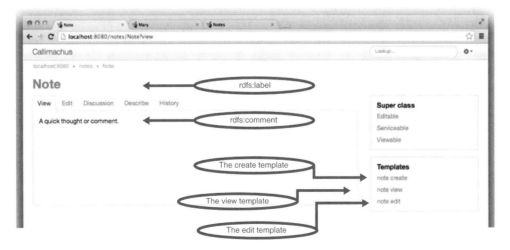

Figure 9.10   Structure of the notes application

9.3.1   Creating a new note

The create template is simply an XHTML page with a form element. Two fields are defined to collect data for an `rdfs:label` and an `rdfs:comment`. The structure is very much like the bonobo view template in listing 9.2. The major differences are the addition of the form and that the `body` tag doesn't need an attribute referring to the URI of the resource (`resource="?this"`) because no resource has been created yet. Instead, the form will be used to create an RDF resource. The following listing shows the contents of the create template. Your create template should be identical (or differ only because of minor version changes in Callimachus). You shouldn't need to modify it.

Listing 9.3   The notes create template

```xml
<?xml version="1.0" encoding="UTF-8" ?>
<html xmlns="http://www.w3.org/1999/xhtml"
    xmlns:xsd="http://www.w3.org/2001/XMLSchema#"
    xmlns:rdf="http://www.w3.org/1999/02/22-rdf-syntax-ns#"
    xmlns:rdfs="http://www.w3.org/2000/01/rdf-schema#">
<head>
    <title>New Note</title>
</head>
<body>
    <h1>New Note</h1>
    <form method="POST" action="" enctype="application/rdf+xml"
typeof="" onsubmit="return
    calli.saveResourceAs(event,calli.slugify($('#label').val()))">
        <fieldset>
            <div class="control-group">
                <label for="label" class="control-label">Label</label>
                <div class="controls">
                    <input type="text" id="label" value=
    "{rdfs:label}" class="auto-expand" required="required"
    autofocus="autofocus" />
                </div>
            </div>
            <div class="control-group">
                <label for="comment" class="control-label">Comment</label>
                <div class="controls">
                    <textarea id="comment"
class="auto-expand">{rdfs:comment}</textarea>
                </div>
            </div>
            <div class="form-actions">
                <button type="submit" class="btn
btn-success">Create</button>
            </div>
        </fieldset>
    </form>
</body>
</html>
```

⮕ ⮕ **A text field for the label, which will create a triple using an rdfs:label predicate**

⮕ **A textarea for the comment, which will create a triple using an rdfs:comment predicate**

Now that you have a create template, you can return to the Note class page and select the link from the main menu in the upper right, Create a New Note. That will bring you to a web page generated from the create template. Fill out the label and comment fields and click the Create button. You'll be prompted to save your new note. Make sure to put it into the notes subfolder to keep things neat.

Callimachus can be configured to allow resources to be automatically saved into a certain directory, but we've omitted that subtlety for brevity. The Callimachus documentation can tell you how to help your users avoid the extra navigation step.

Figure 9.11 shows the note create template in action.

You'll be redirected to a view of your new note as soon as you create it. That view is generated from the view template. You'll get an error that reads "No such method for this resource" if you forget to create your view template. Create a view template if that happens to you.

Figure 9.11 The note create template in action

9.3.2 Creating a view template for a note

The default view template is the same one you used for the bonobos. It shows only a label and a comment. Let's add a couple of items to it that Callimachus already tracks, specifically the name of the user who created or modified the note and the date and time it was last modified.

The next listing shows the view template to use. It contains a few extra lines to include the new information.

Listing 9.4 The notes view template

```
<?xml version="1.0" encoding="UTF-8" ?>
<html xmlns="http://www.w3.org/1999/xhtml"
     xmlns:xsd="http://www.w3.org/2001/XMLSchema#"
     xmlns:rdf="http://www.w3.org/1999/02/22-rdf-syntax-ns#"
     xmlns:rdfs="http://www.w3.org/2000/01/rdf-schema#"
     xmlns:prov="http://www.w3.org/ns/prov#">
<head>
    <title resource="?this">{rdfs:label}</title>
    <link rel="edit-form" href="?edit" />
    <link rel="comments" href="?discussion" />
    <link rel="describedby" href="?describe" />

    <link rel="version-history" href="?history" />
</head>
<body resource="?this">
    <h1 property="rdfs:label" />
    <pre class="wiki" property="rdfs:comment" />
    <hr/>
    <p>Time created: <span rel="prov:wasGeneratedBy">{prov:endedAtTime}</
      span></p>
```

A header based on the object of the rdfs:label triple

A paragraph to show the time the note was created.

"?this" is replaced at execution time with the URI of the requested resource (a particular bonobo).

A preformatted text area based on the object of the rdfs:comment triple

```
    <div rel="prov:wasGeneratedBy" resource="?prov">
        Created by: <span rel="prov:wasAssociatedWith">{rdfs:label}</span>
    </div>
</body>
</html>
```

A division to show the name of the user who created the note

Your users won't need to be authenticated in order to create notes (unless you change the default permissions on the resources—you can see the Callimachus documentation if you want to do that). But only authenticated users will have their names associated with the notes they create or modify.

You should now be able to see notes that look like the one in figure 9.12. You can view your existing notes either by navigating to the notes subfolder and selecting a particular note or by going to the Note Resources link available from the Main Menu on the Note class page and selecting a note from there.

The only thing left to do now is to create an edit template so you can modify your notes after they've been created. Edit templates may seem to be the most complicated of the Callimachus templates, but they're really only a cross between the create and view templates you've already seen.

9.3.3   *Creating an edit template for notes*

Like view templates, edit templates need to have an attribute on the `<body>` tag (`resource="?this"`) so Callimachus can find which note you want to edit. Like create templates, edit templates are XHTML forms and have form elements for each item you want users to be able to edit.

Note that Callimachus offers you complete control over which elements you can create, view, and edit. You can collect more information than you display or restrict editing to just a few fields. It's all up to you.

Listing 9.5 shows the edit template for notes. It should be identical to the default one you already created, so there shouldn't be any need to change it unless you

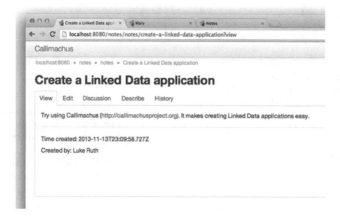

Figure 9.12   A view of a note, generated by the note view template

want to add editable fields later. Try it out by viewing a note and selecting the Edit tab near the top of the page. You'll naturally need to be logged into Callimachus to edit resources.

> **Listing 9.5 The notes edit template**

```
<?xml version="1.0" encoding="UTF-8" ?>
<html xmlns="http://www.w3.org/1999/xhtml"
    xmlns:xsd="http://www.w3.org/2001/XMLSchema#"
    xmlns:rdf="http://www.w3.org/1999/02/22-rdf-syntax-ns#"
    xmlns:rdfs="http://www.w3.org/2000/01/rdf-schema#">
<head>
    <title resource="?this">{rdfs:label}</title>
</head>
<body resource="?this">
    <h1 property="rdfs:label" />
    <form method="POST" action="" enctype=
    "application/sparql-update" resource="?this">
        <fieldset>
            <div class="control-group">
                <label for="label" class="control-label">Label</label>
                <div class="controls">
                    <input type="text" id="label" value=
    "{rdfs:label}" class="auto-expand" required="required" />
                </div>
            </div>
            <div class="control-group">
                <label for="comment" class="control-label">Comment</label>
                <div class="controls">
                    <textarea id="comment" class=
    "auto-expand">{rdfs:comment}</textarea>
                </div>
            </div>
            <div class="form-actions">
                <button type="submit" class="btn
btn-primary">Save</button>
                <button type="button"
    onclick="window.location.replace('?view')"
    class="btn">Cancel</button>
                <button type="button"
    onclick="calli.deleteResource(event)"
    class="btnbtn-danger">Delete</button>
            </div>
        </fieldset>
    </form>
</body>
</html>
```

Note the additional attribute on the `<body>` tag to refer to a particular note, as in the view template.

A text field for the label

A textarea for the comment

Additional buttons to save or cancel the edit and to delete the note

This section showed you how to create a simple Callimachus application without needing to write or read RDF directly. You did need to keep track of some RDF predicates (`rdfs:label` and `rdfs:comment`) in order to make the templates.

The following section shows you how to make a much more complicated application based on the weather application you started to develop in chapter 7.

9.4   Application: creating a web page from multiple data sources

You can extend the weather information collection app from chapter 7 to combine multiple datasets and display the results on a web page. This is a demonstration of retrieving real-world data from multiple sources on the Web, converting it into Linked Data, and making an application using it. This application applies many of the lessons you've learned in this book. You'll extend the application developed in chapter 7 by creating a good-looking web user interface for it. By the end of this section you'll have gone from existing data in CSV and XML that are available from real-world government data sources and ended up with a useful Linked Data application.

The feeds that you'll use come from two U.S. government agencies:

- U.S. Environmental Protection Agency's (EPA) SunWise program[5]
- National Oceanic and Atmospheric Administration's (NOAA) National Digital Forecast Database (NDFD)[6]

The SunWise program is a large effort by the EPA aimed at educating the public on how to protect themselves from the sun. NOAA's NDFD is a collection of digital forecasts of the most relevant weather information from field offices around the United States. This information includes everything from maximum and minimum temperatures to wave height along coastal areas.

Viewing the structure of the weather application in figure 9.13 quickly reveals its components. It comprises basic web tools and techniques including CSS, JavaScript (js/ folder), pictures (media/ folder), and XHTML (index). The bits that are new to web applications are the SPARQL queries (queries/ folder) and the weather data itself (data/folder) represented in Turtle. The landing page file is just an explanation of the application.

Some of the building blocks for this application are outside the purview of this book and therefore won't be explained in depth. For example, there's JavaScript that allows for easier rendering of the page elements and CSS that spruces up the page, but neither relates to the Linked Data aspects of the application. Please see the source code for the weather application at http:LinkedDataDeveloper.com if you're interested in those details.

9.4.1   Making and querying Linked Data from NOAA and EPA

The first step to this application is to adapt the data-collection script from chapter 7 for use with Callimachus. Because Callimachus uses Sesame as its RDF store, we'll no longer need to store the data in Fuseki. Any of the code responsible for starting, loading data into, or querying Fuseki should be removed. Now the script performs the same data retrieval but simply prints the results to an output document. You can then

---

[5]   SunWise, Sun safety for kids and educators, http://www.epa.gov/sunwise/.
[6]   National Weather Service, National Digital Forecast Database, general information, http://www.nws.noaa.gov/ndfd/.

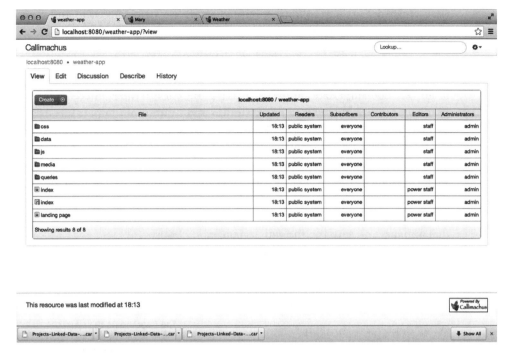

Figure 9.13 Structure of the weather application

load this document into the data directory of the weather application on Callimachus. This can be done in four steps:

1 Navigate to the data folder.
2 Select the upload button (upward-pointing arrow in a circle).
3 Click Choose File and select the output file from the script.
4 Click Upload.

You could also choose to modify the script to upload the contents of the file using the Callimachus REST API. The REST API is described in the Callimachus documentation.

Now that the data is in Callimachus, you can begin to write the supporting code that queries that data, manipulates it as needed, and renders it in the XHTML page. First, you need to extract the data you're interested in. That can be accomplished via a Callimachus feature called a Named Query. A Named Query is a SPARQL query that has been assigned a URL, so the results of the query are returned when the URL is resolved. Looking at our data you can see that there are two distinct datasets we're interested in; one is the temperature data from NOAA and the other is the UV Index data from the EPA. In order to construct a successful query, you must understand the structure of the data and how it will be used in the application. You can see that each URI is unique to the ZIP code and date level by looking at the way the URIs were constructed. The following snippet shows how the ZIP code and date are used to create a unique URI structure for the identification of this data.

```
<http://www.example.com/WeatherHealth/ZipCodes/22401/02-28-2013>
```

This structure indicates that the application must construct this URI from the user's input (ZIP code and date) and issue it as a parameter to the Named Query. You use two predicates to link that URI to its maximum and minimum temperatures: `wh:max_temp` and `wh:min_temp`. As a last step, because you don't know what the temperature's value will be, you want to assign variables to those values (`?maxTemp` and `?minTemp`) for use in the SELECT clause. Now that you have the three pieces of information you need—the subject, predicate, and object—you can construct the query. Navigate to the `queries/` directory and from the Create menu in the top left select More options, More options, then Query. You should type the contents of the following listing into the text editor that appears and save the file with a name you choose.

Listing 9.6   The weather SPARQL query

```
PREFIX rdfs: <http://www.w3.org/2000/01/rdf-schema#>
PREFIX wh: <http://www.example.com/WeatherHealth/Schema#>

SELECT ?maxTemp ?minTemp {
  <$zipDateURI> wh:max_temp ?maxTemp        ◁──
    ; wh:min_temp ?minTemp .
}
```

> The **$** symbol is the syntactic representation of a parameter. The text following the dollar sign will be used as the parameter name in the query URI.

Now you can follow a nearly identical process to create the Named Query for retrieving UV Index data, as shown in the next listing.

Listing 9.7   The UV Index SPARQL query

```
PREFIX rdfs: <http://www.w3.org/2000/01/rdf-schema#>
PREFIX wh: <http://www.example.com/WeatherHealth/Schema#>

SELECT ?value ?alert {
  <$zipDateURI> wh:uv_value ?value
    ; wh:uv_alert ?alert .
}
```

These queries (listings 9.6 and 9.7) as they stand won't return any results unless a value is passed in to satisfy the `$zipDateURI` parameter, which the rest of our application will take care of shortly.

9.4.2   Creating a web page to contain the application

From here you can begin work on index.xhtml, which contains not only HTML but also the JavaScript that will allow you to utilize the queries you just wrote. Before you start collecting data, you need the infrastructure, which will be the HTML, to hold that data on the page and the ability for users to interact with the page. The following listing shows a basic version of the HTML that will serve as the base for the weather application.

Listing 9.8 Stripped-down index.xhtml

```
<?xml version="1.0" encoding="UTF-8" ?>
<html xmlns="http://www.w3.org/1999/xhtml"
    xmlns:xsd="http://www.w3.org/2001/XMLSchema#"
    xmlns:rdf="http://www.w3.org/1999/02/22-rdf-syntax-ns#"
    xmlns:rdfs="http://www.w3.org/2000/01/rdf-schema#">
<head>
<meta charset="utf-8"/>
<title>Linked Data Health App</title>
</head>
<body>
<div id="dashboard">
<div>
<div>
    <div id="location">
<input name="zip" maxlength="5" placeholder="ZIP code" value="" />
<span>Enter a VA ZIP code above</span>
</div>
</div>
<div>
<div id="date">
            <div></div>
              <a></a>
              <a></a>
</div>
        </div>
</div>
<div id="feedback"></div>
<div>
<div>
    <div id="weather"><div>Weather</div></div>
        </div>
        <div>
            <div id="uv-index"><div>UV Index</div></div>
        </div>
        </div>
    </div>
</body>
</html>
```

You'll notice many empty tags here, but this is simply to show the structure of the page before increasing the complexity by adding CSS classes and IDs for use in JavaScript. If you want to style the page using CSS and prepare the HTML to be enhanced via JavaScript, you must add the appropriate classes and attributes to the existing tags. You also need to include the appropriate libraries for your JavaScript and CSS to function. The next listing is the fully described version of listing 9.8 and is only waiting for your custom JavaScript to be put in.

Listing 9.9 Fully described index.xhtml

```
<?xml version="1.0" encoding="UTF-8" ?>
<html xmlns="http://www.w3.org/1999/xhtml"
```

```
    xmlns:xsd="http://www.w3.org/2001/XMLSchema#"
    xmlns:rdf="http://www.w3.org/1999/02/22-rdf-syntax-ns#"
    xmlns:rdfs="http://www.w3.org/2000/01/rdf-schema#">
<head>
<meta charset="utf-8"/>
<title>Linked Data Health App</title>
<style type="text/css" media="all">
@import url(css/bootstrap.min.css);
    @import url(css/weatherhealth.css);
</style>
<script type="text/javascript" src="js/jquery.min.js"></script>
<script type="text/javascript" src="js/date.js"></script>
<script type="text/javascript" src="https://www.google.com/jsapi"></script>
</head>
<body>
<div id="dashboard">
<div class="grid-row location-date">
<div class="w1">
    <div id="location">
<input name="zip" maxlength="5" placeholder="ZIP code" value="" />
<span class="info">Enter a VA ZIP code above</span>
            </div>
</div>
<div class="w1 ml2">
<div id="date">
            <div class="active"></div>
              <a class="alt-1"></a>
              <a class="alt-2"></a>
</div>
            </div>
</div>
<div id="feedback" class="alert alert-info"></div>
<div class="grid-row data" style="margin-left: 200px; margin-right: 200px;">   ◁───┐
<div id="weatherPopover" class="w2" rel="popover" data-placement="top" data-     │
    original-title="Source: NOAA" data-content=                                 │
➡    "This data is provided and published by the National Oceanic              │
➡    and Atmospheric Association (NOAA).">                                      │
        <div id="weather" class="tile"><div class="title">Weather</div></div>  │
          </div>                                                                │
        <div id="uvIndexPopover" class="w2" rel="popover"                       │
➡    data-placement="top" data-original-title="Source: US EPA SunWise">    ◁──┘
            <div id="uv-index" class="tile">
➡    <div class="title">UV Index</div></div>
          </div>
          </div>
      </div>
    <script type="text/javascript" src="js/weatherhealth.js"></script>
<script type="text/javascript" src="js/bootstrap.min.js"></script>
</body>
</html>
```

> **The attributes rel, data-placement, and data-original-title are used for the popover.**

9.4.3   *Creating JavaScript to retrieve and display Linked Data*

Now with the infrastructure in place you can begin to add the JavaScript that will give the page its functionality. The key bit of code uses Google's Visualization API to issue a query and load the results into a variable for manipulation and presentation. The specific function is `google` `.visualization.Query`.

You'll first create the box showing today's high and low temperatures, as shown in figure 9.14. Listing 9.10 uses that API call to execute the query you wrote in listing 9.6 and return the results for manipulation.

Figure 9.14   The temperature box

Listing 9.10   The temperature data-retrieval function

```
function getWeatherData(queryURI) {
google.load("visualization", "1.0", {callback:function() {
new google.visualization.Query("queries/weather.rq?resul
    ts&zipDateURI=" + queryURI).send(
        function(result){
            var data = result.getDataTable();
var rows = data.getNumberOfRows();
if (rows > 0) {
    for (var i=0; i<rows; i++) {
var maxTemp = data.getValue(i,0);
var minTemp = data.getValue(i,1);

wh.renderWeather({value: maxTemp + "&#176;F / " + minTemp + "&#176;F" })
    }
} else {
        wh.renderWeather({value: 'N/A'})
    }
}
);
}});
}
```

Include the appropriate path to the query and structure for passing parameters.

Assign temperature values to maxTemp and minTemp for use throughout the function.

JavaScript function renderWeather() allows for easy display of contents inside the weather tile, and ° is the HTML character encoding for the degrees symbol.

Next, you'll create the box showing today's UV index, as shown in figure 9.15. Listing 9.11 uses the same API call to execute the query written in listing 9.7. You'll then write some custom JavaScript to interpret this data and translate it for interpretation by the CSS definitions.

Figure 9.15   The UV Index box

Listing 9.11   The UV Index data retrieval function

```
function getUVIndexData(queryURI) {
google.load("visualization", "1.0", {callback:function() {
      new google.visualization.Query(
    "queries/uvindex.rq?results&zipDateURI=" + queryURI).send(
function(result){
```

```
var data = result.getDataTable();
var rows = data.getNumberOfRows();
var severity;
for (var i=0; i<rows; i++) {
var index = data.getValue(i,0);
var alert = data.getValue(i,1);

if (index >= 1 && index <= 2) {
    severity = 1;
} else if (index >= 3 && index <= 5) {
    severity = 2;
} else if (index >= 6 && index <= 7) {
    severity = 3;
} else if (index >= 8 && index <= 10) {
    severity = 4;
} else if (index >= 11) {
severity = 5;
} else {
    severity = 0;
}

if (index != "" && index != null && alert != "" && alert != null) {
wh.renderUvIndex({value: index + ' <small>out of 11</small>',
    info: 'Alert: ' + alert, severity: severity })
} else {
wh.renderUvIndex({value: 'N/A', info: 'Unavailable', severity: 0 })
        }
}
}
);
    }});
}
```

Depending on UV index returned, assign appropriate severity level for CSS rules

The functions defined in listings 9.10 and 9.11 are fundamental to the application but need another function to control them and pass in the appropriate parameter. This is done through the construction of an onChange function. The next listing shows this function and how little code is needed here.

Listing 9.12   Function control JavaScript

```
$('body').on('locationChange dateChange', function() {
var queryURI =
    "http://www.example.com/WeatherHealth/ZipCodes/"
    + wh.getLocation() + "/" + wh.getDate();

wh.feedback('The location is ' + wh.getLocation() +
    '. The date is ' + wh.getDate() + '.');

getWeatherData(queryURI);
getUVIndexData(queryURI);
});
```

Build the query string using the user-entered ZIP code and user-selected date.

Show the feedback message to the user displaying the ZIP code and date.

Run the respective JavaScript functions to retrieve weather and UV index data.

9.4.4 Bringing it all together

Now you have a number of snippets of code that all serve their own unique purpose, and it may be a bit tough to keep track of them all, so let's summarize what you've done and how the pieces fit together.

1   Write queries to extract the data you're interested in (listings 9.6 and 9.7).
2   Write the HTML to hold the data you want to display (listings 9.8 and 9.9).
3   Write the JavaScript you need to drive functionality (listings 9.10, 9.11, and 9.12).
4   Put it all together (listing 9.13 and figure 9.16).

The following listing shows the entirety of index.xhtml and includes all relevant JavaScript.

Listing 9.13   Complete index.xhtml

```
<?xml version="1.0" encoding="UTF-8" ?>
<html xmlns="http://www.w3.org/1999/xhtml"
    xmlns:xsd="http://www.w3.org/2001/XMLSchema#"
    xmlns:rdf="http://www.w3.org/1999/02/22-rdf-syntax-ns#"
    xmlns:rdfs="http://www.w3.org/2000/01/rdf-schema#">
<head>
<meta charset="utf-8"/>
<title>Linked Data Health App</title>
<style type="text/css" media="all">
    @import url(css/bootstrap.min.css);
    @import url(css/weatherhealth.css);
</style>
<script type="text/javascript" src="js/jquery.min.js"></script>
<script type="text/javascript" src="js/date.js"></script>
<script type="text/javascript" src="https://www.google.com/jsapi"></script>
<script>
// <![CDATA[
function getWeatherData(queryURI) {
        google.load("visualization", "1.0", {callback:function() {
          new google.visualization.Query("queries/
      weather.rq?results&zipDateURI=
➥     " + queryURI).send(
function(result){
var data = result.getDataTable();
var rows = data.getNumberOfRows();
if (rows > 0) {
for (var i=0; i<rows; i++) {
var maxTemp = data.getValue(i,0);
var minTemp = data.getValue(i,1);

wh.renderWeather({value: maxTemp + "&#176;F / " + minTemp + "&#176;F" })
}
} else {
wh.renderWeather({value: 'N/A'})
} // Close else
}
        );
```

```
}});
}

function getUVIndexData(queryURI) {
google.load("visualization", "1.0", {callback:function() {
        new google.visualization.Query(
➡   "queries/uvindex.rq?results&zipDateURI=" + queryURI).send
➡   (function(result){
var data = result.getDataTable();
var rows = data.getNumberOfRows();
var severity;
for (var i=0; i<rows; i++) {
var index = data.getValue(i,0);
var alert = data.getValue(i,1);

if (index >= 1 && index <= 2) {
severity = 1;
} else if (index >= 3 && index <= 5) {
    severity = 2;
} else if (index >= 6 && index <= 7) {
    severity = 3;
} else if (index >= 8 && index <= 10) {
    severity = 4;
} else if (index >= 11) {
    severity = 5;
} else {
    severity = 0;
}

if (index != "" && index != null && alert != "" && alert != null) {
    wh.renderUvIndex({value: index + ' <small>out of 11</small>',
➡   info: 'Alert: ' + alert, severity: severity })
} else {
    wh.renderUvIndex({value: 'N/A', info: 'Unavailable', severity: 0 })
}
}
}
);
}});
}
// ]]>
</script>
</head>
<body>
<div id="dashboard">
<div class="grid-row location-date">
<div class="w1">
    <div id="location">
<input name="zip" maxlength="5" placeholder="ZIP code" value="" />
<span class="info">Enter a VA ZIP code above</span>
            </div>
</div>
<div class="w1 ml2">
<div id="date">
            <div class="active"></div>
```

```
                <a class="alt-1"></a>
                <a class="alt-2"></a>
    </div>
            </div>
    </div>
    <div id="feedback" class="alert alert-info"></div>
    <div class="grid-row data" style="margin-left: 200px;
➥    margin-right: 200px;">
    <div id="weatherPopover" class="w2" rel="popover" data-placement=
➥    "top" data-original-title="Source: NOAA" data-content=
➥    "This data is provided and published by the National Oceanic
➥    and Atmospheric Association (NOAA).">
        <div id="weather" class="tile"><div class="title">Weather</div></div>
            </div>
            <div id="uvIndexPopover" class="w2" rel="popover"
➥    data-placement="top" data-original-title="Source: US EPA SunWise">
                <div id="uv-index" class="tile"><div class="title">
➥    UV Index</div></div>
            </div>
            </div>
        </div>
        <script type="text/javascript" src="js/weatherhealth.js"></script>
    <script type="text/javascript" src="js/bootstrap.min.js"></script>
    <script>
    // <![CDATA[
    $('body').on('locationChange dateChange', function() {
    var queryURI =
➥    "http://www.example.com/WeatherHealth/ZipCodes/" +
➥    wh.getLocation() + "/" + wh.getDate();

    wh.feedback('The location is ' + wh.getLocation() +
➥    '. The date is ' + wh.getDate() + '.');

    getWeatherData(queryURI);
    getUVIndexData(queryURI);
    });
```

Assign popover functionality to weather tile.

```
    $('#weatherPopover').popover({trigger: 'hover'})
    $('#uvIndexPopover').popover({trigger: 'hover', html: true,
    content: function () {
    return 'This data is published by the US EPA SunWise Program. <img
        src="media/uvindexscale.gif" />';
        }
    })
    // ]]>
    </script>
    </body>
    </html>
```

Display image inside popover.

In a relatively short amount of time and with a small amount of code, you've created a very powerful application. You've now successfully retrieved authoritative government data, turned it into Linked Data, aggregated it easily thanks to the advantages of RDF, and displayed it in an attractive interactive web page for public consumption.

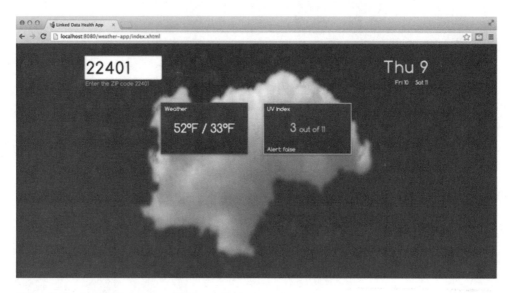

Figure 9.16   Screenshot of the weather application

A live, working example of this application can be found at http://purl.org/net/
LinkedData/WeatherApp.

9.5   *Summary*

This chapter introduced the Callimachus Project, an open source application server
for Linked Data. We showed you how to get started with Callimachus, how to generate
web pages from RDF data, and how to build some applications using it.

We covered three types of Callimachus templates: view, create, and edit. We
showed you how to use those templates to create a Linked Data note-taking application and discussed how to modify it to make it more interesting.

We walked you through an extension of the weather application originally presented in chapter 7. This new weather application looks nice and has functionality you
can actually use. It's based on the RDF data you created from data feeds at a couple of
open data sites provided by the U.S. government.

Don't forget that you can see these applications running and get digital versions of
the source code at the book's companion site, LinkedDataDeveloper.com.

10

Publishing Linked Data—a recap

This chapter covers

- A summary of publishing Linked Data

In this chapter, we'll capture the process of publishing Linked Data from preparation to public publication and highlight critical steps in this process. You want to publish your data using the RDF data model because it is the international standard for representing data on the Web. You want to use the Linked Data principles to describe your data so others can find and reuse it more easily. There are many serialization formats (as described in chapter 2) but only one data model. This standardized model then enables data sources to be

- Easily crawled by search engines
- Accessed using generic data browsers
- Easily integrated with other data from diverse data sources
- Expressed using different schemata
- Expressed using different serialization formats
- Explored by following URIs to additional information
- Published on the Web and easily shared

We've examined each of the steps of this process in previous chapters. But sometimes seeing the big picture is difficult when you're learning individual steps. In this section, we're going to focus on the sequence of steps you'd follow to publish Linked Data. As always, we'll be employing Linked Data publishing best practices, which encompass the Linked Data principles. These principles provide a framework for publishing and consuming data on the Web but don't provide implementation details. The implementation steps are:

1. Prepare your data.
2. Interlink your data to other datasets.
3. Publish your data.

10.1   *Preparing your data*

Prepare your data by transforming data from its existing non-RDF format into one of the RDF formats. You can choose the easiest format for your task, as presented in chapter 2. The transformation is likely to necessitate minting URIs, selecting appropriate vocabularies, and saving the data in your chosen RDF format. Chapters 4, 5, and 6 showed you how to perform those steps.

The final step is deciding which format to use. The most popular choices of serialization formats are RDF/XML, Turtle, RDF/JSON, and RDFa. Don't forget to validate your data and correct any errors prior to exposure. You may choose to store your dataset in an RDF database (chapter 7). The use of an RDF database facilitates SPARQL access to your data.

Chapters 1 and 2 address the Linked Data principles as proposed by Tim Berners-Lee, the inventor of the Web. These principles are:

- Use URIs as names for things.
- Use HTTP URIs so that people can look up those names.
- When someone looks up a URI, provide useful information, using the standards (RDF*, SPARQL).[1]
- Include links to other URIs, so that users can discover more things.

The quality of your data is dependent on you following these principles. Tim Berners-Lee at Gov 2.0 Expo 2010 during his "Open, Linked Data for a Global Community" presentation proposed this quality of data, as depicted in figure 10.1.

Your goal should be to do your best to publish 5-Star data. The process of publishing your data on the Web is multifaceted. In the next sections, we'd like to reinforce some details that we want to be sure you don't overlook.

---

[1]   The term RDF* is sometimes used to refer to the entire family of RDF standards.

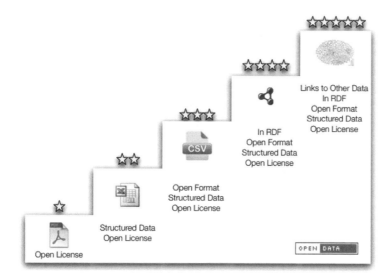

Figure 10.1
5-Star data

10.2 Minting URIs

In brief, you mint URIs by assigning URIs to the resources that you wish to describe. These URIs facilitate two aspects of Linked Data. First, they act as globally unique names for the things you want to describe, and second, by using HTTP URIs, they provide an easy way to link to and access each description online. As we discussed in chapter 2, you need to define your URIs within a publicly accessible HTTP namespace under your control. Use URIs that can be referenced. Avoid exposing implementation details in your URIs. Use short, mnemonic names. You need your URIs to be stable and persistent. Changing your URIs later will break any established links, so devote extra thought to them during the preparation phase.

To prevent problems and confusion in publishing your data, it's beneficial to decide how URIs should be constructed. There are many approaches to structuring URIs and several pros and cons for each. These have been taken into account in the patterns suggested here.

Many of our URIs fall into the following pattern:

```
http://{authority}/{container}/{item_key}
```

- The `authority` part is generally a DNS machine name, optionally with a port. This is necessary for your URL to resolve on the Web. If you're worried about the machine name changing, you might want to use a persistent URL (PURL) instead.
- The `container` part allows you to keep keys separate to each context, avoiding clashes where a number is, for example, an identifier that was originally used in a relational database. Example containers might be `"addresses"`, `"facilities"`, `"people"`, or `"books"`. Naturally, you could use nested containers if you like (such as `/offices/US/NewYork/`).

- The `item` key uniquely identifies a specific resource within that container. For the `item` key you should use clear, human-readable, natural keys that facilitate easy linking by others. So, if your `container` is an address, the `item` key might be a string made up of the address components such as the building number, street name, city, and so on. For people it might be a name. All `item` keys that use natural keys should be URL encoded, of course, or (better yet) just replace spaces with hyphens or something equally readable.

Keep in mind that for each URI pattern you're making three key decisions:

- What is a suitable container name?
- Should the resource be at the root of the data or nested within something else?
- What should form the item's key?

These decisions play a key role in ensuring that URI patterns are robust and allow for extension later.

10.3 *Selecting vocabularies*

Selecting appropriate vocabularies can be challenging. We recommend that you think about the kind of information you're representing. What are you trying to represent? Is it a person? Is it an event? Try to find an existing vocabulary that meets your needs. You want your data to be easily interlinked with other datasets so you need to reuse common vocabularies as much as possible. Table 10.1 contains references to selected vocabularies along with the associated category indicating which terms are best described by those vocabularies. See chapter 2 for a more comprehensive list of common vocabularies. If none of the available vocabularies are sufficient, then try to extend an existing vocabulary rather than creating a vocabulary from scratch.

Table 10.1 Selected vocabularies by category

Groupings	Common vocabularies
Person related	FOAF (http://smlns.com/foaf/0.1/) vCard (http://www.w3.org/2006/vcard/ns#) Relationship (http://purl.org/vocab/relationship)
General purpose	RDF Core (http://www.w3.org/1999/02/22-rdf-syntax-ns#) RDF Schema (http://www.w3.org/2000/01/rdf-schema#) Schema.org (http://schema.org)
Knowledge organization	Simple Knowledge Organization System (http://www.w3.org/2004/02/skos/core#)
Spatial (location)	Basic Geo (http://www.w3.org/2003/01/geo/)
Temporal (things and events)	Dublin Core (http://dublincore.org/documents/dcmi-terms/) Event Ontology (http://purl.org/NET/c4dm/event.owl)
E-commerce	GoodRelations (http://purl.org/goodrelations/v1#)
Graph object	Open Graph Protocol Vocabulary (http://ogp.me/ns#)

Table 10.1 Selected vocabularies by category *(continued)*

Groupings	Common vocabularies
Datasets	VoID (http://rdfs.org/ns/void#)
Open source projects	DOAP (http://usefulinc.com/ns/doap#)
Sitemaps	Sitemaps 0.9 (http://www.sitemaps.org/schemas/sitemap/0.9)

10.4 Customizing vocabulary

When you can't find a vocabulary that fulfills your needs, you can create a customized vocabulary (chapters 2 and 4). We recommend creating an RDF vocabulary. You should consider using a tool like Neologism (http://neologism.deri.ie) to help create and publish your vocabulary. Regardless of method of creation, be sure to pay attention to these guidelines:

- Avoid defining a new vocabulary from scratch, but try to extend an existing vocabulary by publishing terms in a namespace you control.
- Liberally add `rdfs:comments` for each term invented, and always provide an `rdfs:label` property. This will provide for both people and machine consumption.
- Make term URIs referenceable and follow the W3C Best Practice Recipes for Publishing RDF Vocabularies (http://www.w3.org/TR/swbp-vocab-pub/).
- Make use of existing terms or provide mappings to them using `rdfs:subClassOf` or `rdfs:subPropertyOf`.
- Explicitly state all ranges and domains for predicates.

  Here's an example:

  ```
  tri:reporting_year
  rdf:type rdf:Property ;
  rdfs:label "reporting year" ;
  rdfs:comment "Indicates a year when a TRI Report was submitted to the U.S.
      EPA's Toxic Release Inventory system." ;
  rdfs:domain tri:Report ;
  rdfs:range rdfs:Literal .
  ```

10.5 Interlinking your data to other datasets

You can discover other datasets for interlinking by the follow-your-nose method, using a semantic indexer such as Sindice, employing `owl:sameAs`, `rdfs:subClassOf`, or `rdfs:subPropertyOf`, and locating related datasets using SPARQL. Recall that you want to interlink datasets because this aids in the discovery of your data by others and positions your dataset within the Web of Data. These tools and techniques are discussed in chapters 4, 5, 6, and 8.

Be sure to verify by examination or query that the datasets you discovered are indeed relevant and related to your data. Document your dataset by preparing a VoID file (chapter 8) that includes triples that interlink your data with that of others and publish it in the same DNS as your dataset. You should prepare a semantic sitemap (chapter 8) that describes your dataset and publish it in the same DNS as your dataset. Pay special attention to licensing issues, and ensure that you license your data in accordance with how you prefer to share it with others. Proper licensing ensures that others will understand how they may reuse your data.

10.6 *Publishing your data*

Publishing your data can be as simple as storing it in a publicly accessible DNS and ensuring the appropriate permissions are set. If desired and appropriate, you can publish your dataset on the LOD cloud, join Data Hub, register your dataset (chapter 8), and request outgoing links from DBpedia to your dataset. Improving the visibility of your dataset by interlinking and registering it on the LOD cloud facilitates sharing your data with others.

10.7 *Summary*

We've highlighted the process of publishing Linked Data from preparation to public publication. We've identified and tried to clarify easily overlooked steps like minting URIs and customizing vocabularies. We hope that you will find this a helpful reference as you prepare your own datasets for publication.

The evolving Web

11

This chapter covers
- Linked Data and the evolving Web—current state
- Linked Data and the evolving Web—future directions

In our closing chapter, we'll survey the current state of the Semantic Web and the role of Linked Data. We'll identify interesting applications of Linked Data. We'll attempt to predict the direction the Semantic Web and Linked Data will take and look at some emerging applications.

11.1 The relationship between Linked Data and the Semantic Web

Many people assume that the evolving Web of Data is synonymous with the Semantic Web. That's a bit misleading. The original World Wide Web as envisioned by Tim Berners-Lee had semantic hyperlinks. In other words, each hyperlink had meaning. One hyperlink might lead to information about the author of a web page, and another might lead to a description of a particular service. But that's not how the Web evolved. For most of its two decades of existence, hyperlinks on the Web were without any particular meaning. The best that we could say about them was that they meant "look over here."

By the time the term *Semantic Web* was coined in 1999, the discussion was around software agents that would use structured data and artificial intelligence to perform actions on your behalf, such as making a dental appointment or ordering your groceries.[1] We know that hasn't happened yet. Instead, the Web has evolved in different directions. The Web of Data, and specifically Linked Data as envisioned by Tim Berners-Lee in 2005, has grown tremendously. The Linking Open Data project has managed to create a lot of structured data on the Web, and that data is being used in useful ways. Linked Data is as essential to today's Web of Data as hypertext is to the Web of Documents.

The Semantic Web was originally envisioned as an iteration, or evolution, of the World Wide Web in which computers would be able to perform many functions for us automatically by way of understanding shared, structured data. Tim Berners-Lee articulated this vision at the XML-2000 Conference in Washington, D.C., in December 2000. Figure 11.1 illustrates his formulation.

Structured data in the form of RDF would be serialized in an XML format (RDF/XML). The data could be described via various ontologies, and the resulting highly organized information could be reasoned over with a logic engine to produce new, meaningful information that was logically inferred from the underlying statements. This was a vision strong on traditional artificial intelligence techniques that was distributed across the Web. Further, individual data documents would be signed using public-key cryptography methods to allow computers to verify who was claiming what.

We might indeed be able to schedule dentist appointments automatically or have our computers purchase movie tickets for us with a minimum of direction if the Semantic Web had developed that way. But several things about this idea turned out to be rather optimistic. Some of the more obvious ones included the difficulties in combining this vision with deployed information-management technologies; the small number of people who had the skills to build the complicated tools needed; the complexity of the RDF/XML syntax, which hindered adoption; and the difficulties in distributing cryptographic

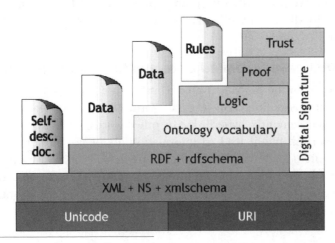

Figure 11.1   The Semantic Web "layer cake" as presented by Tim Berners-Lee, 2000

---

[1] Tim Berners-Lee, et al., "The Semantic Web [Preview]," *Scientific American*, May 17, 2001, http://www.scientificamerican.com/article.cfm?id=the-semantic-web.

keys between individuals and companies. Perhaps more damaging was the lack of a simple, consistent, and easily implementable set of use cases for the idea. Most people just didn't "get it" and were only vaguely interested in having their computers schedule dental appointments for them anyway.

The Semantic Web has not, however, died. It has morphed into several directions as the underlying concepts have been applied to specific problems. Semantics are now a part of mainstream life, at least in the technology-rich parts of the world, and are used daily by people whenever they use Apple's Siri, see Google search results, or "like" a web page. More specialized semantic products assist organizations with information management, inventory control, data collection, and business workflows.

Figure 11.2 illustrates the fragmentation of the Semantic Web and suggests how people pick and choose parts of the technology stack to solve specific problems. Few use all of the possible techniques at once. Even the foundation layers have changed to allow for the internationalization of the Web and deemphasize XML in favor of simpler syntaxes.

We should note that throughout these changes, the data model has remained wholly RDF. The reasons for this are clear: modern computing allows us to operate on a graph data model that more closely resembles the complexity of the real world and the inner workings of the human brain. We're no longer forced to think in hierarchies because of the limitations of our technology. We don't expect that situation to change. Instead, we expect a data model close to or evolving from RDF to become

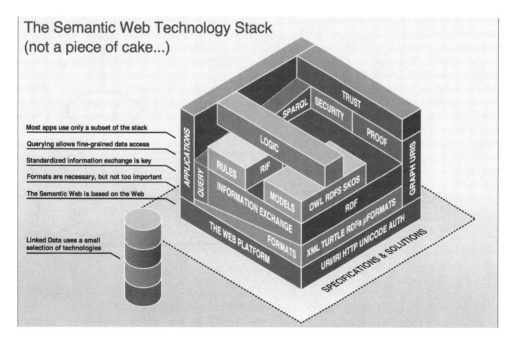

Figure 11.2   Semantic Web—Current State, courtesy of Benjamin Nowack (http://www.bnode.org/). For a full color version of the figure, see http://linkeddatadeveloper.com/Projects/Linked-Data/media/ fig11.2.png.

more important to our society as time passes. After all, the Web is our global repository of knowledge, and it is itself a graph of information.

When you look more closely at figure 11.2 you'll see a small column to the left of the main figure. That column represents the small subset of Semantic Web techniques that are used for Linked Data. Linked Data is built strictly on the Web, uses various RDF formats and the RDF data model, and has a model (the Linked Data principles) layered on top to make it do what we wish it to do. Figure 11.3 visually diagrams the relationships among the Semantic Web, RDF, and various structured data formats. This diagram emphasizes that

- Linked Data is a subset of Semantic Web techniques.
- Linked Data is built upon RDF.
- Structured data includes more than just RDF.
- Schema.org supports two techniques, one of which is Microdata and the other is RDFa.

You're naturally free to bring other parts of the Semantic Web stack to bear on your Linked Data. You may, if you wish, query it with SPARQL, apply rules or a logic engine, cryptographically sign and verify your documents, or build applications on it. But you don't have to do any of this. Linked Data is simple in nature. That, coupled with its clear use cases, is perhaps why it's valuable.

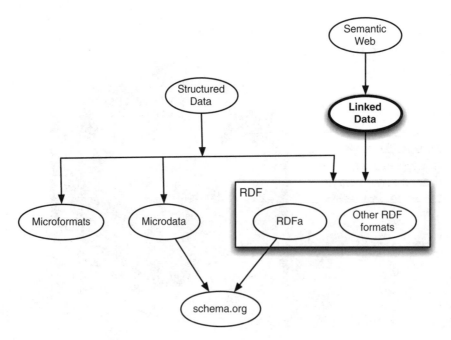

Figure 11.3 The structured data ecosystem

11.1.1 Demonstrated successes

Some of the demonstrated successes of Linked Data are Google rich snippets; schema.org's adoption of RDFa Lite and the GoodRelations vocabulary; increasing use of RDFa in the web pages of companies like Best Buy and Sears; Data.gov; and the continuing growth of the LOD cloud. These successes are difficult to see because Linked Data is "under the hood."

ADOPTION OF RDFA LITE BY SCHEMA.ORG

Search engines exploit semantic data when generating search results. The recent collaboration by Bing, Google, and Yahoo! in forming schema.org demonstrates support for structured data on the Web. As we addressed in chapter 6, schema.org provides schemas for many common domains (http://schema.org/docs/gs.html). Its recent adoption of RDFa Lite further supports the facilitation of sharing data through compatible formats. This adoption is an acknowledgment of the importance of RDFa.

GOOGLE RICH SNIPPETS

Google rich snippets support RDFa along with microformats (http://microformats.org/) and Microdata; see figure 11.3. Rich snippets technology supports numerous vocabularies including GoodRelations and RDF Data Vocabulary (http://rdf.data-vocabulary.org). Many companies are creating rich snippets–enabled pages and benefitting from a higher click-through rate in search results. Websites that don't employ rich snippets may suffer significant sales losses by dropping a position in their search rankings.

PROLIFERATION OF KNOWLEDGE BASES FOR SEARCH ENGINE EXPLOITATION

A knowledge base is an information repository that enables information to be collected, organized, shared, searched, and utilized. It can be either machine-readable or intended for human use. MusicBrainz is one such knowledge base. The major search engines support knowledge bases in specific domains. Bing supports knowledge bases in entertainment, sports, and travel domains. Google through its acquisition of Freebase (http://www.freebase.com) supports Linked Open Data. Google's use of Linked Data extends beyond Freebase. In May 2012, it introduced its Knowledge Graph (http://googleblog.blogspot.co.uk/2012/05/introducing-knowledge-graph-things-not.html). The basis of the Knowledge Graph is the accumulated information about the searches, query sessions, and clicks that searchers perform on the Web each day. Research in this area is ongoing, as evidenced by Microsoft being granted a patent in November 2012 for its process of collecting data on underserved queries.

GROWTH IN THE LINKING OPEN DATA CLOUD

The number of datasets published on the Linking Open Data cloud has grown by a factor of two every year since its inception in 2007. DataHub.io provides a synopsis of the growth of this arena. Perhaps the growth is more apparent when you realize that the Linking Open Data cloud contains more than 31 billion triples. This number grows every day. Table 11.1 contains a summary of some of the more prominent datasets recognized by DataHub.io. There are more than 5,165 datasets as of this writing.

Table 11.1   Selected Linking Open Data datasets

Source	URL
Bioportal	http://datahub.io/group/bioportal
Canadian, citizen-led effort to promote open data	http://www.datadotgc.ca/
Economics	http://datahub.io/group/economics
Linking Open Data cloud	http://datahub.io/group/lodcloud

FACEBOOK'S USE OF RDFA AND ITS CREATION OF RDF DATA

Facebook's Like button generates two sets of RDF triples each time a Like button is clicked. One set is sent to Facebook for its database, and the other set is sent to the company displaying the page. In additional support of Linked Data, Facebook is embedding RDFa using its Open Graph Protocol in company Facebook pages.

USE OF RDFA AND GOODRELATIONS

More and more companies are following Best Buy's example and embedding RDFa in their web pages. Many of these companies are employing the GoodRelations vocabulary to do this. Prominent companies utilizing RDFa include Google, Sears, Kmart, and Facebook. The adoption of this vocabulary by schema.org will further proliferate its use.

OPEN GOVERNMENT DATA

The goal and focus of open government data (OGD) is to facilitate the sharing of machine-readable datasets covering government activity. This is an international effort with the four largest sites being www.data.gov (U.S.), www.data.gov.uk (UK), www.data.gouv.fr (France), and www.data.gov.sg (Singapore.) A list of datasets and catalogs can be found at http://logd.tw.rpi.edu/demo/international_dataset_catalog_search.

Governments prefer releasing data through OGD portals because it is less costly than publishing reports. These sets are often heterogeneous structures and formats (not 5-Star data).

Semantic Community (http://semantic.data.gov) provides support on the use of Linked Data and Semantic Web technologies to improve your ability to use data from http://www.data.gov. You can participate in collaborative government data access, aggregate data from different agencies, transform the raw data into RDF, customize applications, and provide feedback to enhance the quality of published data. www.data.gov enables access to more than 400,000 datasets from 185 U.S. government organizations. The newest communities can be found at www.health.data.gov, www.energy.data.gov, www.law.data.gov, and www.education.data.gov. Open Linked Data is being used in the health and energy sectors. OGD and semantic.data.gov are active initiatives that provide useful information to consumers and the broader community. These organizations have many opportunities for community involvement in providing improved access to available data and the development of specific applications. In fact, the application in chapter 7 accesses and aggregates both EPA and NOAA data from this repository of open government data.

11.2 What's coming

In the early 1990s, we were eager to publish and share documents. Now we're eager to share data. We can see that data is all around us. If we could share that data more easily and integrate large, disparate datasets, there could be huge benefits, and Linked Data is able to fulfill this need. We think it's interesting and relevant to note that semantic technologies have begun to permeate many industries and even consumer products.

Semantic Web technologies are used in situations as diverse as Apple's Siri, IBM's Watson, Google's Knowledge Graph, Facebook's Entity Graph, financial systems, online payment systems, NASA inventory systems, workflows for publishers, drug discovery at pharmaceutical companies, cancer research, government transparency publications, and so on.

In other words, semantic technology is very horizontal. Now, what does that say about Linked Data? Our guess is that it's becoming the basis by which we'll soften (probably not "break") silos on the various social networks. Users clearly want to share data between Google+, Facebook, and Twitter as well as new market entrants that we don't know about yet. These networks have a cross-domain data interoperability problem, and Linked Data is currently the best tool we have to address that problem.

Future uses of Linked Data are already in the planning stages. It's apparent to us that the future of Linked Data will extend well beyond the research community. Here are a few examples.

11.2.1 Google extended rich snippets

Rich snippets are currently displayed based on the content of a single web page. Future extended rich snippets could combine data from multiple sources. The model for this application is called Content-Centric Networking and would employ RDF triples. The resulting rich snippets may contain embedded video, lists of others who are attending an event, and locations where a movie is being shown. Experiments have already demonstrated that Content-Centric Networking is useful when many parties are interested in the same content. This could be fueled by web-scale triple propagation for popular web pages.

11.2.2 Digital accountability and transparency legislation

A future application of the Open Government Data resources would help the United States optimize its federal spending. The Digital Accountability and Transparency Act was considered by the U.S. Congress. Unfortunately, this legislation didn't pass, but it did raise interest and awareness. We'd expect similar legislation to be under consideration in the near future. This act would have established an independent board that would track all federal spending. The sponsors of the 2012 bill, Rep. Darrell Issa of California and Sen. Mark Warner of Virginia, believe such a bill could prevent waste and abuse of federal money. Teradata of Dayton, Ohio, one of the private-sector parties interested in this arena, suggested consolidating datasets from across several federal agencies. This aggregated data could then be analyzed and reviewed. They expect such data would expose abuses in the federal procurement system. Teradata's system is, at the time of this writing, being used in Arizona, Iowa, Maryland, Michigan, Missouri, New Jersey, Ohio, Oklahoma, and Texas, with $1.8 billion recovered.

11.2.3 *Impact of advertising*

In 2011, Facebook realized $3.1 billion in ad revenue for the year. Analysts expect that in 2012, Facebook's ad revenue will have grown to $5.06 billion. Linked Data plays a large role in supporting this effort. The RDF accumulated from Like button clicks can be analyzed so that advertisers can hit their target audience. Similarly, by aggregating and analyzing the data of your browsing habits, advertisers can identify potential customers. Look for more activity in this area.

11.2.4 *Enhanced searches*

Both Google and Facebook are building knowledge bases in preparation for the next-generation search engine. We expect that the next-generation search engine will understand the concepts behind the queries and anticipate what you need before you're able to articulate it. Facebook's Entity Graph and Google's Knowledge Graph are actively acquiring data.

Facebook's Entity Graph is vital to the success of Facebook's Graph Search service. This service isn't yet universally available. Unlike a conventional search engine, Graph Search is designed to understand the meaning of the phrases entered by a searcher and deliver specific results. The results are people, places, books, or movies rather than links to web pages. The Entity Graph describes everything from the restaurants of New York to the concepts of philosophy and the connections between those concepts. Facebook is relying on people for contribution of the data as well as its accuracy. By prompting you to tag duplicate content, Facebook's Entity Graph has "learned" the different ways people refer to the same thing—for example, that NPR and National Public Radio refer to the same thing.

Conventional search engines are based on matching words and phrases and not what the terms actually mean. The Knowledge Graph is a vast database that allows Google's software to identify relationships among data on people, places, and things. Google's Knowledge Graph contains more than 500 million entries, with more than 3.5 billion links among them.

Although Google and Facebook are building their knowledge bases in different ways, both knowledge bases represent Linked Data. Both Google and Facebook are interested in the same result, the next-generation search engine.

11.2.5 *Participation by the big guys*

Large enterprises like IBM, EMC, Oracle, and other large software vendors are currently participating in the Linked Data Platform Working Group at the W3C. In fact, IBM is one of the co-chairs. They're helping to define a common RESTful web services API for the interoperability of enterprise software products. You can find background information on the RESTful web services (API) at http://www.ibm.com/developer-works/webservices/library/ws-restful/.

IBM supports Linked Data in a number of their products. For instance, DB2 version 10 provides support for RDF with a SPARQL engine on top of DB2. EMC uses Linked Data technology in its Big Data open source RDF database platform. Oracle brought an RDF Store to the market as an optional feature in the Enterprise Edition of 11g. These companies are interested in participating on the Linked Data Platform Working Group to enumerate the necessary standards and provide guidance on conventions and good practices. Involvement and agreement from companies like IBM, EMC, and Oracle will simplify deployment by reducing options and increasing interoperability. Defining standards will help the Linked Data community move forward.

11.3 *Conclusion*

Linked Data is being used beyond the LOD cloud, and it's becoming the basis for data sharing in many contexts. We expect that our own interactions with data on the Web will evolve along with new contexts for data sharing. Our belief is that there is no Semantic Web per se, as envisioned by Tim Berners-Lee, et al., nor will there ever be. Instead, we see the Web constantly evolving to include more semantics. Right now we have strong semantics in the hyperlinks used in Linked Data. Hyperlinks in RDF have meaning, and they can both name and define relationships between resources on the Web. Perhaps the future will see those semantics being used more by web browsers and thus enter the mainstream. Only time will tell.

appendix A
Development environments

This appendix covers information regarding setting up the tools and packages used by the examples in this book:

- cURL
- Python
- ARQ
- Fuseki
- Callimachus

A.1   cURL

cURL, a command-line tool for getting or sending files using URL syntax, is a true open source/free software tool that you can modify and redistribute. You may also freely use cURL in your commercial projects. cURL is licensed under an MIT/X derivate license. To download a copy of cURL, point your browser to http://cURL.haxx.se/dlwiz/. We recommend that you select one of the cURL executable packages. Select the curl executable link. This will take you to a site where you can select your OS of choice and download a prebuilt cURL binary for your system. Download and extract the source provided. Be sure to note the path to curl.exe because you may need to navigate to it later. Here are some commands that you might try to ensure that your installation is functioning properly:

- `man curl`—Displays the manual page for cURL.
- `curl http://www.google.com >> ~/google.txt`—cURL resolves the Google home page URL and appends the results to the file google.txt in your home directory.

We suggest that you complete an online tutorial to better understand how to use cURL. Here are two:

- http://quickleft.com/blog/command-line-tutorials-curl
- http://curl.haxx.se/docs/httpscripting.html

A.2   Python

Python is a powerful dynamic programming language that's used in a variety of application domains. Python's notable features include clear, readable syntax; full modularity and supporting hierarchical packages; exception-based error handling; high-level, dynamic data types; extensive standard libraries and third-party modules; and support for all major OSes without need for changes to the source code.

You can download a Python interpreter from Python.org (http://python.org). Follow the guidelines at http://wiki.python.org/moin/BeginnersGuide/Download to select the proper installation package to meet your needs.

You should also download and install the free libraries RDFLib, Lingfo, and html5lib. These libraries can be found here:

- RDFLib—https://github.com/RDFLib/rdflib.
- html5lib—http://code.google.com/p/html5lib/downloads/detail?name=html5lib-0.95.tar.gz.
- Lingfo—http://www.lexicon.net/sjmachin/xlrd.htm. Follow the instructions contained at http://wiki.python.org/moin/CheeseShopTutorial for proper installation.

These library downloads should be stored in [PYTHON HOME]/lib.

A.3   ARQ

ARQ is a SPARQL processor that can be used from a command-line interface. ARQ can be downloaded from the Jena project's site at Apache (http://jena.apache.org). Source and binary executables for various operating systems can be retrieved from http://www.apache.org/dist/jena/. Make sure that you note the directory into which you extract the ARQ files.

Setting up ARQ is straightforward. A single environment variable is used to tell ARQ where its installation directory is located. The next listing shows how that's done on various OSes. In this listing, using Unix-like systems, we're assuming the ARQ files were extracted to /Applications/ARQ-2.8.8. In the Windows system, we're assuming the ARQ files were extracted to c:\MyProjects. You may select different directories, but note the path because you need to set the ARQROOT variable accordingly.

Listing A.1 Setting up ARQ

```
# For Unix-like systems, including Linux and OS X:
$ export ARQROOT='/Applications/ARQ-2.8.8'
$ /Applications/ARQ-2.8.8/bin/arq -h

# For Windows:
set ARQROOT=c:\MyProjects\ARQ
c:\MyProjects\ARQ\bat\arq.bat /h
```

Getting help for ARQ

Setting up the ARQ environment

You can verify the correct installation and setup of your ARQ environment by navigating to the ARQ directory and executing a prevously saved SPARQL query (for example, sample.rq) on previously saved RDF data (sampleData.rdf):

```
/bin/arq --query sample.rq --data sampleData.rdf
```

A.4 *Fuseki*

Fuseki is a lightweight, in-memory database suitable for working with small amounts of RDF data. Fuseki implements SPARQL query and update protocols that can present RDF data and answer SPARQL queries over HTTP. Fuseki also implements the SPARQL Graph Store HTTP Protocol.

Additional documentation and Fuseki installation and execution instructions are available from http://jena.apache.org/documentation/serving_data/index.html. Installation procedures vary, so we recommend you follow the instructions relevant to your OS.

A.5 *Callimachus*

Developers refer to Callimachus as a Linked Data management system. You may think of it as an application server for Linked Data. Callimachus is open source software released under the Apache 2.0 license. Callimachus provides browser-based development tools to easily create web applications using RDF data. Callimachus allows you to navigate, visualize, and build applications upon Linked Data. The data may be stored locally or gathered from the Web and may even be converted as it's brought into Callimachus.

You can download the most recent release and documentation from the project's website, http://callimachusproject.org. Installation and configuration instructions are in the file README.txt in the Callimachus distribution. Start the server and resolve the service's URL in your web browser. You'll see the Callimachus welcome screen following a successful installation.

appendix B
SPARQL results formats

This appendix covers

- SPARQL XML results format
- SPARQL JSON results format
- SPARQL CSV and TSV results format

This appendix explores the different output formats available for SPARQL queries. These formats allow for a high level of flexibility when using SPARQL in your applications. We cover the general structure of each format and where to find more detailed information about each.

All of the example results in this appendix are based on the first SPARQL query example shown in chapter 5 (listing 5.1). Keep in mind that this is a very simple query, and as queries become more complex, so do their results. For your convenience, the following listing is a copy of the SPARQL query from listing 5.1.

Listing B.1   SPARQL query from listing 5.1

```
prefix foaf: <http://xmlns.com/foaf/0.1/>
prefix pos: <http://www.w3.org/2003/01/geo/wgs84_pos#>
```

```
select ?name ?latitude ?longitude
from <http://3roundstones.com/dave/me.rdf>
from <http://sw-app.org/foaf/mic.rdf>
where {
  ?person foaf:name ?name ;
          foaf:based_near ?near .
  ?near pos:lat ?latitude ;
        pos:long ?longitude .
}
LIMIT 10
```

B.1 SPARQL XML results format

The SPARQL query results in XML format is a W3C Recommendation. The full specification is available online at http://www.w3.org/TR/rdf-sparql-XMLres/. It's a standard for the representation of the results of a SPARQL query in XML syntax. It consists of two main sections: a head section and a results section; both are wrapped in a SPARQL definition. From that point there are many options for further definition and representation, but here we'll cover only the basics.

All SPARQL XML results must be wrapped in a SPARQL document element, as outlined in the next listing.

Listing B.2 SPARQL XML document element

```
<?xml version="1.0"?>
<sparql xmlns="http://www.w3.org/2005/sparql-results#">
  ...
</sparql>
```
⟵ The head and results elements will appear here, within the **SPARQL** document element.

Within the SPARQL document element there must be two additional elements: a head section and a results section. For SELECT queries that return a series of variables, all variables must be defined in the order in which they're requested in the SELECT statement of the query. The example query we're using throughout this appendix (listing 5.1 in chapter 5) selects ?name, ?latitude, and ?longitude in that order. The relationship is established via variable tags with a name attribute corresponding to the variable name from the query. The listing that follows shows the document element from listing B.2 now including the head element.

Listing B.3 SPARQL XML head element

```
<?xml version="1.0"?>
<sparql xmlns="http://www.w3.org/2005/sparql-results#">
  <head>
    <variable name="name"/>
    <variable name="latitude"/>
    <variable name="longitude"/>
  </head>
  ...
</sparql>
```
⟵ The results element will appear here.

The second element contained within the SPARQL document element is the results element, which contains the actual results of the query. Each value retrieved from the query's SELECT statement is described using a results element within the parent results element. These results are bound to the variables delineated in the head element described earlier in the SPARQL document element via a binding tag with a name attribute that matches the variable name. The next listing shows a full example of a SPARQL XML result set including variable definitions and results bound to those variables.

Listing B.4   Complete SPARQL XML result set

```
<?xml version="1.0"?>
<sparql xmlns="http://www.w3.org/2005/sparql-results#">
  <head>
    <variable name="name"/>
    <variable name="latitude"/>
    <variable name="longitude"/>
  </head>
  <results>
    <result>
      <binding name="name">Michael G. Hausenblas</binding>
      <binding name="latitude">47.064</binding>
        <binding name="longitude">15.453</binding>
    </result>
    <result>
      <binding name="name">David Wood</binding>
      <binding name="latitude">38.300</binding>
        <binding name="longitude">-77.466</binding>
    </result>
  </results>
</sparql>
```

Result bindings can be further specified with the use of different document element tags within the binding element. Results can be typed as URIs (`<uri>`), literals (`<literal>`), literals with language tags (`<literal xml:lang="…">`), typed literals (`<literal datatype="…">`), or blank nodes (`<bnode>`). The next listing shows an example using the `<binding>` tag.

Listing B.5   SPARQL XML results binding type example

```
<?xml version="1.0"?>
<sparql xmlns="http://www.w3.org/2005/sparql-results#">
  ...
    [[
    <binding name="name"><literal>David Wood</literal></binding>
    ]]
  ...
</sparql>
```

For further references, explanation, and examples, see the full specification online (http://www.w3.org/TR/rdf-sparql-XMLres/).

B.2   *SPARQL JSON results format*

The SPARQL query results in JSON format is a W3C Proposed Recommendation. The full specification in its current state is available online at http://www.w3.org/TR/sparql11-results-json/. It's in the process of becoming a standard for the representation of the results of a SPARQL query using JSON syntax. Just as with the XML formatting, it consists of two main sections: a head section and a results section. Both of these are contained within a single parent JSON object. From that point there are many options for further definition and representation, but here we'll cover only the basics.

The parent JSON object contains two member objects, head and results. The listing that follows shows an example head section.

Listing B.6   SPARQL JSON head element

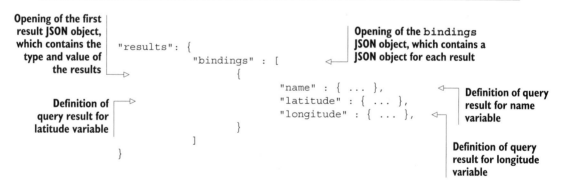

Once the variables are defined, the results of the query can be described appropriately. This is where the results member appears. The results member object contains a bindings member array, which creates a JSON object for every result from the query. The next listing shows an example of the bindings array.

Listing B.7   SPARQL JSON results element

Opening of the first result JSON object, which contains the type and value of the results

Definition of query result for latitude variable

Opening of the bindings JSON object, which contains a JSON object for each result

Definition of query result for name variable

Definition of query result for longitude variable

```
"results": {
              "bindings" : [
                  {
                     "name" : { ... },
                     "latitude" : { ... },
                     "longitude" : { ... },
                  }
              ]
}
```

The results are bound to the variables defined in the head element by the key of the key-value pair defined in each JSON object. At this point, these two elements can be combined within the parent JSON object to form a complete example of a SPARQL JSON result set. The following listing shows this full example.

Listing B.8   Complete SPARQL JSON result set

Opening of the parent JSON object, which contains head and results members

Opening of the head JSON object, which declares the variable names

```
{
    "head": { "vars": [ "name" , "latitude", "longitude" ]
    } ,
    "results": {
        "bindings": [
            {
                "name": {"type": "literal" , "value": "Michael G. Hausenblas
                "latitude": {"type": "literal" , "value": "47.064"},
                "longitude": {"type": "literal" , "value": "15.453"}
            },
            {
                "name": {"type": "literal" , "value": "David Wood"},
                "latitude": {"type": "literal" , "value": "38.300"},
                "longitude": {"type": "literal" , "value": "-77.466"}
            }
        ]
    }
}
```

Opening of the results JSON object, which contains query results

Definition of query result for longitude variable

Definition of query result for name variable

Definition of query result for latitude variable

As you can see, the elements used in the JSON formatting are identical to the formatting of XML results with only minor syntactic differences. The head element contains variable definitions, the results element contains the results of the query, and variables are bound within binding elements, which can define both their type and value.

B.3   *SPARQL CSV and TSV results format*

The SPARQL query results in CSV (comma-separated value) and TSV (tab-separated value) format are a W3C Proposed Recommendation. The full specification in its current state is available online at http://www.w3.org/TR/sparql11-results-csv-tsv/. It's in the process of becoming a standard for the representation of the results of a SPARQL query using CSV and TSV structure.

The formatting for SPARQL CSV results is quite different from either XML or JSON. Due to its inherent structure, all of the information encoded in RDF can't be transferred successfully to CSV. Whereas XML and JSON can encode types for the values returned from the query, CSV can only return a string literal and the type must be inferred. The syntax and structure are identical to any other CSV file, where the first line defines the variables in the order in which they were gathered from the SELECT clause. Each line after the first line represents a result from the query bound to the columns defined in the first line by their relative position. The next listing shows an example CSV result set.

Listing B.9   Complete SPARQL CSV result set

First line denoting
the variables. This
order applies to all
subsequent lines.

```
name, latitude, longitude
Michael G. Hausenblas, 47.064, 15.453
David Wood, 38.300, -77.466
```

The first value is for the
variable name; the second for
the variable latitude; the third
for the variable longitude.

TSV is identical in structure to CSV but allows for the serialization of RDF types using the same syntax as SPARQL and Turtle. If the value is a URI, it's enclosed in angle brackets (`<URI>`). If the value is a literal, it's enclosed in either single or double quotes (`"literal"`) with the option to add a language tag (`@lang`) or a data type (`^^`). The following listing shows an example of a TSV SPARQL result set. `<TAB>` is used in place of an actual tab character.

Listing B.10   Complete SPARQL TSV result set

First line denoting
the variables. This
order applies to all
subsequent lines.

```
name<TAB>latitude<TAB>longitude
"Michael G. Hausenblas"@en<TAB>47.064<TAB>15.453
"David Wood"@en<TAB>38.300<TAB>-77.466
```

The first value ("name") is a literal with an
English language tag; the second and third
values are bare strings without a type. An
XSD:datatype could be added if desired.

XML, JSON, CSV, and TSV all have similarities and differences when it comes to structure, syntax, and application. The key is to choose which serialization is appropriate for your application.

glossary

This appendix covers common Linked Data terms and their definitions. Terminology is constantly growing and evolving, and as Linked Data continues to expand, so too will the language around it.

APACHE JENA
An open source software implementation of a Semantic Web development framework. Supports the storage, retrieval, and analysis of RDF information. See http://jena.apache.org.

CALLIMACHUS
A Linked Data management system (or application server for Linked Data). Supports the building of Linked Data applications. See http://callimachusproject.org.

CONNEG
See *content negotiation.*

CONTENT NEGOTIATION
In HTTP, the use of a message header to indicate which response formats a client will accept. Content negotiation allows HTTP servers to provide different versions of a resource representation in response to any given URI request.

CONTROLLED VOCABULARIES
Carefully selected sets of terms that are used to describe units of information; used to create thesauri, taxonomies, and ontologies.

CSV
See *comma-separated values format.*

COMMA-SEPARATED VALUES FORMAT
A tabular data format in which columns of information are separated by comma characters.

cURL
A command-line open source/free software client that can transfer data, including machine-readable RDF, from or to a server using one of its many supported protocols.

DATA MODELING

The process of organizing data and information describing it into a faithful representation of a specific domain of knowledge.

DATASET

A collection of RDF data, comprising one or more RDF graphs that are published, maintained, or aggregated by a single provider. In SPARQL, an RDF dataset represents a collection of RDF graphs over which a query may be performed.

DBPEDIA

An RDF representation of the metadata held in Wikipedia and made available for SPARQL queries on the World Wide Web.

DCMI

See *Dublin Core Metadata Initiative*.

DIRECTED GRAPH

A graph in which the links between nodes are directional (they only go from one node to another and not necessarily in reversed order). RDF represents things (nouns) and the relationships between them (verbs) in a directed graph. In RDF, the links are differentiated by being assigned URIs.

DUBLIN CORE METADATA ELEMENT SET

A vocabulary of 15 properties for use in resource descriptions, such as can be found in a library card catalog (author, publisher, and so on). The most commonly used vocabulary for Semantic Web applications.

DUBLIN CORE METADATA INITIATIVE

An open international organization engaged in the development of interoperable metadata standards, including the Dublin Core Element Set and Dublin Core Metadata Terms. See http://dublincore.org.

DUBLIN CORE METADATA TERMS

A vocabulary of bibliographic terms used to describe both physical publications and those on the Web. An extended set of terms beyond those basic terms found in the Dublin Core Metadata Element Set. See http://dublincore.org/documents/dcmi-terms/.

ENTITY

In the sense of an entity-attribute-value model, an entity is synonymous with the subject of an RDF triple. See *triple*.

FOAF

See *Friend of a Friend*.

FRIEND OF A FRIEND

A Semantic Web vocabulary describing people and their relationships for use in resource descriptions.

GRAPH

A collection of objects (represented by nodes), any of which may be connected by links between them. See also *directed graph*.

INTERNATIONALIZED RESOURCE IDENTIFIER

A global identifier standardized by joint action of the World Wide Web Consortium and Internet Engineering Task Force. An IRI may or may not be resolvable on the Web. A generalization of URIs that allows characters from the Universal Character Set (Unicode). Slowly replacing URIs. See also *URI, URL.*

IRI

See *internationalized resource identifier.*

JavaScript Object Notation

A language-independent data format for representing simple data structures.

JavaScript Object Notation for Linking Data

A language-independent data format for representing Linked Data, based on JSON. JSON-LD is capable of serializing any RDF graph or dataset, and most, but not all, JSON-LD documents can be directly transformed to RDF.

JSON

See *JavaScript Object Notation.*

JSON-LD

See *JavaScript Object Notation for Linking Data.*

Linked Data

A pattern for hyperlinking machine-readable datasets to each other using Semantic Web techniques, especially via the use of RDF and URIs. Enables distributed SPARQL queries of the datasets and a browsing or discovery approach to finding information (as compared to a search strategy). See http://www.w3.org/DesignIssues/LinkedData.html.

Linked Data API

A REST API that allows data publishers to provide URLs to lists of things and allows clients to retrieve machine-readable data from those URLs.

Linked Data client

A web client that supports HTTP content negotiation for the retrieval of Linked Data from URLs and/or SPARQL endpoints.

Linked Data Platform

A specification that defines a REST API to read and write Linked Data for the purposes of enterprise application integration. Defined by the World Wide Web Consortium (W3C).

Linked Open Data

Linked Data published on the public Web and licensed under one of several open-content licenses permitting reuse.

Linked Open Data cloud

A colloquial phrase for the total collection of Linked Data published on the Web.

Linking Open Data cloud diagram

A diagram representing datasets published by the Linking Open Data project from 2007 to 2011. The diagram stopped being updated when individual datasets could no longer be meaningfully represented in a single diagram because of the number of total data-sets. See http://lod-cloud.net/state/.

LINKING OPEN DATA PROJECT
An open community project to interlink data on the Web using URIs and RDF.

LINKSET
A collection of RDF links between two datasets.

MACHINE-READABLE DATA
Data formats that may be readily parsed by computer programs without access to pro-prietary libraries. For example, CSV, TSV, and RDF formats are machine-readable, but PDF and Microsoft Excel are not.

METADATA
Information used to administer, describe, preserve, present, use, or link other infor-mation held in resources, especially knowledge resources, whether physical or virtual. Metadata may be further subcategorized into several types (including general, access, and structural metadata).

N-QUADS
A line-based format to encode an RDF dataset (possibly consisting of multiple RDF graphs). Defined by the World Wide Web Consortium. See http://www.w3.org/TR/n-quads/.

N-TRIPLES
A subset of Turtle that defines a line-based format to encode a single RDF graph. Used primarily as an exchange format for RDF data. Defined by the World Wide Web Con-sortium. See http://www.w3.org/TR/n-triples/.

NAMESPACE
See *namespace IRI*.

NAMESPACE IRI
A base IRI shared by all terms in a given vocabulary or ontology.

OBJECT
The final term in an RDF statement. See *triple*.

ONTOLOGY
A formal model that allows knowledge to be represented for a specific domain.

PERSISTENT UNIFORM RESOURCE LOCATOR
URLs that act as permanent identifiers in the face of a dynamic and changing web infrastructure. PURLs redirect to the current location of or proxy specific web content.

PREDICATE
The middle term (the linkage, or verb) in an RDF statement. See *triple*.

PROVENANCE
Data related to where, when, and how information was acquired.

PROTOCOL
A set of instructions for transferring data from one computer to another over a network. A protocol standard defines both message formats and the rules for sending and receiving those messages. One of the most common internet protocols is the Hypertext Transfer Protocol (HTTP).

PURL
See *persistent uniform resource locator.*

QUAD STORE
A colloquial phrase for an RDF database that stores RDF triples plus an additional element of information, often used to collect statements into groups.

RDF
See *Resource Description Framework.*

RDFA
See *Resource Description Framework in Attributes.*

RDF DATABASE
A type of database designed specifically to store and retrieve RDF information. May be implemented as a triple store, quad store, or other type.

RDF/JSON
A simple serialization of RDF triples in JSON. See also *JSON-LD.*

RDF LINK
An RDF triple whose subject and object are contained in different datasets. The datasets may be found on different servers.

RDF SCHEMA
See *Resource Description Framework Schema.*

RDF/XML
An RDF syntax encoded in XML. A standard of the World Wide Web Consortium.

REFERENCEABLE URIs
URIs that are used as identifiers in RDF graphs and that also may be resolved as URLs on the Web.

REQUEST
An action requested by a client using a particular protocol to request a response from a server. In HTTP, a request is synonymous with the term *URL resolution.* See also *response.*

RESOURCE
In an RDF context, a resource can be anything that an RDF graph describes.

RESOURCE DESCRIPTION FRAMEWORK
A family of international standards for data interchange on the Web produced by the World Wide Web Consortium.

RESOURCE DESCRIPTION FRAMEWORK IN ATTRIBUTES (RDFA)
An RDF syntax encoded in HTML documents. It's a standard of the World Wide Web Consortium.

RESOURCE DESCRIPTION FRAMEWORK SCHEMA (RDFS)
A standard of the World Wide Web Consortium and the simplest RDF vocabulary description language. It provides much less descriptive capability than the Simple Knowledge Organization System (SKOS) or the Web Ontology Language (OWL).

RESPONSE
An action by a server taken as the result of a request by a client. In HTTP, a response provides a resource representation to the calling client. See also *request*.

REST
See *Representational State Transfer.*

REPRESENTATIONAL STATE TRANSFER
An architectural style for information systems used on the Web. It explains some of the Web's key features, such as extreme scalability and robustness to change.

REST API
An API implemented using HTTP and the principles of REST to allow actions on web resources. The most common actions are to create, retrieve, update, and delete resources.

SEMANTIC WEB
An evolution or part of the World Wide Web that consists of machine-readable data in RDF and an ability to query that information in standard ways (for example, via SPARQL).

SINDICE
A search engine for Linked Data. It offers search and querying capabilities across the data it knows about, as well as specialized APIs and tools for presenting Linked Data summaries. See http://sindice.com.

SPARQL
See *SPARQL Protocol and RDF Query Language.*

SPARQL ENDPOINT
A service that accepts SPARQL queries and returns answers to them as SPARQL result sets.

SPARQL PROTOCOL AND RDF QUERY LANGUAGE
A query language standard for RDF data on the Semantic Web; analogous to the Structured Query Language (SQL) for relational databases. A family of standards of the World Wide Web Consortium. See http://www.w3.org/TR/sparql11-overview/.

SUBJECT
The initial term in an RDF statement. *See triple.*

TAB-SEPARATED VALUES FORMAT
A tabular data format in which columns of information are separated by tab characters.

TRIG
An extension of Turtle to encode an RDF dataset. Defined by the World Wide Web Consortium. See http://www.w3.org/TR/trig/. See also *N-Quads* and *Turtle*.

TRIPLE

An RDF statement, consisting of two things (a subject and an object) and a relationship between them (a verb, or predicate). This subject-predicate-object triple forms the smallest possible RDF graph (although most RDF graphs consist of many such statements).

TRIPLESTORE

A colloquial phrase for an RDF database that stores RDF triples.

TSV

See *tab-separated values format*.

TURTLE

An RDF syntax intended to be readable by humans. It's a standard of the World Wide Web Consortium. See http://www.w3.org/TR/turtle/.

UNIFORM RESOURCE IDENTIFIER

A global identifier standardized by joint action of the World Wide Web Consortium and Internet Engineering Task Force. It may or may not be resolvable on the Web. See also *IRI* and *URL*. See http://tools.ietf.org/html/rfc3986 and http://www.w3.org/DesignIssues/Architecture.html.

UNIFORM RESOURCE LOCATOR

A global identifier for web resources standardized by joint action of the World Wide Web Consortium and Internet Engineering Task Force. A URL is resolvable on the Web and is commonly called a web address. See also *IRI* and *URI*.

URI

See *uniform resource identifier*.

URL

See *uniform resource locator*.

VOCABULARY

A collection of terms for a particular purpose, such as RDF Schema, FOAF, or the Dublin Core Metadata Element Set. The use of this term overlaps with ontology.

VOCABULARY ALIGNMENT

The process of analyzing multiple vocabularies to determine terms that are common across them and to record those relationships.

VoID

Vocabulary of Interlinked Datasets, an RDF Schema vocabulary for expressing metadata about RDF datasets and a standard of the World Wide Web Consortium.

WEB OF DATA

A subset of the World Wide Web that contains Linked Data.

WEB OF DOCUMENTS

The original, or traditional, World Wide Web in which published resources were nearly always documents.

index

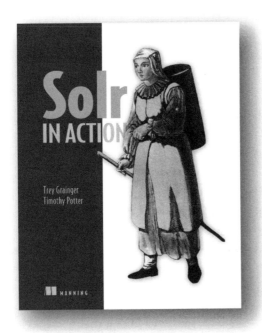

Solr in Action

by Trey Grainger
    Timothy Potter

ISBN: 978-1-617291-02-9
600 pages
$49.99
January 2014

Big Data
Principles and best practices of
scalable realtime data systems

by Nathan Marz
    James Warren

ISBN: 978-1-617290-34-3
425 pages
$49.99
March 2014

For ordering information go to www.manning.com

MORE TITLES FROM MANNING

Taming Text
How to find, organize, and manipulate it
by Grant S. Ingersoll
   Thomas S. Morton
   Andrew L. Farris

  ISBN: 978-1-933988-38-2
  320 pages
  $44.99
  January 2013

Making Sense of NoSQL
A guide for managers and the rest of us
by Dan McCreary
  Ann Kelly

  ISBN: 978-1-617291-07-4
  312 pages
  $34.99
  September 2013

For ordering information go to www.manning.com

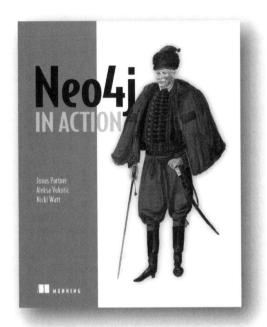

Neo4j in Action

by Jonas Partner
    Aleksa Vukotic
    Nicki Watt

ISBN: 978-1-617290-76-3
350 pages
$44.99
March 2014

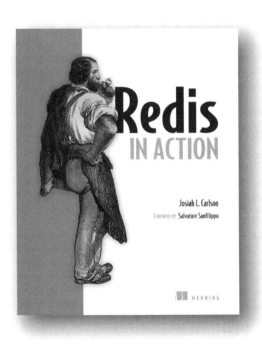

Redis in Action

by Josiah L. Carlson

ISBN: 978-1-617290-85-5
320 pages
$44.99
June 2013

For ordering information go to www.manning.com

MORE TITLES FROM MANNING

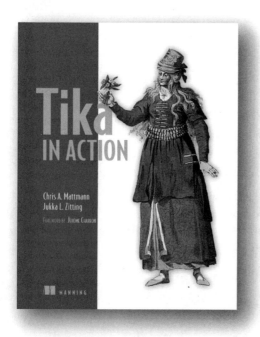

Tika in Action

by Chris A. Mattmann
   Jukka L. Zitting

   ISBN: 978-1-935182-85-6
   256 pages
   $44.99
   November 2011

The Quick Python Book,
Second Edition

by Naomi R. Ceder

   ISBN: 978-1-935182-20-7
   360 pages
   $39.99
   January 2010

For ordering information go to www.manning.com